How NATO Adapts

THE JOHNS HOPKINS UNIVERSITY STUDIES IN
HISTORICAL AND POLITICAL SCIENCE
132nd series (2017)

1. *How NATO Adapts: Strategy and Organization
in the Atlantic Alliance since 1950*
Seth A. Johnston

How NATO Adapts

Strategy and Organization in the
Atlantic Alliance since 1950

SETH A. JOHNSTON
US Military Academy, West Point

Johns Hopkins University Press
Baltimore

The views expressed are those of the author and do not necessarily reflect those
of the US Military Academy, US Army, or any other agency.

Johns Hopkins University Press
2715 North Charles Street
Baltimore, Maryland 21218-4363
www.press.jhu.edu

Library of Congress Cataloging-in-Publication Data

Names: Johnston, Seth A. (Seth Allen), 1981– author.
Title: How NATO adapts : strategy and organization in the Atlantic Alliance
since 1950 / Seth A. Johnston.
Description: Baltimore : Johns Hopkins University Press, 2017. | Includes
bibliographical references and index.
Identifiers: LCCN 2016022028| ISBN 9781421421988 (pbk. : alk. paper) | ISBN
9781421421995 (electronic) | ISBN 1421421984 (pbk. : alk. paper) | ISBN
1421421992 (electronic)
Subjects: LCSH: North Atlantic Treaty Organization—History.
Classification: LCC UA646.3 .J5688 2017 | DDC 355/.031091821—dc23
LC record available at https://lccn.loc.gov/2016022028

A catalog record for this book is available from the British Library.

*Special discounts are available for bulk purchases of this book. For more
information, please contact Special Sales at 410-516-6936 or specialsales@press
.jhu.edu.*

Johns Hopkins University Press uses environmentally friendly book materials,
including recycled text paper that is composed of at least 30 percent
post-consumer waste, whenever possible.

To the soldiers of Task Force Zabul, International Security Assistance Force IX. Their adaptability and determination in Afghanistan embodied the most admirable and enduring qualities of the Alliance.

CONTENTS

ACKNOWLEDGMENTS

NATO is a remarkably adaptable institution. Insofar as this study's many revisions are comparable, I gratefully acknowledge those who contributed to its better points and lessened the shortcomings for which I remain responsible.

This project began at Oxford, where Professor Sir Hew Strachan supervised its development with wisdom and generosity. Professor Richard Caplan's support ranks indispensable since my first years as a graduate student. Professors Duncan Snidal, Jennifer Welsh, Anand Menon, Sibylle Scheipers, Rob Johnson, Patricia Owens, Hartmut Mayer, Valerie Worth, Stephen Fisher, Michael Beloff, and Sir Ivor Roberts exceeded every expectation of endowment and civility for which this institution is rightly known.

I am equally indebted to my colleagues at West Point and the Department of Social Sciences in particular. Brigadier General Cindy Jebb, Colonel Suzanne Nielsen, Colonel Tania Chacho, and Dr. Scott Silverstone were my professors as an undergraduate and perhaps even more instructive as leaders of junior faculty. Work on this book paralleled the development of new courses on international organization and European politics for cadets, whose energy and determined service testifies to their character every day. Fellow faculty members Nelly Lahoud, Hugh Liebert, Jordan Becker, Rachel Sondheimer, Thomas Sherlock, Ruth Beitler, Aaron Miller, Brandon Archuleta, Susan Carter, Lissa Young, Matt Cavanaugh, Brian Retherford, Brian Forester, Brian Babcock-Lumish, Keith Benedict, Ben Mitchell, Rob Person, Robert Chamberlain, Joe Da Silva, Raven Bukowski, Mike Rosol, Scott Handler, Charlie Faint, and Bonnie Kovatch, among others, inspired by their editorial hand and professional example.

Research about NATO would not have been possible without official assistance from several quarters, including the NATO Archives, International Staff, Public Diplomacy Division, and Supreme Headquarters Allied Powers Europe. I am especially obliged to Brigadier General John Adams and the US Delegation to the Military Committee for treating me as one of their own, and to Colonel Jonathan Freeman, Brigadier General Peter Zwack, Lieutenant General David Hogg, and Lieutenant General Robert Caslen for the professional latitude and support to see the Alliance in action.

The Marshall Aid Commemoration Commission of the British government, Atlantic Council of the United States, Harry S. Truman Scholarship Foundation, Saltzman Institute of War and Peace Studies at Columbia University, Merrill Center for Strategic Studies at the Johns Hopkins School of Advanced International Studies, Rupert H. Johnson Grand Strategy Program at West Point, US Air Force Institute for National Security Studies, American Council on Germany, Council on Foreign Relations' Academic Outreach Initiative, Wertheim Study at the New York Public Library, and Trinity College, Oxford, generously supported work leading to this endeavor.

The fellowship of scholars and practitioners who offered feedback on drafts of these pages further include David Blagden, Joe Cerami, Sewell Chan, Samuel Charap, Eliza Gheorghe, Benoît Gomis, Cristina Gonzalez, Ron Granieri, Julian Gruin, Michael Jago, Sarwar Kashmiri, John Keeling, Sam Kleiner, Jeff Larsen, Travers McLeod, Kate Millar, Tristen Naylor, Claire Palmer, Suwita Hani Randhawa, Ruben Reike, Emile Simpson, Michael Urban, Vinícius Rodrigues Vieira, Jiajun Xu, and Makio Yamada. I owe a particular debt to Stan Sloan, whose helpfulness as a reviewer of this manuscript and guest lecturer in the West Point course on European politics are matched only by his class as a gentleman.

Elizabeth Sherburn Demers, Juliana McCarthy, Andre Barnett, Nicole Wayland, and the entire team from Johns Hopkins University Press could not have been more obliging, efficient, or thorough in bringing this work to print.

To have a professional editor, publisher, or librarian in the family is an advantage in a project like this, but to have all three in my mother, Darcie Conner Johnston, was monumentally fortunate. Geo. Allen Johnston, my father, has always matched respect for the past with optimism for the future; his inspiration is written on every page. Thanks to all of my family and friends for their support, encouragement, and understanding of long hours and absences.

ACT	Allied Command Transformation
AWACS	Airborne Warning and Control System
BERCON	Berlin contingency plan
CAOC	Combined Air Operations Centre
CENTO	Central Treaty Organization
CFE	Treaty on Conventional Armed Forces in Europe
CFSP	Common Foreign and Security Policy
CJTF	Combined Joint Task Force
CSCE	Conference on Security and Cooperation in Europe
CSTO	Collective Security Treaty Organization
DPC	Defence Planning Committee
DSACEUR	Deputy Supreme Allied Commander Europe
EAPC	Euro-Atlantic Partnership Council
EC	European Communities
ECSC	European Coal and Steel Community
EDC	European Defence Community
EEC	European Economic Community
EPC	European Political Cooperation
ESDI	European Security and Defence Identity
FEB	Financial and Economic Board
GDR	German Democratic Republic
ICBM	intercontinental ballistic missile
IFOR	Implementation Force
IMS	International Military Staff
IO	international organization
IPP	Individual Partnership Programme
IRBM	intermediate-range ballistic missile

ISAF	International Security Assistance Force
MAD	mutually assured destruction
MLF	Multilateral Force
NAC	North Atlantic Council
NACC	North Atlantic Cooperation Council
NDAC	Nuclear Defence Affairs Committee
NPG	Nuclear Planning Group
NPT	Treaty on the Non-Proliferation of Nuclear Weapons
NRF	NATO Response Force
NTM-A	NATO Training Mission-Afghanistan
OSCE	Organization for Security and Cooperation in Europe
PfP	Partnership for Peace
PJC	Permanent Joint Council
PRT	Provincial Reconstruction Team
SACEUR	Supreme Allied Commander Europe
SEATO	Southeast Asia Treaty Organization
SFOR	Stabilization Force
SHAPE	Supreme Headquarters Allied Powers Europe
SLBM	submarine-launched ballistic missile
SRG	Strategy Review Group
START	Strategic Arms Reduction Treaty
TCC	Temporary Council Committee
UNPROFOR	United Nations Protection Force
WEU	Western European Union

How NATO Adapts

CHAPTER ONE

Introduction

[Lord Ismay, the North Atlantic Treaty Organization's first secretary-general,] famously described NATO's [founding rationale to "keep the Americans in, the Russians out, and the Germans down."] Would Lord Ismay recognize NATO today? In its seventh decade, NATO's missions, functional scope, size, and membership are profoundly different from those of its origins. NATO entered its first major ground war and longest-ever conflict in Afghanistan, far outside its traditional geographic area and with a coalition of more than forty countries that would have astounded the Washington Treaty's twelve original signatories in 1949. An [offer of membership to Montenegro in 2015 meant an alliance of twenty-nine full members,] several of which were once part of the Warsaw Pact or even the Soviet Union. Yet NATO's adaptation is [not exclusive] to the twenty-first century. Ismay's formulation would seem equally dated to observers of Germany's rearmament within the Alliance after 1955, a scant six years after its founding, or of Russia's inclusion in post–Cold War political overtures like the Partnership for Peace and NATO-Russia Council. Indeed, NATO undergoes significant change with some regularity.

The fact of these changes and their boldness and frequency over a period of nearly seventy years distinguish NATO from other international institutions. Among post–World War II bodies with similar longevity to NATO, others reflect the international politics of their founding era more closely. Global institutions such as the United Nations Security Council have retained more consistent membership and organization. Regional alliances expressly modeled after NATO, such as the [Southeast Asia Treaty Organization (SEATO)] and [Central Treaty Organization (CENTO),] have long ceased to exist, while others, such as the [Western European Union (WEU),] fell into institutional obscurity, even though their member countries remained aligned. Yet both [adaptation and endurance characterize NATO.]

Neither change nor longevity is inevitable, however. NATO is frequently said to be in crisis, its internal politics frustrating and inefficient, and its external policies and strategies suboptimal. Russia's aggression against Georgia in 2008 and Ukraine in 2014 highlighted the potential for political split among Alliance members with dissimilar attitudes toward Russia while also generating military and strategic urgency after years of declining defense investment in Europe. Previous crises, from the withdrawal of France from NATO's integrated military structure in 1966 to the membership enlargement debates of the 1990s, further illustrate the often-difficult struggles through which NATO has attempted to meet new security challenges.

A common feature of NATO crises has been the possibility or proposal of alternative institutional arrangements outside NATO for meeting the new challenges. Whether, for example, through the assertion of national independence in nuclear deterrence, supranational solutions for European security, or ad hoc "coalitions of the willing" for expeditionary operations, the reinvention of NATO to address new security challenges is rarely an automatic or uncontested development. As a result, the considerable, frequent, and effective adaptation of NATO is puzzling.

The NATO Literature

NATO's survival is the central concern of other works, from Ronald Steel's *The End of Alliance* to the more recent *Why NATO Endures* by Wallace J. Thies.[2] The present study differs from these other works in its emphasis on NATO institutions. This emphasis relies on a distinction between the [Alliance as a treaty-based agreement among states and *NATO* as a formal international institution.] Rather than a focus on why the alignment of European and North American states persists, this study accepts the existence of the Alliance but explores the fact that it continues to find institutional expression in the organization known as NATO. Given the changes in the international system since its founding and the proposal or creation of other regional defense and security institutions, how NATO adapts and remains the institutional embodiment of the transatlantic Alliance remains an important question.

Among those works that document changes in NATO, this study goes further in providing long-term historical context for theorizing NATO adaptation. The pioneering works of Robert S. Jordan were among the first to draw attention to the roles of institutional leaders in NATO's development, but they stop short of generalizable insights for institutional theory.[3] Although other works such as David Yost's *NATO Transformed* and Rebecca Moore's *NATO's New Mission* assess changes after the Cold War, this study examines a broader scope of cases, addressing both the Cold War record and the contemporary patterns of NATO's institutional adaptation.[4]

The Argument

NATO is a highly adaptive institution. This study advances two main theoretical claims about how NATO adapts. First, institutional adaptation can be understood using an analytical framework based on recent advances in the study of institutions in political science and international relations. But doing so entails a conception of NATO not just as an alliance among states but also as a formally organized international institution. Second, although states maintain considerable power over international institutions, the latter have autonomous capacities and can play consequential roles in facilitating their own adaptation. This study finds consistent adaptation of NATO across multiple periods of Alliance history and in its contemporary affairs, as well as regularity in the processes of how that adaptation occurs. Plausible alternatives to NATO have surfaced regularly during contingent periods of institutional instability, but NATO has ultimately adapted and endured. Institutional actors—that is, those representing NATO itself, not necessarily its member-states—have played underappreciated and consequential roles in facilitating adaptation.

Sources and Methods

This study draws on the literature in historical institutionalism to develop a framework for the analysis of challenges to NATO's endurance based on "critical junctures"—significant relaxations of the structural constraints on institutional stability. Such crises or junctures constitute the challenges that threaten institutional endurance. By disrupting institutional stability, these conditions can make institutional change more likely, but critical junctures are not synonymous with change nor do they necessarily involve it. While this study finds evidence of NATO adaptation across cases, the critical juncture framework allows for two other possible outcomes in institutional analysis, namely continuity in NATO (i.e., the preponderance of stability over change) and the adoption of non-NATO alternatives for organizing cooperation among states.

The critical juncture framework also allows for an analysis of the key actors and events in how NATO adapts. The process tracing method is used to show the causal path through which actors facilitate institutional adaptation.[5] In order to guide the analysis and structure comparison across cases, this study focuses on adaptation of NATO's internal organization and external strategy. Chapter 3 also advances a set of propositions about the mechanisms by which institutional actors facilitate this adaptation. Although states heavily constrain institutional action, these mechanisms indicate the consequential autonomy and capability of institutional actors.

The sources for this study consist of official documents from NATO and some of its member-states, as well as correspondence and interviews with officials in the NATO organization, national missions to the Alliance, and the military forces involved in NATO plans and operations.[6] Where this study seeks to establish a basis for adaptation in historical context, secondary literature is used to identify important developments in NATO that merit further examination of primary sources. Speeches, diplomatic correspondence, and contemporaneous national discourse supplement official texts where useful.

Aims and Contributions

The original contributions of this study are both practical and theoretical. In order to illustrate the process of adaptation in NATO, ideas about institutions and strategy developed for other uses will be applied to NATO. The use of historical institutionalism and the critical juncture framework is an alternative to the main theoretical schools of thought in international relations, which do not consistently explain NATO's regular pattern of behavior in response to new challenges. Most theories of international relations conceptualize NATO through the lens of interstate alliance politics. This study does not set out to show that traditional international relations theory is unhelpful or wrong in describing why NATO endures. Rather, the purpose is to show how it adapts, which involves focusing on process and locating the importance of institutional actors within the broader knowledge of NATO. By examining institutional adaptation through critical junctures, this study emphasizes institutions' potential to exercise independent, autonomous powers. This approach has implications for knowledge of both NATO and international institutions in general.

A practical contribution of this study is to inform understanding of NATO's contemporary endeavors and future challenges. NATO's involvement in the 2011 Libyan civil war and its aftermath, renewed deterrence of Russia, a training mission in Iraq, and advisory assistance to the African Union, among other operations, has involved the Alliance in a relatively unprecedented range of global challenges.[7] Noting NATO's latest organizational and strategic behavior provides an opportunity to identify continuities in the context of historic challenges to NATO's institutional endurance. It also provides an opportunity to show whether or how peace and wartime security challenges may be different in defining the range of feasible external strategies available to NATO. These observations have obvious implications for NATO's future tasks and missions.

A further practical contribution of this study is to illuminate the kinds of institutional arrangements that suit transatlantic security and defense cooperation. Each case in this study features proposals for serious non-NATO institutional alternatives to cooperation, usually in the form of bids for relatively greater European autonomy. This study offers insight into the institutional characteristics of cooperation that NATO states prefer, which has implications not only for transatlantic alliance politics within NATO but also for continuing efforts to institutionalize defense cooperation in the European Union (EU).

Case Selection and Outline

This book comprises three case studies of critical junctures in NATO, as well as an assessment of the argument's applicability to contemporary challenges. The primary criterion in the selection of cases is the significance of the challenge to NATO's institutional endurance.[8] Accordingly, the cases comprise momentous crises from throughout NATO's history, including the first and second Berlin crises, France's partial withdrawal, and the end of the Cold War. Although there are other cases to which this approach to the study of NATO institutions could apply, a selection of the most challenging critical junctures from different periods offers the potential to identify patterns of adaptation without engaging in an exhaustive history of the Alliance, of which there are already several.[9]

The fact that this study only considers cases in which NATO endures is both inevitable and defensible. There are no cases of NATO's breakup to study. All cases of NATO in crisis conclude with the institution's continuing endurance, so this common outcome is an inexorable feature of any study of NATO. Fortunately, this does not pose significant problems for the research design. Each case shows significant variation in the substance of the crises facing NATO, allowing for multiple applications of the congruence method.[10] Moreover, each case also offers sufficient data to permit process tracing in order to demonstrate the applicability of the theory and argument.[11]

A consideration in the selection of these cases is the variation of antecedent conditions present across the different time periods studied. Among other things, the international system structure, the degree of historically rooted patterns of cooperation among Alliance members, the potential for cumulative bureaucratic inertia, the changing character of warfare, and the prevailing ideological discourses in politico-military affairs vary substantially from the time of NATO's early history to its twenty-first-century reality. This variance strengthens the case selection method insofar as it helps to emphasize the potential importance of consistent patterns of NATO's adaptation.[12]

The first case concerns [NATO in the early 1950s, when the Cold War was emergent and the outbreak of war in a divided Korea raised fears of war in a divided Europe] too. This period saw a reevaluation of Germany's role in the post–World War II order and the rise of the "O" in NATO. Although institutional arrangements such as the European Defence Community represented real alternatives to the institutionalization of the Alliance, NATO adapted vastly to increase the organization of its military and political cooperation as well as to incorporate West Germany into the Alliance. In terms of key institutional actors, Chairman of the North Atlantic Council Deputies Charles Spofford played a particularly influential role in these developments.

The second case concerns the [early 1960s, when the Cuban Missile Crisis and détente raised questions about the credibility of American nuclear deterrence] and eased the structural tensions in the international system. National alternatives to collective defense, including the development of independent nuclear forces in France and Britain and the withdrawal of France from NATO's integrated military system, achieved greater traction than the supranational alternatives of the previous decade. But NATO adapted by developing the Nuclear Planning Group, the strategy of "flexible response," and an increased political dimension embodied in the Harmel Report. Supreme Allied Commander General Lyman Lemnitzer and Secretaries-General Dirk Stikker and Manlio Brosio played important roles in moderating these adaptations.

The third case begins with the [collapse of the Cold War order in Europe and of the Soviet Union]. While not a direct military crisis, the political upheaval engendered by these developments was perhaps NATO's best-known critical juncture. With its main adversary apparently gone, NATO's purpose was unclear. Alternative institutional arrangements for making Europe whole and free existed in the newly branded EU and the Organization for Security and Cooperation in Europe. NATO adaptation and strategy-making turned to membership enlargement, political engagement, and crisis management in the former Yugoslavia. Key institutional actors included Colonel Klaus Wittmann of NATO's International Military Staff, Assistant Secretary-General Michael Legge, and Secretaries-General Manfred Wörner and Willy Claes.

The pattern of how NATO has endured historical challenges also offers insight into explaining the institution's twenty-first-century trials. A fourth empirical chapter assesses the applicability of the overall argument for explaining NATO's contemporary challenges and demonstrates congruence with the critical juncture framework and NATO's adaptation after the 1999 Kosovo air campaign and the terrorist attacks of September 11, 2001, especially with respect to NATO's involvement in Afghanistan. This chapter demonstrates the plausibility that institutional actors continued to play consequential roles in facilitating organizational and strategic adaptations, contributing to conclusions about directions for future research. Although NATO's future remains a topic of sometimes acrimonious debate, the consistency of NATO's contemporary experience with previous challenges suggests cause for optimism. Plausible institutional alternatives to NATO have regularly surfaced in the aftermath of critical junctures, but NATO has ultimately adapted in ways that have promoted its endurance. Institutional actors have played consequential, if not always leading, roles in facilitating how NATO adapts.

PART ONE

THINKING ABOUT ADAPTATION AND NATO

CHAPTER TWO

Historical Institutionalism and the Framework of "Critical Junctures"

What is NATO? Most international relations scholarship treats NATO as an alliance among sovereign states. This study departs from the state-centric focus by emphasizing NATO's character as an international institution. The institutional conception offers potential to examine questions of how NATO adapts with specific insight into the roles of bureaucratic actors in those processes. Because the existing scholarship conceptualizing NATO as an institution is underdeveloped, this chapter introduces a framework for the study of adaptation to address some of the gaps in previous institutional approaches. This framework draws on the concept of "critical junctures" from the literature on historical institutionalism. Critical junctures have not been used previously in a major study of NATO, so their use here contributes to knowledge about international institutions generally and NATO in particular.

Conceptualizing NATO as an Institution

The North Atlantic Treaty (known as the Washington Treaty) of 1949 established an alliance among its signatory states in Europe and North America. By itself, this treaty fits traditional conceptions of alliance formation as the result of agreement among sovereign states. Such alliance-making is commonplace as a practice and as a topic of theorizing in the academic discipline of international relations. As one noted scholar exemplified, "Alliances are central to international relations: they are the primary foreign policy means by which states increase their security."[1] An important aspect of this conception is that states are the key actors in international relations, and alliances are thus a function of *policy* made by *states*. These foreign policy agreements are the essential constitution of alliances, regardless of whether they are formalized in treaties or institutionalized in any other way.

On this point of institutionalization, of course, NATO emerges as something more than simply an agreement among states. For most of its history, the Atlantic Alliance has exhibited a much higher degree of formal institutionalization than most other alliances.[2] Although its formal institutions have changed and developed over time, NATO has included from a very early stage a permanent administrative bureaucracy with independent agencies; an integrated multinational military command structure; and common standards, doctrine, and procedures, among other formal structures. These structures constitute more than an intergovernmental policy agreement. Thus, although the North Atlantic Treaty created an alliance in the traditional sense, NATO is also an international organization. Such organizations are explicitly more formalized and institutionalized than other international agreements, including alliances.[3] Although international organizations are generally established by states and count states among their members, they are "sufficiently institutionalized to include some sort of centralized administrative apparatus with a permanent staff."[4] NATO clearly meets this standard of institutionalization.

Some precision is warranted, however, as notions of institutions vary, and international institutions themselves can assume several forms. The most important definitional matter is the distinction between formal and informal institutions. Traditional conceptions of institutions focus primarily on formal organizations: explicitly established groups with specific purposes, such as businesses or public bureaucracies.[5] International organizations such as the International Monetary Fund or the Organization for Security and Cooperation in Europe fit this conception of institution as formal organization (as does NATO). A definition of informal institution, by contrast, focuses not only on formal organization per se but rather on routinized practices, rules, and/or norms, and draws from various academic disciplines in the social sciences.[6] An important point here is that formal institutions also tend to manifest informal institutions. Informal institutions can arise spontaneously and so do not necessarily entail any formal organization. But formal organizations do regularly develop embedded norms, values, practices, and other informal institutions. Thus, while several different definitions of institutions exist in ideal type, institutions in the real world often embody more than one such classification.

NATO exemplifies this variation in the definition of institutions and in the various forms institutions assume in the real world. For some, NATO is simply and literally what the acronym implies, that is, the formal North Atlantic Treaty *Organization.* This includes the NATO secretariat, bureaucracy, integrated military command, and other structures, as well as the formal rules and procedures defined in the North Atlantic Treaty and other NATO agreements. For others, *NATO* is [shorthand for the informal institutions of a transatlantic group of North American and European states that have joined in order to facilitate their common security, interests, values, or identity.] This latter definition is closer to the conception articulated by state-centric alignment theories of alliances and also bears resemblance to what Karl Deutsch termed [a *pluralistic security community*.] Both the formal and informal institutional definitions are useful conceptions. But for clarity during the course of this study, *NATO* will be used in the strict sense of the term as referring most directly to the formal organization.[9] In contrast, the terms *Atlantic Alliance*, or *the Alliance*, can be seen to embody the collection of member-states or the broader informal institutions they share.

Although this study is most directly concerned with NATO's formal organization, this focus does not deny the existence or importance of the Alliance's informal institutions or of the member-states. On the contrary, states and the informal institutions that shape their relations are part of the background story as to why the Alliance exists.[10] But the functions of NATO's formal institutions have played a consequential and largely underappreciated role in how NATO works and adapts. A focus on formal institutions distinguishes this study from previous investigations into NATO adaptation and also more generally distinguishes the institutional approach from state-centric international relations theories, which emphasize the effects of institutions on interstate cooperation while downplaying the active and independent roles of the institutions themselves as key actors.[11] An institutional approach to an examination of how NATO adapts therefore has the potential to expand knowledge of NATO as well as institutions generally.[12]

Conceptualizing NATO as an institution allows for the examination of the precise mechanisms of how it adapts. These processes occur within the context of organizational politics and interstate alignments that organization theories and traditional international relations address, but this institutional approach allows for a greater focus on the mechanisms of *how* things happen. Following the work of Robert McCalla in his study of NATO after the Cold War, this study also adopts an institutionalist perspective that "looks at the interaction of NATO's organizational interests and its members' interests."[13] States matter, but international organizations do, too. Both are important in institutional analysis.

Two further points about the specific character of NATO institutions are worth mentioning. First, international formal institutions embody important aspects of public sector bureaucracy.[14] As James Wilson points out, public institutions have greater external constraints than private (e.g., business, social) institutions because public institutions do not fully control their own institutional priorities and allocation of resources; in bureaucracies, "control over revenues, productive factors, and agency goals is all vested to an important degree in entities external to the organization."[15] Insofar as international formal institutions also depend on member-states for resources, such institutions share important features with government bureaucracies that they do not share with other large organizations. Following Michael Barnett and Martha Finnemore's pathbreaking work explicitly conceptualizing international institutions as bureaucracies, this study articulates specific mechanisms for how international institutions generally and NATO in particular exercise power, autonomy, and adaptation.[16]

A final point of conceptualization is that military and security institutions such as NATO can be distinguished from standard bureaucracies in the martial character of their purposes. Militaries are a distinctive sort of institution in that they are instruments of violence and are, as Barry Posen puts it, "endowed with all sorts of resources, and masters of a particularly arcane technology."[17] Steven Rosen further argues that it is vital to "regard military organizations as complex political communities . . . [that] have this political character to a greater degree than other bureaucratic organizations."[18] International formal security institutions, especially highly militarized ones, are likely to share this political character insofar as they are concerned with the high-stakes realm of violence and survival, and possess related resources, as NATO does.[19]

Institutional Approaches to NATO Adaptation

Notwithstanding their potential, institutional studies of NATO are relatively few when compared to the larger literature in international relations alliance theory. Perhaps as a result of the comparatively underdeveloped condition of the institutional literature, previous institutionalist analyses of NATO reveal a variety of gaps and limitations that could benefit from further development.[20]

One shortcoming has been a relatively greater focus on the structure of institutions and an accordingly underdeveloped analysis of the role of agency in institutional analysis. Celeste Wallander, for example, makes an important contribution to the literature in describing the concept of "asset specificity." She argues that a framework for assessing the character of an institution's assets as general or specific "provides a basis for predicting when states will choose to maintain existing institutions as opposed to abandoning them entirely or creating new, more costly ones."[21] But although Wallander acknowledges that "a complete account of any case requires both structure and agency," she admits that her own approach is "dependent on structural incentives and opportunities."[22] Moreover,

Wallander's acknowledgment of agency remains limited to a state-centric conception that does not address the potential for institutional actors themselves to exercise agency independent of states: "International institutions play a role in security relations by reducing transaction costs and making it possible for states to cooperate when it is in their interests to do so."[23] Institutional accounts that explore agency should be clear about identifying the key actors and open to the idea that nonstate institutional actors may play autonomous and consequential roles.

A second limitation of previous institutional accounts has been their tendency to focus on institutional stability as a source of endurance without adequately allowing for the prospect of institutional adaptation or change. As Anand Menon and Jennifer Welsh indicate, "many studies of NATO's persistence after the Cold War have tended to equate organizational persistence with institutional stability. This logic is misleading because, in NATO's case, the former has in fact been the result of far-reaching institutional change that has seen the alliance fundamentally transform itself."[24] Indeed, this criticism is not limited to analyses of the post–Cold War period or to analyses of NATO among other international institutions.[25] As shown in this study, adaptation has been a consistent feature of NATO since its earliest days in the 1950s. Institutional approaches to explaining NATO endurance should thus be able to incorporate the role of change as well as stability.

Third, previous institutional approaches have tended to overlook the role of conflict in explaining institutional dynamics. Just as some state-centric international relations theories have emphasized the prospects for interstate cooperation over conflict, so have institutional accounts that emphasize structure and stability also minimized the importance of conflict.[26] Yet, particularly as crisis and conflict have appeared to be persistent characteristics in NATO, institutional approaches to explaining endurance should be able to account for them. Conflict does not necessarily affect or undermine institutional performance but rather only implies that institutionalist approaches should be able to account for the dynamics of power and politics that accompany agency and potential for institutional change.[27]

Critical Junctures: A Refined Framework for the Study of Institutional Adaptation

In refining an institutionalist approach to the examination of how NATO adapts, the concept of critical junctures allows for the development of a conceptual framework that benefits from the insights of previous work while also addressing some of their limitations. This framework allows for a methodologically precise institutional analysis that captures the roles of both structure and agency, offers a sophisticated way of treating cooperation and conflict through considerations of power, and allows for institutional change without requiring it tautologically.

The concept of critical junctures is associated with the "historical" branch of scholarship sometimes known as the new institutionalism.[28] Historical institutionalist analyses generally advance a view that the normal condition of an institution is one of path-dependent stability. Path dependence is the idea that history matters because past events shape the present reality by constraining today's choices.[29] Because this concept of path dependence implies relative stability, explanations of meaningful change in historical institutionalism often focus on critical junctures in history during which change may occur and new path dependencies emerge.

A leading and precise definition by Giovanni Capoccia and R. Daniel Kelemen describes critical juncture as "a situation in which the structural (that is, economic, cultural, ideological, organizational) influences on political action are significantly relaxed for a relatively short period, with two main consequences: the range of plausible choices open to powerful political actors expands substantially and the consequences of their decisions for the outcome of interest are potentially much more momentous."[30] Capoccia and Kelemen's definition builds on similar definitions from James Mahoney, who defined critical junctures as "choice point[s] when a particular option is adopted among two or more alternatives" and "moments of relative structural indeterminism when wilful actors shape outcomes in a more voluntaristic fashion than normal circumstances permit."[31] Although the concept of critical junctures and its conceptual antecedents have been widely used in studies of international relations and political science,[32] many analyses have focused more attention on the path dependencies surrounding these events than on the critical junctures themselves, or have used definitions of critical junctures that are not widely generalizable or methodologically rigorous. Mahoney, Capoccia, and Kelemen offer important contributions to resolve these issues in their definitions.[33]

Use of the term *critical juncture*—as opposed to *crisis* or another more casual term—allows for some precision of the concept and its essential features. One such essential point is that a critical juncture needs a unit of reference. Unlike a general social upheaval or period of turmoil, the concept of a critical juncture is used with reference to a specified institutional context (i.e., NATO, for our purposes). The same structural influences on political action in the world may affect different institutions differently. Thus, a critical juncture for one institution may not be a critical juncture for another. Some institutions may weather periods of general instability without undergoing a critical juncture, while in other cases an institution may undergo a critical juncture even though the world may be generally stable in other respects.[34]

Critical junctures allow for the importance of both structural factors and the agency of institutional actors. On the one hand, critical junctures arise out of structural conditions. It is the relaxing of constraints on action and the resulting circumstances of "relative structural indeterminism" that precipitate critical junctures.[35] On the other hand, while the initial conditions of a critical juncture are largely structural, the consequences of a critical juncture are primarily the expansion of the range of available choices and the importance of such choices among actors. Analysis of critical junctures thus also involves an important role for agency. The window of opportunity created for agents, in terms of both their available choices and the impact of such choices on the creation of path-dependent futures, distinguishes critical junctures from times of normal institutional operation.[36]

The importance of agency and choice also means that power is an important ingredient in the institutional analysis of critical junctures.[37] The asymmetries and dynamics of power among institutional actors are central to the identification of the actors and choices that are the most influential in determining the causal process of an institution's course through a critical juncture. Unlike some economic analyses of path dependence that tend to emphasize chance or randomness in the "lock-in" of certain institutional developments, power plays an important role in the political analysis of institutions.[38] Random chance has a role to play in any event, but power matters in politics. As Kathleen Thelen and Sven Steinmo write: "Groups and individuals are not merely spectators as conditions change to favor or penalize them in the political balance of power, but rather strategic actors capable of acting on 'openings' provided by such shifting contextual conditions in order to enhance their own position."[39] The identification of the key events, institutional actors, and the decisions these actors make is an essential task for institutional analysis of critical junctures.

Process tracing is therefore a particularly useful method of institutional analysis of critical junctures.[40] Process tracing allows for an analysis of how structural considerations give rise to a critical juncture within a given institutional context; the identification of the key events, actors, and decisions regarding the institution in view of the critical juncture; and the consequences of those decisions with respect to the institution. Theoretical propositions can play a role in guiding the narrative and further organizing the analysis.

An important element of any such analysis is contingency. Contingency is important in two ways. First, contingency implies that the choices made during a critical juncture were not the only possible choices, and that other options were available. These other available alternatives should be explored. This may involve counterfactual analysis or, depending on the data available, an assessment of the real options considered.[41] In this study, real-world institutional alternatives to NATO perennially arose during critical junctures in NATO, and both NATO and non-NATO institutional choices will be assessed in each case study. Either way, regarding institutional analysis in general, the identification of alternative choices is important for demonstrating that a crisis really was a critical juncture.

A second element of contingency is the implication that a critical juncture does not necessarily involve institutional change but merely the possibility or likelihood of change.[42] This second aspect of contingency has important implications for research design. A model of institutional process that insisted on change risks inserting an element of selection bias or tautology into the analysis.[43] Instead, rather than selecting for change, the use of this model of critical junctures in historical institutionalism allows us to focus on cases in which NATO's path-dependent stability is interrupted, and then to test whether a hypothesized theory of institutional adaptation occurs. Moreover, the critical juncture framework also reinforces the criteria used for case selection (i.e., selecting cases of serious challenges to NATO rather than serious changes in it). Although institutional adaptation is one possible outcome of a critical juncture, this framework allows for two other outcomes that could falsify such expectations: the possibility that institutional stability rather than change predominated during a critical juncture and the possibility that real contingency during a critical juncture leads to state preferences for institutional alternatives to NATO. By allowing for the possibility that institutional change might not occur at a critical juncture, such a view of critical junctures reduces the risk of selection bias among cases on the basis of change and allows for the possibility of negative cases in which change did not occur.[44]

A conceptual framework grounded in historical institutionalism and emphasizing the importance of critical junctures avoids the limitations of both traditional international relations theory and previous institutional accounts in the examination of how NATO adapts. The concept of critical junctures offers a starting point for explaining the institutional basis of adaptation: a critical juncture relaxes the structural constraints on action within the Alliance by challenging NATO's competence or relevance. The resulting expanded range of choice and potential for momentous change introduces an element of contingency in which alternative institutional arrangements are plausible and pursued. This contingency gives rise to a variety of choices for NATO (including adaptation or maintenance of a stable status quo), as well as the possibility that entirely different, non-NATO institutional alternatives are pursued. Figure 2.1 shows the process of how a critical juncture unfolds in NATO and specifies possible outcomes. This study traces this process in order to determine outcomes. Where adaptation occurs, this framework allows for assessment of the key actors.

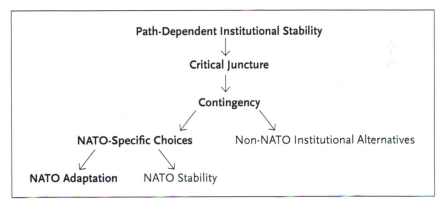

Figure 2.1. NATO critical juncture process and possible outcomes

CHAPTER THREE

Institutional Actors and the Mechanisms of NATO Adaptation

What are the specific processes of adaptation in NATO, and who are the key actors in these developments?[1] The adaptive mechanisms identified here focus on the roles of bureaucratic or "institutional" actors, meaning those actors who represent NATO itself and not its member-states or other stakeholders. This focus qualifies a key finding of this study that institutional actors have played a consequential and underappreciated role in how NATO adapts. Internal changes to NATO's formal organization and external changes to its "strategy" serve as units of analysis for what kinds of adaptation occur. These ideas proceed according to five points.

First, institutions resist adaptation. This resistance is a source of stability but also a starting point for explaining how adaptation occurs. Environmental uncertainty, organizational traits such as standardized routines, and sociological influences all serve as sources of resistance to change. Institutional change is therefore not trivial or automatic, and these sources of stability provide clues into how actors overcome resistance in the processes of institutional adaptation.

Second, power is central to explaining how institutional adaptation occurs. This point builds on concepts from historical institutionalism and involves five detailed claims: (1) adaptation is a political process in which the dynamics of power are essential, (2) institutions structure the power relations of states and other actors, (3) adaptation involves bargaining and negotiation, (4) history affects how an institution adapts, and (5) a multiplicity of interests expands opportunity for political influence.

Third, although institutions structure the power relations of states and other actors, they also have powers of their own. These powers, which are related to institutions' bureaucratic nature, allow institutional actors to exercise autonomy and independence. Although states may constrain institutional actors and retain considerable powers of their own, institutional actors can play consequential roles in facilitating adaptation. This point is essential to the finding that institutional actors indeed have played such roles in NATO.

Fourth, institutional actors facilitate adaptation through specific mechanisms, which include convening, agenda-setting, delegating, information-sharing, delaying, moderating, and co-opting. These mechanisms may be pursued alone or in combination and depend on the independent agency of institutional actors, as well as the constraining influences of structure, member-states, and other actors.

Finally, an important characteristic of institutional adaptation is that it can have internal and external dimensions. Internal adaptation concerns changes to the bureaucratic or organizational structure of the institution, while external adaptation relates to changes in the institution's output and impact on its environment. For security institutions like NATO, the concept of strategy is introduced as the unit of analysis for external institutional output.

Institutional Resistance to Adaptation

The sources of institutional stability are foundational to analyses of institutional change. The regular practices and rules of institutions are a form of social order, of which the reduction of uncertainty through stability is a core purpose. Even institutions that are meant to promote change (or innovation, transformation, etc.) tend to do so in a relatively stable manner.[2] Therefore, in order to understand change, it is useful to understand the forces of stability that must be overcome.[3] Although stabilizing forces are not always strong enough to prevent change, they may act as a countervailing pressure against change even as it is occurring. An institution's stability is thus both a source of resistance to change and a characteristic of any change process.

Uncertainty plays a key role in the stability of institutions. As rational choice approaches in institutionalism describe, institutions reflect patterns of regular behavior. Institutions are stable because actors cannot improve their situation by making other choices within the given institutional setting.[4] Stability does not imply satisfaction, however. Actors may not be able to achieve their optimal preference because of the constraining preferences of other actors and/or because of the rules of the institution. Rational actors incorporate expectations about the behavior of other actors in their calculations of how to maximize the attainment of their preferences. Stable institutions reduce uncertainty, which leads to more accurate expectations of other actors.[5] Proposed changes to institutions upset these expectations and increase uncertainty. Consequently, even if an actor is likely to benefit from a proposed change, the actor may be reluctant to support the change because it is difficult to predict how institutional change will unfold once begun. Actors may therefore prefer the imperfect status quo to the uncertainty of institutional change.[6]

Uncertainty is important not only to internal interactions among actors within the institutional context but also to the external impacts of the institution's wider environment. As James Thompson explained in his seminal work, formal institutions often attempt to reduce uncertainty by establishing a division of labor in which certain bureaus manage issues directly related to the external environment, while others concentrate on the internal and technical aspects of organizational management, planning, and control.[7] Within NATO's contemporary International Staff, for example, the Public Diplomacy Division may engage with the external environment through media and other outlets, while the Office of the Financial Controller may focus more on internal organizational management. Divisions of labor such as these insulate the various institutional partitions, isolating them from adaptation schemes and serving as further sources of stability.

In complex formal institutions, the forces of stability are likely to be compounded by the size and complexity of the organizational structure. Graham Allison's organizational process model highlights the extent to which regular patterns of behavior (e.g., standard operating procedures and routines) complicate processes of change in large organizations.[8] According to this model, large organizations standardize routines in order to coordinate the efforts of disparate actors across the organization. Divisions of labor and the resulting isolation of different institutional partitions generate the need for such standardization. But such standardization and division impose constraints on administrative feasibility, limit flexibility, and contribute to an overall resistance to deviation from the established routines.[9] These dynamics do not preclude change but instead emphasize that change in large formal institutions does not occur "quickly or easily."[10]

In addition to these rational choice and formal organizational impediments to institutional change, sociological approaches to the study of institutions further highlight the stabilizing potential of embedded informal institutions.[11] Social influences on formal institutions can be normative or cognitive. Normative influences guide how individuals believe they should act given their particular role in an institutional context. These influences can be prejudicial to doing things in new or different ways. The rationale to continue a certain practice because "that's the way we've always done it" reflects this kind of normative influence. Cognitively, institutions may affect not only what individuals believe they should do but also the possibilities regarding what they could do. In other words, such "cognitive scripts" reduce the likelihood that new ideas will occur to anyone in the first place—"I didn't even think about doing things that way!" Institutions thus have both normative and cognitive influence that may guide preferences and the awareness of possible alternatives.[12] Informal institutions therefore promote continuity and stability and are thus a further source of resistance to institutional change.

Power and Institutional Adaptation

Given the array of factors that promote institutional stability, it is by no means trivial that institutional change occurs at all. But in the way that rational choice approaches offered a starting point for analysis of institutional stability, historical and sociological institutionalism offer useful insights for the examination of sources and characteristics of change. Central to these explanations of institutional change are considerations of power.[13]

The idea that power relations among institutional actors is a starting point for understanding institutional change has its origins in historical institutionalism.[14] This focus on power relations stands in contrast to rational choice approaches, which often deemphasize the political nature of institutions and potential for change in them.[15] Power, broadly defined as the capacity to impose one's will on others, is essential in any political process.[16] Sources of actors' power may reflect material capability and resources, social capabilities such as information or relationships, or normative biases such as trust and credibility. Rather than a "game" among "rational" actors with fixed and given preferences, institutions can be conceptualized as political environments in which actor preferences derive from an assessment of interests and outcomes derive from power interactions. Adaptation is accordingly a function of power politics.

Institutions structure power relations. Historical institutionalism emphasizes how institutional rules, procedures, and norms structure power relations by privileging certain actors over others or certain sources of power over others.[17] Consider, for example, the "veto power" of the permanent five members of the United Nations Security Council compared to the "consensus rule" in the North Atlantic Council (NAC). The veto power, which derives from the Security Council's voting rules, establishes a power structure in which some states are privileged over others. By contrast, the consensus rule for making decisions in the NAC also structures power, but does so in a way that equilibrates rather than differentiates the power of states. Thus, according to the rule, the votes of Iceland and Albania in the NAC carry the same weight as the United States or

France, for example.[18] Moreover, this consensus rule also mitigates power derived from noninstitutional sources (e.g., material wealth or military capability), underlining the importance of institutional rules. Institutional procedures and norms also structure power relations. For another NATO example, consider the "silence procedure," which involves the distribution of a proposed decision and a specified time after which silence is deemed to communicate assent.[19] Such a procedure entails costs for opposing a decision or change, thus empowering the administratively competent and the well resourced. Moreover, such a procedure also creates norms against "breaking silence," for which opposition is expected to be nontrivial and violations may entail negative diplomatic or social consequences.

Power affects the ability of actors to mobilize others to support or oppose change and involves bargaining and negotiation. Bargaining power is partially a function of the substance of the issue being negotiated. As anyone who has tried to buy a used car or obtain a favor from a coworker knows, the more imperative a proposed change is to a given actor, the less bargaining power that actor may have in a negotiation. Conversely, an actor that is indifferent to change may exercise greater bargaining power relative to other actors.

But bargaining power can also derive from negotiating style and skill. Even when the substance of a negotiation does not favor the bargaining position of an actor, a skilled negotiator may be able to achieve collective gains by identifying areas of mutual advantage.[20] This is especially the case given a collective action problem, which arises when group benefits are possible but difficult to realize.[21] Skilled negotiators may employ techniques such as building coalitions in order to stimulate collective action, which can be formalized through adaptations in institutions that promote continuance of the collective action.[22] Bargaining and negotiation style thus reflect the power relations among actors in processes of institutional adaptation.

The politics of negotiation and bargaining have an especially important role when proposed institutional adaptations involve multiple interests. These situations complicate actor preferences and create greater room for bargaining and negotiation to influence preference formation and decision-making.[23] Actor preferences regarding a proposed change are likely to have multiple sources according to the multiple interests at stake. This is common in complex, real-world institutional settings. Actors may have interests that are largely internal to the institution, such as the maximization of power or influence relative to other actors. Yet actors may also have interests related to the external capacity of the organization, such as the efficient accomplishment of tasks delegated to the organization. Such multiple interests are not always aligned. Conflicting interests imply ambiguous preferences with respect to a proposed institutional change. For example, in considering the NATO proposal to remilitarize Germany less than a decade after the end of World War II, France had a strong incentive to prevent the rearmament of its former wartime enemy yet also possessed an interest in encouraging German rearmament in order to strengthen Cold War defenses. Bargaining and negotiation may emphasize the importance of certain interests over others, influencing the preferences and decisions of actors with respect to proposed institutional adaptations.

Finally, historical patterns of power relations and previous instances of change within a similar institutional context also structure power relations among actors. In particular, history exerts a strong influence on the social and normative aspects of power. Sociological institutionalism stresses that norms and identities affect institutional politics because actors interpret proposed changes in terms of institutional norms. An actor's preference for or against institutional change may be based not only on an assessment of material interest but also on norms of fairness with regard to the distribution of gains and the sharing of burdens and risks.[24] For example, debates within NATO regularly invoke the concept of "burden-sharing" in discussing the relative contributions of NATO members to contemporary expeditionary operations.[25]

Power is thus an essential element in institutional change. Institutions structure power relations among actors. Power manifests itself in the ability of actors to mobilize others to support or oppose change, and change necessarily involves bargaining or negotiation. The importance of bargaining and negotiation is especially crucial when the multiple interests of actors complicate preferences and expand openings for politics to influence preference formation. Historical patterns of power relations, norms, and other informal institutions also play specific roles in the processes of institutional change. However, it is important to add one qualification: although this analysis identifies power relations among actors as essential to understanding institutional adaptation, it does not specify which actors are likely to be most important. An empirical and historical approach remains necessary to identify key actors in the specific circumstances of a given case.

The Sources of Institutional Power, Independence, and Agency

Institutions structure power relations among actors. But institutions may also themselves be actors. The politics of institutional adaptation involve power relations among the members of an institution. Institutional actors themselves possess power and have interests at stake in the institution. The power and interest of the institution give it the capacity to exercise autonomous, independent agency in addition to structuring the power relations of others. A key finding of this study is that NATO's institutional actors have played consequential and largely underappreciated roles as independent actors in precisely this way.

The observation that institutions have the capacity for independent agency is an important conceptual departure from theories that view institutions only as forums or structures for the configuration of sovereign states. This structural view treats institutions as locations in which others act but assigns no independent capacity for action to the institution itself.[26] Such structural approaches allow for uncomplicated and elegant analyses, but at the risk of oversimplification.[27] As Michael Barnett and Martha Finnemore report in their empirical studies, "Yes, IOs [international organizations] are constrained by states, but the notion that they are passive mechanisms with no independent agendas of their own is not borne out by any detailed empirical study of an IO that we have found."[28] In fact, the multiple interests, agendas, and sources of power and agency may be especially acute in larger and more complex institutions, such as NATO with its permanent secretariat and international staffs; the integrated military structure; the professional communities of military officers, diplomats, and civil servants; and beneficiaries of and participants in NATO programs, among other potential actors. In other words, the simplifying assumption that institutions are a neutral forum for states alone discounts the potential and observed truth that institutional actors may exercise independent agency.

An understanding of how international institutions exercise independence requires further consideration of power. As previously described, institutions can be thought of as political environments in which actor preferences derive from an assessment of interests and outcomes emerge from power interactions. Just as states serve as actors in this political environment, so can institutions exercise independent agency in their own setting.

A key difference between state and institutional actors, however, lies in the sources of their power. The sources of state power arise largely outside the institutional context, even though institutions may further structure their relations. State power derives importantly from material capabilities such as population, geography, economic wealth, and military capability; social resources such as diplomacy, governmental leadership, and information; and norms such as state sovereignty.[29] International institutions do not share the same sources of power as states. Rather, institutional power is largely constituted in the institution itself. The institution's very existence and control over its own processes are essential sources of institutional power. As Barnett and Finnemore explain, international institutions "can become autonomous sites of authority, independent from the state 'principals' who may have created them, because of power flowing from at least two sources: (1) the legitimacy of the rational-legal authority they embody, and (2) control over technical expertise and information."[30] Because these two sources of power are part of what characterizes the existence of an institution in the first place (i.e., institutions have these things by definition), such powers can be understood as an effect of the way institutions are constituted. This constitutive effect lends institutions the power necessary for autonomous action.

Max Weber's classic study of bureaucracy offers important insights into these two sources of institutional power. A bureaucracy, like any formal institution, is an established organization with specific purposes. Weber noted that the rational, legal basis of bureaucratic authority is viewed as particularly legitimate in modern civilization.[31] The impersonal "rule of law," as opposed to the subjective rule of a prince or tyrant, is the basis of modern authority. Because bureaucracies embody rules and rational processes, people view them as legitimate and submit to their authority. As Weber describes, "in legal authority, submission does not rest upon the belief and devotion to charismatically gifted persons . . . or upon piety toward a personal lord and master. . . . Rather submission under legal authority is based upon an *impersonal* bond to the generally defined and functional 'duty of office.' The official duty . . . is fixed by *rationally established* norms, by enactments, decrees, and regulations in such a manner that the legitimacy of the authority becomes the legality of the general rule."[32] Bureaucracies are thus powerful when they are exercising their "official duty" by following procedures or regulations and enforcing rules.

Weber argues that a second source of institutional power derives from information and expertise, and the special control that institutional actors possess in these respects. Details relating to institutional rules and procedures are more familiar to institutional actors than to actors outside the institution. Knowledge of these rules, already important as a source of legitimacy, constitutes a specialized technical expertise not available to others.[33] This expertise extends not only to procedural competence gained from training and experience but also to knowledge of the substantive content of bureaucratic activity. In other words, bureaucrats are knowledgeable about *how* the bureaucracy works and also about *what* the bureaucracy is working on. Weber acknowledged that expertise and control of information provides a technical function in helping a bureaucracy operate efficiently but that these features also invest bureaucrats with power over other actors.[34]

These two sources of power allow institutions to act in an independent way. In relating these powers and the concept of independence to IOs, Kenneth Abbott and Duncan Snidal explain that "independence produce[s] political effects. . . . Independence, in particular, enables IOs to shape understandings, influence the terms of state interactions, elaborate norms, and mediate or resolve member states' disputes. The acts of independent IOs may be accorded special legitimacy, and they affect the legitimacy of members' actions."[35] Thus the legitimizing authority that derives from the appearance of impersonal and apolitical functions results ironically in the accumulation of significant political power in international institutions.[36]

Institutional powers are not necessarily strong or unconstrained, however. Whatever the constitutive sources of institutional power and independence, it is important to recall that institutional powers operate in the context of a wider external environment that may serve to either further enable or constrain autonomy. In particular, the power and autonomy of international institutions does not deny the substantial power and agency of states.[37] States and external circumstances may serve to further promote or constrain the independence of international institutions. Whatever the sources of institutional independence, institutional power and agency do not exist in a vacuum, and external factors therefore limit the degree of institutional independence and autonomy.

These insights provide a way to understand the sources and characteristics of independent power and autonomy in international institutions. The legitimacy of an international institution's rational-legal authority gives it the power that is independent of the states or other actors that created it. In exercising the institution's independence, institutional actors also benefit from their possession of expert information about the character of the institution, as well as privileged information about the substantive content of the institution's activities. States and noninstitutional actors retain important powers of their own, but institutional actors also possess certain powers, including those to facilitate and shape other actors' behavior.

The Institutional Mechanisms of Adaptation

Through their own power and autonomy as actors, international institutions can play independent and even consequential roles as actors in facilitating their own adaptation. The various sources of institutional stability suggest a number of obstacles that actors would need to surmount in adapting institutions, such as the resistance to change engendered by uncertainty. As discussed previously, it is essential to appreciate the role of power relations in institutional adaptation, particularly as it relates to bargaining and negotiation, the expectations derived from historical incidences of change, and the potentially diverse interests of actors. The specific sources of institutional power, namely rational-legal legitimacy and control over technical expertise and information, suggest several mechanisms through which international institutions may act to facilitate their own adaptation.

Convening

Institutional actors convene other actors—member-states, other institutional actors, or external players—to locations for discussion or decision-making. Convening is sometimes significant for the very fact that actors meet at all, especially when conflict or other circumstances decrease its likelihood. In other cases, convening affects the way actors interact, even down to details such as the speaking order or shape of a conference table. In any event, convening actions structure ensuing discussion and decision-making to some degree.

Agenda-Setting

Institutional actors shape the substantive content of what states and other actors do and do not address. This is especially likely in instances where institutional actors have also employed the convening mechanism. Like other institutional functions, agenda-setting powers may be formally described in an institution's charter or other agreements, or they may develop informally.

Delegating

Institutional actors refer work, issues, or discussion to different institutional settings or actors. In a sufficiently large organization, delegating may occur exclusively among various institutional actors. In other cases, institutions may also be able to delegate to states or other actors. Delegating sometimes implies the creation of new institutional settings, which may entail formal and lasting organizational reform or informal, ad hoc working groups or task forces with only limited mandates.

Information-Sharing

Institutional actors facilitate the sharing of information that is directly relevant to bargaining and negotiation. The institution's control over technical expertise and information is especially pertinent in this regard. The sharing of information directly militates against the uncertainty that serves as a source of resistance to institutional change. Furthermore, the selective use of information-sharing in bargaining and negotiation may play a determining role in preference formation among actors with multiple interests at stake.

Delaying

Paradoxically, institutional actors may facilitate adaptation by slowing it. Especially when combined with agenda-setting, delaying may be a deliberate tactic to avoid discussions or decision-making until conditions for change become favorable. Whether deliberate or due to the unavoidably gradual nature of organizational processes, delays also allow actors to prepare for and accept change. All other things being equal, rapid change is more alarming than slow change. Time may allow actors to "warm up to" or "get used to" proposals for change. In other words, delays maximize opportunities for information-sharing and reducing uncertainty, which may be particularly acute during periods of rapid change.

Moderating

Institutional actors temper conflict among other actors and minimize the apparent significance of acrimony and crises. Moderating plays an important role in bargaining and negotiation and reinforces the rational-legal legitimacy of the institution. Moderating may also increase the political time and space available for the implementation of institutional adaptations. This political effect reduces the urgency and the likelihood of uncompromising opposition to adaptation or to the institution itself.

Co-opting

Institutional actors may appropriate the resources (e.g., material, social, or normative) of states or other institutions. Co-opting may be formal and publicly acknowledged, such as when one institution absorbs the legacy structures and responsibilities of another. This formal co-opting is a kind of institutional adaptation unto itself. Alternatively, co-opting may also be informal and generally unacknowledged. In these cases, institutional actors may leverage the resources of states or other independent actors in pursuing institutional activities.[38] This informal co-opting is particularly likely when institutional actors are "dual-hatted," meaning they have more than one identity or role insofar as they are both institutional actors and actors of some other institution or state.[39]

Institutional actors may pursue these mechanisms alone or in combination in order to facilitate institutional adaptation. However, independent institutional action in accordance with these mechanisms does not guarantee that adaptation will occur. Empirical, process-tracing analysis remains suitable for demonstrating whether and to what extent these mechanisms have causal impact.

Units of Analysis in Institutional Adaptation: Organization and Strategy

Although the institutional mechanisms of adaptation suggest how actors might facilitate adaptation, they do not specify what kinds of adaptation might occur. Adaptations correspond to the kinds of things that institutions are and do, and can be conceptualized in two dimensions: internal and external. Institutions have a substantially procedural internal dimension and an external dimension that relates to the institution's impact on its wider environment. Adaptation, therefore, can be internally related to an institution's structure or organizational processes and externally concerned with changes to institutional outputs. This distinction may be more conceptual than real, as a single program of institutional adaptation may have both internal and external dimensions. However, the conceptual distinction is nonetheless important because it allows for the identification of specific units of analysis in institutional adaptation and their systematic evaluation in each of the cases. For NATO, the unit of analysis for internal adaptation is its formal organization, while NATO strategy serves as the unit of analysis for external adaptation.

Identifying internal institutional adaptation is relatively straightforward. These adaptations relate to how an institution is constituted and its institutional ways and means, rather than its ends and purposes. Examples include changes to the bureaucratic or organizational structure of the institution; the specific tasks that are the basis of the institution's rational-legal authority and specialized expertise; and the institution's processes, including rules, routines, and standard operating procedures. Adaptations concerning the internal aspects of the formal organization are the most unambiguous to ascertain, although instances of adaptation may also affect embedded norms or other informal institutions.

Identifying external institutional adaptation is less straightforward because of the potential difficulty of identifying institutional effectiveness. If formal institutions are established with specific purposes, the most intuitive way to assess outcomes would be to measure the extent to which the institution's purposes are obtained. However, this approach tends to elide an institution's causal role in outcome achievement and risks mistaking correlation for causation. Outcomes may be the product of institutional performance but are also affected by other factors, such as the size and material resources of the institution, the scale of institutional goals and mission, and the wider environment, including the activities of other actors or institutions.[40] If the purpose of an institution is to maintain peace in Europe, for example, the incidence of peace in Europe is not necessarily a consequence of institutional performance. Outcomes may be a result of institutional efforts, but they may equally or even principally derive from other factors. Measuring outcomes is especially difficult for international institutions with purposes that are difficult objectively to define or measure (e.g., peace, security, stability).

A better way to identify external institutional adaptation is to focus on changes in the specific *outputs* of institutions. Whereas "outcomes," in the sense of broad achievement of institutional purposes, may be the result of both institutional and noninstitutional factors, "outputs" refer specifically to the products of an institution's processes and capacities. They are the intermediate observable effects of institutions, if not necessarily the determining causes of achievement or disappointment in the realization of broad issue outcomes.[41] Examples of outputs for international institutions might include the publication of new institutional goals or purposes, or the extent to which states or other actors participate in or comply with institutional initiatives. An institution's external adaptations can be more clearly identified when measuring changes to these observable outputs rather than changes in the wider environment.

The concept of strategy is useful when examining institutional outputs for NATO. Although strategy is a particularly relevant concept in studying security institutions, the term enjoys such broad contemporary usage that institutions of almost every kind are said to employ it.[42] J. C. Wylie, an important twentieth-century writer on military strategy, provides a useful definition of the term: "A plan of action designed in order to achieve some end; a purpose together with a system of measure for its accomplishment."[43] The essential insight in this definition is that strategy is about the connection between means and ends. Wylie was not the first to highlight the means-ends logic of strategy, but his definition captures the soundness of Clausewitz and others while expressing the relationship in highly general terms.[44] Strategy in this conception is a helpful concept when interpreting the intermediate observable effects that connect an institutional process to a particular outcome in an institution's environment. Strategy may or may not be the main causal factor in the outcome, but changes in strategy can be seen as evidence of external adaptation.

Strategy, therefore, will serve as the main unit of analysis signifying external adaptation in NATO. Strategy is a contested concept, but there are three reasons why its use in this sense is appropriate. First, strategy as conceived here is an unambiguous institutional output. Wylie's definition treats strategy as a product, a plan that is the result of some kind of activity. Other theorists define strategy not as a product but as an evolving process in which "no plan survives first contact with reality" and that needs constant revaluation.[45] Process-oriented strategic thinkers treat actual plans as subordinate to strategy or as the intermediate outputs of a larger strategy-making process. Either way, though, plans are made in strategy, and the use of these plans in this study as an institutional output does not deny ongoing processes but rather allows for the specification of precise, discrete units of analysis.

Second, this use of strategy is substantively and historically suitable. NATO is a security institution with its historical origins in the early Cold War. This is the time and focus of Wylie's writing and does not require the transposing of concepts from alien historical periods or types of activity. Wylie's definition is not based on observations of war in ancient China or Napoleonic Europe, nor is it a reflection of contemporary business literature.[46] This is most significant in the sense that military strategy is usually conceived with respect to a single country. The experience of World War II and subsequently in NATO, however, showed that strategy could be aggregated among countries in a coalition or alliance. Strategy is always aggregated at some level (e.g., among the various military departments and political authorities of a single state), so acknowledging strategy at the level of an international institution reflects its modern character.[47]

Third, and most important, is that NATO is conscious of strategy and intentionally views the making of strategy to be a core institutional task. Some theorists, such as those who examine the concept of strategic culture, consider strategy to be the inevitable or even unintentional result of actors in strategic situations.[48] Such views of strategy risk vagueness and errors of interpretation that are not necessary. NATO has endeavored intentionally to make strategy. The institution set out to devise plans of action with respect to its purposes; articulated means, ends, and the ways that connect them; and committed these plans explicitly to paper, often with the title "Strategic Concept." For clarity and precision, the present volume refers to these plans in the same way NATO does: as strategy.

Although processes of institutional adaptation can be ideally conceptualized as internal or external, real-world adaptations do not necessarily fit only one of the ideal types. Some adaptations involve both internal processes and external outputs. Strategy, especially, tends to blur perfect theoretical distinctions between internal processes and external outputs. Because strategy is, by the definition adopted here, a device that connects internal processes and means to external ends and purposes, it is neither exclusively internal nor external when put into practice.[49] The implementation of external strategic goals is likely to involve internal procedural adaptations and vice versa. For instance, institutional membership is a clear example of a real-world adaptation that has both internal and external dimensions. A change in institutional membership involves internal changes to an institution's organizational structure and processes yet also affects the institution's external environment and purposes. However, the conceptual distinction is nonetheless important because different kinds of adaptation may involve different configurations of power and interests among actors. An examination of changes in organization and strategy allows for a systematic analysis of how adaptation occurs.

Adaptation Processes and Units of Analysis in NATO

The literature on institutional adaptation provides a number of general insights from which this chapter has drawn theoretical propositions about the processes of adaptation in NATO, as well as specified its units of analysis. The sources of institutional stability provide foundational insights into how adaptation occurs. The rational choice literature introduces uncertainty as a potential obstacle to change, suggesting that adaptation may be more likely when actors have greater information about its implications. Organization theory shows that the more highly institutionalized an organization is, the more likely adaptation is to be slow and difficult, if accomplished at all. Historical institutionalism introduces power as the fundamental concept in explaining how adaptation occurs. Weberian conceptions of bureaucracy contribute to the idea that international institutions like NATO can have independent power and autonomy. Table 3.1 summarizes the specific mechanisms through which institutional actors use these powers to facilitate adaptation. Table 3.2 shows the units of analysis this study will use for internal and external adaptation in NATO.

TABLE 3.1.
How Institutional Actors
Facilitate Adaptation

Mechanisms
Convening
Agenda setting
Delegating
Information sharing
Delaying
Moderating
Co-opting

TABLE 3.2.
Units of Analysis for Institutional Adaptation

Adaptive Dimension	Generic Institutional Units of Analysis	NATO-Specific Units of Analysis
Internal	Formal organization	International staff/secretariat, committee structure, NATO agencies, Integrated military structure, etc.
External	Observable institutional output	NATO strategy & "strategic concept"

PART TWO

CASE STUDIES OF
NATO ADAPTATION

CHAPTER FOUR

The West German Question in the Early Cold War, 1950–1955

No sooner had the North Atlantic Treaty been signed in 1949 than the outbreak of the Korean War in 1950 gave new urgency to the problems of the Cold War in Europe. At this first critical juncture in the Atlantic Alliance were questions about not only the security of the established treaty powers but also how to deal with the possibility of German rearmament in the context of an intensifying Cold War. The strategic challenge of addressing Germany's role in European security during a period of cooling relations with the West's erstwhile wartime Soviet ally also accompanied an organizational challenge to NATO in the form of the European Defence Community (EDC), because intra-European solutions served as a potential institutional alternative to transatlantic answers to the German question.

Ultimately, NATO adapted to address the internal imperatives of the original treaty powers while bolstering its external strategic credibility. The inclusion of West Germany as a member of the Alliance added that country to the military balance in favor of the allies in the Cold War, while institutionalization of NATO's formal organizations, such as the integrated military command, reflected concerns about the need for strategic readiness and the requirement to provide an internal check on the rearmament of Germany. However effective, this compromise was long and slow in the making, such that five years would transpire between the initial cause for urgency in the Korean War and the resulting organizational and strategic adaptation in NATO.

Several factors stand out in this case of how NATO adapted. In terms of key actors, both the positions of supreme allied commander in Europe (SACEUR) and secretary-general were developed during this period, though it was the chairman of the North Atlantic Council Deputies, Charles Spofford, who played a particularly active institutional role in NATO's initial developments. The early creation of various functional capacities within the Council Deputies fore-shadowed the burgeoning of future NATO bureaucracy, though growth of the international staff was balanced against a close guarding of national sovereignty and decision-making authority in the Council of member-state governments. Institutional actors thus exercised important powers of convening, agenda-setting, and delegating, which allowed them to pursue organizational and strategic adaptation while moderating conflict among state actors. Institutional actors often benefited from being "dual-hatted" with national responsibilities as well, allowing them to invoke national credibility, prestige, and power in the service of their NATO-specific institutional duties. The laborious informal and backchannel institutional negotiations within NATO dramatically lengthened the process of institutional adaptation but also ensured that officially proposed changes would enjoy broad and durable coalitions favoring change.

The Alliance and the West German Question in Early Cold War Europe

In the emerging Cold War structure of European security, the so-called German question remained one of the most important unresolved structural issues in 1950. In the five years since the end of World War II, a system of postwar European relations had become otherwise clear. Politically, the East-West divide in Europe was entrenched. Whereas Winston Churchill had publicly proclaimed the existence of an Iron Curtain in 1946, the United States' launch of the containment policy and the Truman Doctrine in 1947 had made the division a matter of official policy.[1] The West would not interfere in East European affairs, such as when the communists effected a coup in Czechoslovakia in February 1948. But communist expansion in the West would be contained, as was the case with American military aid to Greece and Turkey.[2]

In economics, the Marshall Plan was providing development assistance for economic recovery in sixteen West European countries, including the western parts of Germany.[3] According to President Truman, the Marshall Plan and the Truman Doctrine were "two halves of the same walnut," which is to say that both were elements of the containment strategy.[4] While the Truman Doctrine was a program of military aid, the Marshall Plan reflected an economic approach to containment, with the assumption that economic distress fostered political unrest and communism. Moreover, participation in the Marshall Plan required a capitalist, market-based economy with transparency and currency exchange arrangements that were only compatible with the Western system.[5]

Regarding security arrangements, the successive Anglo-French Dunkirk (1947), five-power Brussels (1948), and North Atlantic (1949) treaties provided classic military alliance guarantees for, in the latter case, twelve West European and North American countries.[6] In the event of renewed conflict in Europe, an attack against any one signatory to these treaties would be considered an attack against all.

The Soviet Union, of course, represented the greatest potential adversary of the Western powers. The Red Army was the largest in the world, mechanized, experienced, in occupation of vast territory in Eastern Europe, and much larger than the Western armies that had dramatically reduced in size since World War II. Moreover, Soviet behavior gave increasingly threatening meaning to its foreign policy intent. Marxist revolutionaries were active in several West European countries, particularly France and Italy. Communists in Czechoslovakia overthrew the pro-Western leader Jan Masaryk on February 25, 1948, and killed him two weeks later. The British Embassy in Washington sent a secret message the following month informing the United States that the Soviet Union was aggressively pressuring Norway to conclude a security pact.[7] And the 320-day Berlin blockade, among the Cold War's first major crises, began on June 24, 1948. The Western system of alliances, which developed in response to these events and culminated in the North Atlantic Treaty, provided politico-military solidarity in the West and served as a warning against potential aggression from the East.

Yet these alliances represented security guarantees not only against the threat of Soviet aggression but also quite explicitly against the possibility of a resurgent Germany. With World War II not long over, concern about Germany's future figured prominently in the security agenda of Western powers, and for understandable reasons. The 1940 campaign in World War II represented the third time in seventy years that Germany had invaded France. Belgium and Holland had likewise been in the path of advancing German armies. Britain and the United States had twice been drawn into great wars on the continent. The recent war was only the latest reminder of the consequences that flowed from a failure to answer the German question: how could this large and powerful country located in the center of Europe be integrated into a sustainable European order?[8]

The original intention among some of the victorious allies was that Germany should be kept permanently weak and demilitarized. The Morgenthau Plan of 1944, for example, specifically envisioned a Germany with no heavy industry capable of sustaining a modern mechanized military.[9] The Monnet Plan of 1946 (named for Jean Monnet, the same French statesmen better known for his later contributions to European integration) sought to place industrial areas on the Ruhr and Saarland under French control in order to reduce German economic capacity both absolutely and relative to France.[10] Although the Western powers ultimately rejected punitive economic approaches in the style of Versailles, German rearmament or inclusion in postwar Western alliances was initially out of the question. Quite the reverse, the Treaty of Dunkirk was explicitly directed against Germany, with signatories "[d]etermined to collaborate in measures of mutual assistance in the event of any renewal of German aggression . . . with the object of preventing Germany from becoming again a menace to peace."[11] The Treaty of Brussels and the North Atlantic Treaty became progressively more general and comprehensive in the language of the treaty text, but the Brussels Treaty also dealt specifically with Germany and began with a resolve to "take such steps as may be held to be necessary in the event of a renewal by Germany of a policy of aggression."[12] The North Atlantic Treaty did not specify any particular adversary, but the official negotiations leading to it included only the Brussels Treaty powers plus Canada and the United States.[13] Thus, unlike economic initiatives such as the Marshall Plan, Germany was initially and expressly excluded from postwar military alliances.

Taken together, the situation in 1950 was such that the German question remained a significant, unresolved structural issue in early Cold War Europe. General developments had established the East-West political, economic, and military rivalry of the Cold War with a divided Germany and Berlin perhaps its most emblematic features. The establishment of two rival German states, the western Federal Republic (from May 23, 1949) and the eastern Democratic Republic (from October 7, 1949), did as much to underscore questions about Germany's role as it did to resolve them. Precisely how the two Germanys would fit into this new order remained unsettled. In the West, Germany's role remained incongruous: economically welcome in the Western system but pointedly excluded from its military security arrangements. This situation was untenable, since political stability, economic vitality, and military strength were all necessary resources for the Western strategy of containing communism, but this otherwise comprehensive approach to European security only partially included Germany. If ambivalence prevailed as to whether the most significant threat was in Germany or in the Soviet Union, later events in 1950 would force the West to take up the remaining aspects of the German question with greater conclusiveness.[14]

Meanwhile, in the Alliance, development of any standing organization or strategy had initially proceeded at a relatively incremental pace of path-dependent stability. The text of the North Atlantic Treaty did not call for the creation of the complex international organization into which NATO would grow. Rather, the treaty's organizational prescriptions mostly reflected traditional notions of military alliances as foreign policy commitments rather than formal organizations. An exception to this is the treaty's Article 9, which established "a Council" (i.e., the North Atlantic Council) and empowered it to "set up subsidiary bodies as may be necessary; in particular it shall establish immediately a defence committee which shall recommend measures for the implementation of Articles 3 and 5."[15] But this did not imply that NATO would one day need to create a burgeoning organization. Indeed, the treaty did not even insist that the Council be a permanent or continuously operating institution, but merely that it "shall be so organized as to be able to meet promptly."[16]

It is in some ways remarkable that any permanent structure existed at all in view of the treaty's limited organizational provisions. To be sure, NATO organization that did exist in 1950 was disparate and uncoordinated. But it had taken shape to fulfill those provisions of the North Atlantic Treaty that called for organization. During its first meeting in September 1949, the Council dutifully established the Defence Committee, to consist ordinarily of defence ministers, as stipulated under the treaty. It also established the Military Committee, to be composed of chiefs of staff or other senior military representatives of each member-state. This first Council also set up a "Standing Group" of the Military Committee, which consisted of military representatives from only France, the United Kingdom, and the United States, and which was to function, remarkably, in a continuous fashion in Washington, DC. Finally, the first Council also established five Regional Planning Groups to "develop and recommend to the Military Committee, through the Standing Group," respective regional defense plans. The second North Atlantic Council in November 1949 went further in organizational development by creating the Defence Financial and Economic Committee and the Military Production and Supply Board. Both of these organizations were to have permanent working staffs in London. This trend continued in May 1950, when the Council established a permanent, continuously operating civilian body to carry out the work of the Alliance, known as the Council Deputies (i.e., representatives of each of the member-states' ordinary Council representatives, the foreign ministers). The Council Deputies were to create a "suitable full-time organization composed of highly qualified persons contributed by member governments," which later represented the beginnings of an international civilian staff. Thus, by the end of its first year, NATO consisted of a number of suborganizations, convened at various locations, with some working permanently or continuously and staffed with national representatives and also some international NATO organizational personnel. It is fair to characterize this system of committees as an international institution (as opposed to merely an alliance in the traditional sense of foreign policy commitments) at this stage. But it is also worth mentioning that many of the NATO structures and offices of later years did not yet exist; there was no secretary-general or secretariat, no supreme allied commander, no integrated military structure or military staff, and no coordinated system for aligning the efforts of the committees in place.[17]

Strategically, the Alliance had decided on a concept and adopted a tentative plan with important implications for Germany as a likely battleground. But action to implement the plans was neither swift nor undertaken with much urgency. The Defence Committee, meeting in Paris in December 1949, adopted a strategic concept laying out the general principles for an "integrated defence of the North Atlantic area."[18] This concept stressed the need for peacetime military and economic cooperation with a view toward deterrence and the interoperability of forces if hostilities proved unavoidable. But the North Atlantic Council, in approving the concept in its Washington, DC, session of January 1950, emphasized that all of this was to be done on an intergovernmental basis in line with the treaty principles of "self-help and mutual aid" rather than through the development of any specific organization. A subsequent document that came to be known as the "Medium Term Defence Plan," adopted by the Defence Committee in April 1950 at The Hague, further detailed the policy, strategy, and concept of operations that NATO would plan to have in place by 1954. Significantly, this plan called for the Alliance to do as much as possible to avoid relinquishing territory to an enemy advance, to defend as far east as possible, and, specifically where Western Europe was concerned, to "hold the enemy as far to the east *in Germany* as possible."[19] Thus peacetime preparations in western Germany for defense against possible Soviet aggression would be an unavoidable part of NATO's strategy.[20]

The Medium Term Defence Plan also made clear that the military means required to implement the strategy and concept of operations it envisioned were not available in the spring of 1950. Indeed, the "requirements to meet the 1954 [Medium Term] Defense Plan" called for more than eighty divisions of land forces and ten thousand combat aircraft.[21] At that time, the allies had approximately fourteen divisions and fewer than one thousand aircraft on the continent of Europe. The Soviet Union, by contrast, maintained twenty-five divisions and six thousand combat aircraft forward-based in Eastern Europe, with the further bulk of its armed forces behind its recently enlarged borders.[22] Moreover, NATO forces in Europe were then organized for postwar occupation and administration rather than defense. Several British and American military units in Germany were positioned to the west of their main supply lines and depots (and thus to the rear of any front line in a contest with Soviet forces), for example, and none were deployed in coordinated defensive postures. Reflecting on the disposition of Western forces in a report to the Brussels Treaty powers on June 15, 1950, Field Marshal Montgomery's assessment was thus: "As things stand today and in the foreseeable future, there would be scenes of appalling and indescribable confusion in Western Europe if we were ever attacked by the Russians."[23]

Despite this lack of conventional military preparedness, and despite the fact that the Soviet Union had ended the American monopoly on nuclear weapons with its own test of an atomic device nearly a year earlier on August 29, 1949, swift action to implement the new NATO strategy was not forthcoming. The North Atlantic Council stressed that movement toward the Medium Term Defence Plan goals would occur not as a matter of urgent business but rather with "balanced collective forces in the progressive build-up of defence" from 1950.[24] As Lord Ismay explained: "This reflected the rather leisurely pace of Western rearmament during that period. Clearly the NATO countries intended to take their time about rebuilding their armed strength; and each of them, before deciding on costly and somewhat unpopular measures, had a tendency to 'wait and see what the other fellow was doing.'"[25]

Critical Juncture: The Korean War

The "other fellow," as it turned out, may not have been in other Western European countries but on the Korean peninsula. After years of inconclusive tension over the postwar fate of a divided Korea, Soviet-backed communist North Korean forces began an invasion of US-aligned South Korea on June 25, 1950. This event immediately and profoundly influenced NATO, disrupting the leisurely, path-dependent approach to its organizational development and strategy, and representing a critical juncture for the institution. A communist-initiated war in Asia gave urgency to the real and increased possibility of a similar Cold War conflagration in Europe. If NATO's conventional military readiness had been low prior to the Korean War, the commitment of American conventional forces to Asia crushed any illusions that Alliance-wide weaknesses could be quickly rectified in the event of war in Europe. The inadequacy of NATO's internal organization and external strategy was brought into high relief. This turn of events loosened the constraints on action for powerful actors within the Alliance and meant this equivocation on the German question was no longer an affordable luxury. The decisions taken during this time were likely to be more momentous for NATO than everyday business, not only because NATO was relatively new and young but because settlement of the German question was likely to have long-standing repercussions for European security in the Cold War.

Almost overnight, the outbreak of the Korean War appeared to increase the likelihood of war in Europe. Despite the entrenchment of Cold War tensions in Europe, the prevailing consensus in the West had been that armed hostilities in a "hot" war remained unlikely.[26] This consensus optimism about war's avoidability was at the center of NATO's decision to proceed with slow and progressive development despite its acknowledged military weakness. The Korean War dashed this optimism. It showed, in the first instance, that war was yet possible despite the damage still felt from World War II and the increased hazard of conflict in the nuclear age. But, even more, the particular analogy of Korea to Germany was impossible to avoid: if war would come to a Korea divided by the Cold War, would it happen over a divided Germany too? German Chancellor Konrad Adenauer, for whom the parallel with Korea must have been especially disconcerting, declared: "The fate of the world will not be decided in Korea but in the heart of Europe. I am convinced that Stalin has the same plan for Europe as for Korea. What is happening there is a dress-rehearsal for what is in store for us here."[27] Lord Ismay, writing later, after he became NATO's first secretary-general, generalized somewhat less dramatically: "It was obvious that the sort of outrage which had taken place in far-away Korea could easily be repeated elsewhere. For NATO the period of cautious optimism and slow methodical progress was over."[28]

Korea not only made the prospect of war in Europe seem more likely, but it also made the task of defending Europe appear more difficult. Whereas contemporary NATO strategy emphasized political solidarity and the progressive development of national capabilities that could be organized as needed at a later time, the first few weeks of fighting in Korea demonstrated the limitations of such an approach. The initial Western reaction to the outbreak of war in Korea had been swift and united, but the actual fighting went poorly. The United Nations Security Council decided to support South Korea within two days of the invasion.[29] The United States independently committed its air and naval forces to the defense of South Korea on the same day as the Security Council's decision, and its ground forces arrived within one week under the United Nations mandate. But, in a direct parallel to the potential situation that Western occupation troops would face in Germany, the American units deployed to Korea from postwar occupation duty in Japan were ill-equipped and unprepared for wartime action. Notwithstanding often-heroic resistance and terrible losses, United Nations forces suffered repeated defeats and were pushed to the "Pusan Perimeter" on the tip of the Korean peninsula after just two months of fighting.[30] This turn of events suggested that contemporary NATO assumptions about the ease of preparing and organizing for a defense of Europe were overly optimistic.

An essential lesson from Korea was the centrality of conventional military forces, even in the nuclear age. The conventional fight in Korea showed that NATO could not rationalize its military weakness in Europe by assuming that American strategic air forces could hold back an invading Soviet army from its bases in Britain and North Africa while NATO organized the conventional defense of continental Europe.[31] Massive American air and naval power in the Korean conflict did not prevent early losses, and President Truman firmly rejected proposals to use the atomic bomb in the Korean War.[32] The speed and ease with which North Korean forces had swept through the South's defenses implied the need for better peacetime conventional defenses in Europe, as neither the time necessary to generate them nor the assuredness of nuclear weapons could be counted on to compensate in case of actual hostilities across the Iron Curtain. Especially if NATO's strategy was to hold back Soviet forces as far to the east as possible, a strong conventional military defense would need to be in place at the outbreak of hostilities. All of this served to further increase the salience of the German question insofar as German territory and material resources would be vital to any conventional defense of Europe.

Furthermore, with the United States leading the UN effort in Asia and committing its economic and conventional military resources there,[33] the likelihood of being able to rely on additional American conventional forces in the event of war in Europe was also open to question. Notwithstanding the relatively new North Atlantic Treaty commitments, United States foreign policy had historically been ambivalent about military ties to Europe: from the early days of the American republic and George Washington's farewell advice against entangling alliances, through the isolationism of the 1930s and its reluctance to join the fight against Nazi Germany, even after the fall of France in 1940. Many of the most pressing Cold War concerns for the globally interested superpower were in Asia. The "loss" of China in the formation of the communist People's Republic in 1949 stood as a major setback and seemed to hold the risk of Indochina and other countries "falling like dominos" in similar contests for post–World War II governance in Asia.[34] Efforts to cultivate Japan as a peaceful and friendly country were still fledgling.[35] The outbreak of the Korean War urgently heightened these concerns. Whatever the Korean War indirectly signaled for the risk of an analogous conflict in Europe, the war was obviously a more direct and urgent problem in Asia. As a matter of strategic means, the orientation of American political, economic, and military resources toward Asia limited the resources that the United States might be able to bring to the defense of Europe and entailed the more general risk that the United States might consider its alliance commitments in Europe a second-tier priority.

In addition to the aforementioned strategic problems, the United Nations' experience in Korea had negative implications for NATO's organizational functions and capabilities. Where the UN had achieved swift political action and solidarity (among noncommunist states, at least) in resolving to contest aggression, it lacked the independent organizational capacity to follow through on its resolution. The Security Council almost immediately delegated execution of its efforts in Korea to the United States, and requested other countries to "make such forces and other assistance available to a unified command under the United States of America."[36] But if any questions existed about whether the United States would be politically and militarily willing and able to do the same in Europe, then the UN model in Korea was not one NATO could hope to emulate. At the outbreak of the Korean War, however, NATO's organizational capacity may not have offered any other choice. NATO organizationally consisted of several committees and working groups directed at the aims of policy and alliance solidarity but possessed no organization for the military means needed to defend Europe.

The Korean War had thus shown the inadequacy of NATO strategy and its organization. The need for greater conventional military means and the organization for those means in Europe was clear. The perceived urgency and increased likelihood of war in Europe loosened the existing constraints on thinking and action within the Alliance, opening the door to powerful actors to seek new courses of action, specifically with respect to the German question. Military analysts in France, Britain, and the United States had concluded as far back as 1948 that the rearmament of Germany would be essential for the defense of Western Europe.[37] The critical juncture of the Korean War helped overcome the political obstacles to that eventuality. As Georges-Henri Soutou wrote of France, the place where political obstacles to movement on the German question were strongest: "Now was the time of reckoning: German rearmament was the price to be paid for Western solidarity, for a bigger American involvement in Europe, for an American supreme commander for NATO forces (all things for which the French had been clamouring since 1948). The pretence that the Western alliance was useful as much against Germany than against the Soviet Union (a presence that had been helpful to get French public support for the 1947–9 shift) had outlived its usefulness and had now to be discarded."[38]

The outbreak of the Korean War had been a critical juncture for NATO. By increasing the perceived likelihood of a European war and the apparent difficulty of defending Europe in the event of war, the North Korean invasion disrupted the path-dependent stability of NATO's then-leisurely organization and strategic development by showing its current state to be inadequate to the new assessment of threat. This forced a reckoning with the unpleasant reality that the Alliance could no longer keep the Germans down while also credibly preparing to keep the Russians out, and even suggested that more might have to be done to keep the Americans in, too. The critical juncture significantly loosened the structural constraints on action within the Alliance as to how the German question could be addressed, introducing contingency into the developments that followed. The question then became how this would occur: Would the North Atlantic Treaty Organization endure as the institutional framework for an answer to the German question?

Contingency

Possible, plausible, and considered responses to the challenge of the Korean War's outbreak in Europe involved proposals both within NATO and outside it. Initial proposals in NATO focused on the internal organizational development of military structures and a strategic proposal to rearm Germany within NATO. Non-NATO proposals focused on the pursuit of supranational European plans for communal defense, namely the European Defence Community. This real possibility of non-NATO solutions to the problems raised by the critical juncture meant that NATO's own endurance was by no means a foregone conclusion.

The first proposal for an institutional solution to the German question arose during a meeting of the Council of Europe. The debate that opened in the Consultative Assembly of the Council of Europe on August 9, 1950, featured, as its most important proposal, a plan for a supranational European solution to the German rearmament question. Winston Churchill, then out of office but always a leading figure, dominated the debate with a speech on August 11 advocating a European Army. Churchill argued that a European initiative to even out the conventional military balance in Europe would be the surest means "not only of saving our lives and liberties, but of preventing a third world war."[39] He continued, "We should make a gesture of practical and constructive guidance by declaring ourselves in favour of the immediate creation of a European Army under a unified command and in which we should bear a worthy and honourable part."[40] Churchill's proposal met with approval in the Council of Europe, where the final resolution of the debate read: "The Assembly, in order to express its devotion to the maintenance of peace and its resolve to sustain the action of the Security Council of the United Nations in defence of peaceful peoples against aggression, calls for the immediate creation of a unified European Army, under the authority of a European Minister of Defence, subject to proper European democratic controls and acting in full co-operation with the United States and Canada."[41]

Such a proposal for a supranational solution to the German question followed in the spirit of European federalism that was already finding expression in proposals for integration in other areas. Following discussions with Chancellor Adenauer, French Foreign Minister Robert Schuman proposed at a press conference in May 1950 that the coal and steel industries of France and Germany be placed under a supranational authority in what would be a "first step in the federation of Europe."[42] The Schuman Declaration, as it came to be known, reflected the emergence of a growing group of European federalists that included such notable figures as Jean Monnet as well as Churchill, who had also once called for a "United States of Europe."[43] Notwithstanding the April 1951 Treaty of Paris, in which six continental states acceded to the European Coal and Steel Community (ECSC), Churchill's supranational inclinations did not enjoy support, particularly at home where the attitude of the British government under Prime Minister Clement Atlee reflected a broader aversion to supranationalism.[44]

Within NATO, the response to the Korean War's outbreak came in two varieties. First, institutional actors inside NATO's formal organization began to gather information and develop scenarios for institutional adaptation. Second, proposals for institutional adaptation came from national representatives of Alliance member-states acting within the intergovernmental forum that NATO provided. Member-state decisions would be necessary for any political decision on resolving the German question within NATO, and so national representatives to NATO constituted powerful actors within the Alliance. But the persistent and enterprising activities of internal institutional actors would prove instrumental in positioning NATO as a durable institutional arrangement.

The leading institutional actors inside NATO's formal organization quickly emerged among the Council Deputies. The first meeting of the newly appointed Council Deputies occurred on July 25, 1950, under the chairmanship of Ambassador Charles M. Spofford, who had been selected by the other deputies to preside over the group while serving concurrently as deputy for the United States. Spofford, a prominent New York lawyer who had been awarded the French Legion of Honour and the Order of the British Empire as an army staff officer in the North African and Mediterranean theaters of World War II, had departed his law firm earlier in 1950 for what would amount to a two-year assignment at NATO.[45] While dangling the possibility of increased military aid from the United States,

Spofford requested all other deputies collect and return information from their member governments on their willingness to take steps toward more rapid re-armament. In a sign of the sense of urgency, all replies were delivered in just four weeks.[46] NATO countries quickly complied with the information-sharing effort. But although the Korean War had generated evidence of a desire to work together, it did not generate any consensus on precisely what to do, especially in-sofar as the German question was concerned. The grand proposals at the Coun-cil of Europe were political bombshells that stirred passions and brought forth divisions both domestically and internationally. The approach taken in NATO through the Council Deputies offered a more subtle approach. By judging the prevailing attitudes of countries during this information-gathering process, it was possible not only to judge the positions and seriousness of the Alliance members about addressing the German question but also to confirm their will-ingness to work within the NATO institution toward an eventual solution.[47] The information-sharing initiative allowed members to engage in a cooperative ef-fort within NATO, even if their initial positions revealed substantive differences that would take some time to resolve.

In contrast to the subtle or delicate institutional approach of the Council Dep-uties, the first firm national proposals made at the North Atlantic Council had more in common with the bombshell approach. US Secretary of State Dean Acheson dominated the Council meeting in New York beginning on Septem-ber 15, 1950, with a sweeping proposal on the future of NATO's organization and Germany's role in it.[48] On organization, Acheson proposed the creation of an integrated military structure for NATO whereby member-states would con-tribute units and a central military organization would administer, train, and command those forces.[49] The question of German participation, according to Acheson, depended on what was necessary given the integrated force concept he described. The United States viewed German participation as essential, and Acheson therefore proposed rearming Germany with its own military units that would participate in the integrated NATO structure he outlined.

Acheson's proposal during these North Atlantic Council proceedings caught the other national representatives off guard. The prospect of a rearmed Ger-many with independent national armed forces, however rational from the Amer-ican point of view, was still politically taboo in Europe and sparked immediate controversy in the Council. Debate on Acheson's proposal was fierce but incon-clusive since most representatives did not have instructions from their home governments about how to respond to such a proposal.[50] Two exceptions were the United Kingdom and France. France was totally opposed to the idea of German rearmament, with members of the French delegation being "shocked" at the very idea.[51] The United Kingdom largely supported the American view, with Ernest Bevin being "outraged" by the intransigence of the French delegation under Schuman.[52] The proceedings had to be suspended for several days in order for representatives to consult with their home governments.

Negotiations in the Council dragged on for about two weeks but concluded with a final communiqué on September 26 that reflected continuing disagreement. For France, the American proposal seemed an expedient but ill-conceived solution to the short-term problem of America's global military commitments, especially in Korea. France did not want European security subordinated to America's global considerations.[53] Moreover, solving the German question through NATO threatened the primacy of the European integrationist approach, in which France was the leading state and Schuman himself an important individual contributor. The September 26 communiqué simply recommended studying the matter of German participation in European defense, with the resolution that the issue would be taken up again at the NATO Defence Committee meeting on October 28.[54] France was therefore faced with a dilemma and a deadline of one month in which to propose an alternative.

Two months after the outbreak of the Korean War, path-dependent stability in the slow or incremental development of the Atlantic Alliance had been upset, but contingency prevailed on how the strategic challenge would be addressed. The critical juncture had exposed the inadequacy of the Alliance's defenses and loosened the structural constraints on action to address the German question, but no immediate consensus existed as to what to do. Powerful actors pursued different courses of action. Within NATO, the leading proposals involved the creation of an integrated military structure and the rearmament of Germany under the Federal Republic. Outside NATO, supranational ideas for a common European army enjoyed nascent support. Both sets of proposals offered possible and plausible ways to involve Germany, and both proposals would be pursued in the effort to settle the German question in early Cold War Europe.

The European Defence Community Institutional Alternative

The European Defence Community was the most serious institutional alternative to NATO for addressing the German question in early Cold War Europe. Despite the ultimate failure of the EDC treaty ratification in 1954, the four-year period between its proposal and its eventual demise at the hands of the French National Assembly revealed the EDC to be a possible and plausible arrangement that was seriously pursued. In the first instance, the EDC episode highlights some of the substantive interests of the foreign policy priorities of states that would also bear on NATO's own efforts at institutional adaptation. Second, the process-tracing of the EDC's proposal and failure offers some ability to contrast the causal mechanisms that led to the adoption of one institutional form over another. Finally, the EDC proposal and treaty allows for a comparison of institutional characteristics with NATO.

The EDC as a Plausible Institutional Arrangement

Jean Monnet was aware of Dean Acheson's proposal at the North Atlantic Council in September 1950, and he was aware of the impasse over the German question. Writing to Schuman before he left New York, he said: "There seem to be three possible courses to take. To do nothing—but is that possible? To treat Germany on a national basis—but that would stop the Schuman Plan and the building of Europe. Or to integrate Germany into Europe by means of a broader Schuman Plan, taking the necessary decisions within a European Framework."[55] Agreeing on the third course of action, Monnet and Schuman, with the blessing of Prime Minister René Pleven, quickly assembled many of the same authors of the Schuman Plan to set about the formulation of a plan that would enlarge the scope of the "European Framework" to include defense issues. By October 14, basic points for their proposal were taking shape. The first point was that France opposed the re-creation of a German army as a threat to both French and European security. Second, the integrationist supranational model put forth in the Schuman Plan for coal and steel could be applied to military affairs. In this case, a European army with a single command and common equipment would be placed under the control of a supranational authority that would also control funding. Third, German units could be slowly integrated into this supranational European army. And fourth, so as not to jeopardize the other efforts at European integration, the European army proposal would not be adopted until the Schuman Plan for coal and steel had been put into effect.

On October 24, Pleven introduced this proposal in a speech to the French National Assembly. Placing his proposal in the context of Churchill's proposal at the Council of Europe, the speech outlined what would be called the Pleven Plan and argued that the NATO members

> have recognized the need to defend the Atlantic community against any possible aggression, on a line situated as far to the East as possible. . . . Germany, which is not a party to the Atlantic Treaty, is nevertheless also destined to enjoy the benefits of the security systems resulting therefrom. It is consequently right that it should make its contribution towards setting up a system of defence for Western Europe.

Consequently, before opening discussions on this important problem in the Assembly, the government has decided to take the initiative of making the following declaration. . . . It proposes the creation, for our common defence, of a European Army tied to political institutions of a united Europe. This suggestion is directly inspired by the recommendations adopted on 11 August 1950 by the assembly of the Council of Europe.[56]

Pleven went on to propose under this plan integrated units at the lowest possible level, a European Minister of Defence, common funding mechanisms, compatibility under the NATO unified command system, and an invitation to the United Kingdom and other European states to join the plan. From the French perspective, the Pleven Plan offered the advantage of delaying the rearmament of Germany until the new European army was established, especially since German units would only be incorporated slowly into that system. In essence, the idea of a European army in which Germany contributed units seemed less dangerous than pure German rearmament.[57] By echoing Churchill's call for a European army, adopted at the Council of Europe, the Pleven Plan was familiar to many Europeans. Because it offered some plan by which Germany could contribute to European security, Britain and the United States were at least open to giving the idea further study. Although many questions needed to be answered, the French proposal had met the deadline for proposing an alternative in time for the October 28 NATO Defence Committee meeting, and momentum had been built for a European solution to the German rearmament question.

Negotiations for the establishment of the EDC began in February 1951 with Belgium, France, Italy, Luxembourg, and West Germany acting as full participants. The Netherlands, initially represented by an observer, became a full participant in October 1951, while Denmark, Portugal, and the United Kingdom remained observers. The resulting EDC Treaty was signed in Paris on May 27, 1952, by the same six countries that had formed the ECSC and was to last fifty years.

The main body of the EDC treaty consisted of 132 articles and 12 protocols, plus three additional conventions dealing with the EDC and NATO; the EDC and Britain; and the EDC, Britain, and the United States. According to the treaty, the EDC was to be a "supranational European organization . . . supranational in character, comprising common institutions, common armed forces, and a common budget."[58] Rather than an international or intergovernmental organization, the EDC would act independently of the member-states, and its decisions would be binding. Rather than the close coordination of national armed forces, the EDC would fuse them into one force.

The institutional structure of the EDC would consist of a supranational Board of Commissioners, with nine commissioners serving six-year terms as the executive body of the EDC. Rather than dealing directly with the member-states, the Board of Commissioners would receive instructions from the EDC Council. The Council would consist of representatives from the member-states and would make policy that would ideally balance both national and European interests. Voting in the Council would be proportional to a member-state's military contribution to the EDC. This was the intergovernmental part of the EDC. The EDC would also share an Assembly with the ECSC, except that France, Italy, and West Germany would receive three additional seats. The Assembly would provide oversight and could force the resignation of the Board of Commissioners, but the Assembly was also responsible for trying to coordinate the aims of the EDC within the context of the ECSC and other efforts at European integration. The EDC would operate from a common budget, made up of contributions from the member-states and foreign aid.

The structure of the armed forces under the EDC would be combined—that is, multinational—at the higher echelons, where logistics and general staffs would be integrated. The operational military units, however, would be composed of soldiers, sailors, and airmen of the same country. After an adjustment period, the Board of Commissioners would facilitate recruiting, mobilization timetables, common doctrine, the positioning of forces, and common equipment, weapons, logistics, and infrastructure. Only Germany had to accept the unequal conditions that it would not develop weapons of mass destruction (atomic, biological, or chemical), missiles, large naval vessels, or military aircraft.

The Politics of EDC Rejection as a Viable Institutional Solution to the German Question

The dissolution of national armed forces and the pooling of forces among former enemies such as France and Germany challenged the idea of national identity and sovereignty.[59] The critical juncture of 1950 had made such bold, radical proposals as a supranational European military authority conceivable. By the time the EDC treaty was nearing completion, coming as it did on the heels of the launch of the ECSC on July 25, 1952, the integrationist spirit in Europe ran high, and the potential for EDC success was real. Moreover, the prospective EDC members had begun talks with other Council of Europe members on the possibility of a European Political Committee that would further integrate Western Europe through the harmonization of foreign policy, which was seen as an important corollary to the EDC since irreconcilable foreign policy disputes could bode negatively for the EDC's effectiveness where decisions about the use of military force were concerned.[60]

Belgium, Luxembourg, and the Netherlands ratified the EDC treaty fairly quickly. The decision was uncontroversial in Luxembourg. The Netherlands felt that, although a NATO solution would be best, the EDC was a necessary compromise in order to ensure French participation in any comprehensive plan to involve Germany in West European defense. Questions of constitutionality were raised in Belgium, where the supranational character of the EDC conflicted with the Belgian notion of sovereignty regarding war and peace, but the vote in Belgium was ultimately overwhelming in favor of the EDC.

In West Germany, Chancellor Adenauer had been privy to the initial idea of the Pleven Plan and had supported involvement in European organizations as a way to root West Germany in the Western European system, thereby reducing the risk of incorporation into the Soviet bloc. Adenauer was cautious not to appear too enthusiastic but realized that participation could be linked to the recovery of Germany's sovereignty. Moreover, Adenauer also saw cooperation with France as a way to ease historic tensions between the two countries.[61] But the EDC encountered resistance in Germany, especially among the opposition in the Social Democratic Party, who cited deficiencies such as the unequal restrictions on Germany's involvement in the EDC, questions about the efficacy of rearmament under such conditions, the dubious effectiveness of the EDC's military capabilities, and concerns about the EDC's effect on future German reunification. Moreover, it was constitutionally unclear whether membership in the EDC was compatible with the portions of German Basic Law that restricted foreign policy decisions on the use of force in international relations. But in the elections of September 1953, Adenauer's Christian Democratic Party increased its share of seats in the Bundestag by enough to give it a sufficiently commanding majority over the opposition Social Democrats to pass changes in the Basic Law and ratify the EDC Treaty.[62]

Despite the fact that the EDC had been a French proposal, the treaty was not sent after its signing to the French National Assembly for several months. The reason for this delay is unclear, although the notoriously unstable political climate of the French Fourth Republic certainly contributed to the difficulty of projects like the EDC, the negotiations for which outlasted successive governments.[63] An initial French National Assembly vote in early 1952 had expressed support for the principle of the EDC under the conditions that there be a strong American troop presence in Europe, close participation of the United Kingdom in the project, and the creation of a supranational political structure to govern defense policy.[64] As the EDC's inability to meet the 1952 conditions became increasingly clear, important French public figures turned against the EDC for many of the same reasons that other European countries had expressed reservations about the plan (even while the other countries were signing up to the EDC in order to mollify France). Charles de Gaulle fervently opposed the EDC, entering the debate in characteristically bold style during a press conference on February 25, 1953, stating that the treaty "was based on untrue assumptions. The army it would create would not be European. It would not guarantee American support. It would not increase security. It would not safeguard France's position in the world. . . . A team of persons had been at work to foist the EDC on France exploiting the present mood of extreme national depression, widespread ignorance and much illusion, with the help of official and semi-official propaganda, money and foreign support."[65] Doubts and concerns in France about the EDC grew as the debate over ratification drew near. Jules Moch, a prominent politician since 1928, rapporteur of the assembly's Foreign Affairs Committee, and indeed the defense minister in 1950–1951 who had introduced the Pleven Plan at NATO, published a book condemning the EDC as the debate was heating up in 1954.[66] Fears about German rearmament even within the context of a supranational organization, the loss of France's own armed forces, and the effectiveness of a European force in stopping a Soviet attack formed the core arguments of the opposition in France to the EDC. Opponents echoed de Gaulle's argument that neither the United States nor the United Kingdom were substantially involved, and that France had to give up much by way of its national forces and identity without gaining in terms of material benefits to its security. Moreover, since France was becoming increasingly embroiled in the Indochina conflict, moves to disband France's continental army would potentially have meant fewer forces available for action there and in other parts of the world where French interests were at stake. Ultimately, the matter of ratification in the French National Assembly was not even taken up for consideration but was blocked on August 30, 1954, by a procedural motion as inappropriate for debate. This blockage rendered the remaining unfinished Italian parliamentary ratification debate irrelevant and signaled the defeat of the EDC proposal.[67] In a strange turn of events, France had defeated its own proposed institutional alternative to NATO for dealing with the German question in early Cold War Europe.

Comparing and Contrasting the EDC with NATO

There are several noteworthy features of the EDC treaty and the formal institutions it proposed to create. The most obvious contrast between the EDC and

NATO was in the supranational character of the former. Although the EDC treaty included standard alliance collective defense guarantees, EDC members would have had to give up a certain measure of policy decision-making authority about defense to the EDC commissioners and Council. Because the Council would vote on a proportional basis, EDC members would risk not being able to veto EDC action in the way that NATO's consensus method allowed. Moreover, rather than assigning independent national forces to an integrated command as in NATO, states would have had no independent control over the European army except through EDC institutions. If states wanted to pursue independent military operations or guard unique overseas interests, they would need to create entirely separate forces outside the EDC. This surrender of power to supranational institutions contrasts with the practice that would evolve in NATO of delegating the staffing of various cooperative initiatives down to the institution while retaining the sovereign decision-making independence of the states.

A second important characteristic of the EDC was that its institutions were articulated in great detail and enshrined in a very specific treaty that sought to comprehensively address the political and organizational issues in its 132 articles and additional protocols and conventions. Although this exhaustiveness may have given states clarity on what they might have been signing up to, it also left little room for flexibility of interpretation and gave actors many details over which to object or find concern. The EDC treaty contrasted with the comparatively short and vague North Atlantic Treaty, which expresses a number of principles but leaves the details of Alliance organization and decision-making to be determined outside the specific provisions of the treaty.

Finally, the EDC foresaw a different configuration of states and state power than did NATO. In contrast to NATO's institutions giving equal institutional voting rights to all members, not all EDC members would have equal status under the EDC, with Germany in particular being subject to certain limitations on the character of its military contributions to the European army, even if Germany, France, and Italy would rate additional representation in the Assembly. To be sure, leading states would fill a disproportionate number of influential positions within NATO, too, but these inequalities in NATO came about through the exercise of politics rather than through the enshrining of differential status in the treaty. Moreover, on the important question of resources and capabilities, the United States and the United Kingdom were conspicuously absent from the EDC. This allowed a measure of autonomous continental European organization but risked creating a structure that would not guarantee the substantial material resources of the noncontinental powers so important to the credible defense of Europe. For all the costs to independent national sovereignty that the EDC would entail, it might not be able to deliver the requisite security benefits on its own.

NATO's endurance following the critical juncture of the Korean War was not a foregone conclusion, and the EDC represented a plausible institutional alternative. However, the EDC proved a flawed institution, demanding much in terms of a detailed submission of state sovereignty in the sensitive area of military affairs while not convincingly mustering the material capabilities that would be needed to mount a credible European defense. Moreover, the process by which the EDC was proposed and debated reflected a strangely insular political odyssey—first proposed in the French National Assembly but ultimately rejected in the very same domestic legislature—evidence of insufficiently broad or durable coalitions for such significant proposals. The impact of these contrasts would be felt as answers to the German question developed in NATO.

NATO Organization and Strategic Adaptation

The EDC exercise came about as a result of the impasse over the initial proposals in NATO to include German rearmament as part of NATO's response to the critical juncture of the Korean War. Although the question of German rearmament was the most contentious issue at hand and was resolved only after the EDC proposal had run its course, other aspects of NATO's organizational and strategic adaptation continued and did much to position the Alliance for the ultimate resolution of the German question in the Cold War in 1955. Following the outbreak of the Korean War, NATO pursued the adaptation of its internal institutions and its strategy with the aim of addressing the challenges brought about by the Korean War within the bounds of what NATO members would find politically acceptable. Internal institutional actors, especially in the Council Deputies and the integrated military structure, played key roles in setting the agenda for adaptation, promoting consensus, and shifting contentious issues around different parts of the organization, all the while seeking to ensure that NATO remained the leading institutional arrangement for addressing the wider issues that the critical juncture had raised.

The North Atlantic Council meeting in September 1950 was a key event from which the broad outlines of NATO organizational and strategic adaptation over the next four years would develop. The importance of this meeting may not have been apparent at the time, however, as its content revealed deep differences among the members. Dean Acheson's proposal for German rearmament had been a rare instance in which a significant issue was brought to the Council floor without having been informally deliberated and tested for feasibility prior to formal session. The primary reason why the Council session dragged out for an uncharacteristically long period (September 15–26) was that the session had to be interrupted after the first three days of debate in order to allow Council members to undertake the kind of informal discussions and consultations that normally preceded the formal Council sessions.

Just as the North Atlantic Council heard the American proposal for German rearmament without prior informal discussion, NATO's Defence Committee meeting of October 28, 1950, featured the equally unfamiliar French proposal for what became the EDC.[68] With Prime Minister Pleven having unveiled this idea to the French National Assembly only four days earlier, there had been no time for informal discussions of the Pleven Plan within NATO prior to its being brought up at the Defence Committee session. Accordingly, the Defence Committee was at a similar impasse after the French proposal as the Council had been after the American proposal for German rearmament one month earlier. With neither consensus on the principle nor time to assess the detailed particulars of the new French proposal, the Defence Committee referred the matter to the Military Committee and the Council Deputies for further study. In the absence of agreement, the Defence Committee's postponement of the decision and referral of the issues to other elements of the NATO organization echoed the Council's own action in deferring the Acheson proposal to the Defence Committee in the first place and foreshadowed a regular pattern in which NATO shifted contentious issues around to different parts of the institution.

Meanwhile, institutional actors within NATO were also hard at work. Just as Ambassador Charles Spofford had led the initial effort within NATO to share information about immediate responses to the outbreak of the Korean War during the summer of 1950, Spofford was again the leading figure in the work that had been delegated to the Council Deputies, facilitating discussion and compromise with the Military Committee and between the differing French and American proposals on the German question that emerged during the autumn.[69] These discussions culminated in a joint meeting of the Council Deputies and Military Committee on December 13, 1950, during which the two bodies were able to agree on a report to the Defence Committee and North Atlantic Council recommending an acceptable way ahead.[70] The key finding of Spofford's report was a reaffirmation of the centrality of Germany's importance to NATO's strategy: "an acceptable and realistic defence of Western Europe and the adoption of a forward strategy could not be contemplated without active and willing German participation."[71] The report further specified that "any system of German participation must be within the NATO structure." As to the details of how this would be accomplished, the report offered a variety of technical recommendations on the sizes and capabilities of German military units and defense industries but ultimately remained agnostic as to whether the organization of German rearmament should take place as part of the integrated NATO force (i.e., the US proposal) or as part of a unified European army (the French proposal).

The Spofford report recognized which aspects of the German question's resolution remained contentious and stopped short of overreaching recommendations. But, significantly, the Spofford report had found consensus on the ideas that Germany would be rearmed somehow and that NATO would be the supreme institutional umbrella under which Western defense would develop (even if a unified European army was established to handle the German contributions). Moreover, the Spofford process also signaled an ability for actors within NATO to effectively lead negotiations among Alliance members, even (or perhaps especially) on highly contentious issues.[72] Following the Spofford report, the North Atlantic Council agreed in December 1950 that the three occupying powers (i.e., Britain, France, and the United States) should begin direct consultations with the Federal Republic of Germany on politically acceptable ways to achieve German rearmament, while NATO turned its attention to the adaptation of its internal organization.[73]

These initial reactions in NATO to the critical juncture of the Korean War's outbreak demonstrate a number of themes that would resonate throughout its organizational and strategic adaptation during the course of its effort to resolve the German question. The first was a careful setting of agendas, in which NATO took up action and adaptation on issues where agreement was within reach, such as in the commitment to the integrated military structure, while putting off decisions on other issues. Second was an early commitment to the principle of pursuing comprehensive solutions to issues within the NATO framework, as in the Spofford report and accompanying North Atlantic Council meetings of December 1950. A third related theme was the model of negotiation that sought consensus only on general points while delegating the sorting out of detailed plans and unfinished business to subsequent meetings or other institutional settings. Throughout, internal institutional actors played important roles in gathering information, setting agendas, building consensus, and moving action around various committees and institutional locations.

NATO Organizational Adaptation, 1951–1954

If the political dimensions of Germany's rearmament remained a subject of diplomacy among the leading states at the end of 1950, the mandate for organizational adaptation of NATO was clear and vigorously pursued. In September 1950, the North Atlantic Council agreed to Dean Acheson's other proposal to create an integrated military command structure.[74] Unlike the new and more controversial US and French proposals of September and October 1950, the desire to establish an integrated military command structure was a well-known idea that already enjoyed wide support prior to the September meeting. In announcing the agreement on the integrated force, the Council had already specified that the Military Committee would oversee the strategic direction and priorities of the integrated force; the Defence Committee would establish details for the organization of the force and the contributions of the member-states, and recommend changes necessary to bring the force in line with the Alliance's strategic concept; and a supreme allied commander would be appointed, supported by an international civilian and military staff, to provide training in peace and command in war.[75] Significantly, the Council also resolved that the integrated forces should be "adequate to deter aggression and ensure the defence of Western Europe, *including Western Germany*," affirming its commitment to addressing the German question, even if the particulars were still in contention.[76]

The North Atlantic Council meeting of December 1950 in Brussels carried forward the results of both the Spofford report on German participation in Western defense and the development of the NATO integrated force under a designated supreme commander. According to Lord Ismay: "The words 'integrated force' and 'supreme command' at once brought to mind the name of Dwight D. Eisenhower. . . . It was indeed fortunate for the free world that a man of General Eisenhower's unique prestige, qualification and experience was available at this critical juncture. His name was associated with victory in the minds of millions and millions of people, and his appointment was a tremendous psychological asset to the Alliance."[77] The Council reached an easy consensus on Eisenhower as the first supreme allied commander and accordingly appointed him to the post after receiving approval from US president Truman.[78]

The extraordinary decision to create an integrated international military force in peacetime, and the subsequent rapid installation of a significant international figure in General Eisenhower as its commander, accelerated the process of internal organizational adaptation within NATO. The development of the integrated force was itself a significant organizational process, but a correspondingly robust consolidation of NATO's civilian structures also occurred as NATO internalized the lessons from the Spofford report on the importance of competent institutional leaders in generating consensus among Alliance members on decisions required for NATO's further organizational development.

At the same North Atlantic Council session in December 1950 in which General Eisenhower had been identified as the future supreme allied commander, the Council also undertook several organizational reforms that were meant to increase the level of coordination within NATO and to institutionalize that behavior in permanent, continuously operating bodies. A committee of military representatives from each NATO member-state was to be established in Washington and would be subordinate to the NATO Military Committee. The task of determining for the Military Committee the future requirements of the newly formed integrated force was delegated to the Standing Group, and a Standing Group Liaison Office was to be established in London in order to facilitate closer work with the Council Deputies and other organs of NATO.[79]

The burgeoning growth of the NATO organization during this period served not only to institutionalize cooperation among Alliance member-states but also to cement NATO as an international organization. In order to simplify NATO workings, and to consolidate control of its operations, organizational adaptation tended to feature the creation or growth of international organization while replacing or deemphasizing forums that had been composed of representatives reporting directly to member-states. For example, NATO announced in May 1951 that the Defence Committee and the Defence Financial and Economic Committee would be discontinued and their responsibilities incorporated into the North Atlantic Council.[80] Whereas the Defence Committee had seated defense ministers and the Defence Financial and Economic Committee had seated finance ministers, the Council would become the "sole ministerial body" in NATO. It would therefore "be a Council of governments, not one of individual [Foreign] Ministers."[81] While the number of NATO bodies hosting member-state government ministers was reduced, new bodies were created to emphasize international work. Although the Council Deputies remained representatives of their governments, because of the newly expanded portfolio of the Council they became, de facto, "the permanent working organization of the North Atlantic Council."[82] More significantly, a truly international NATO staff, paid for from a common budget funded by contributions from all member-states, was established under the chairman of the Council Deputies, the already influential Charles M. Spofford.[83] Finally, a new organization called the Financial and Economic Board (FEB) was set up to replace all other existing NATO groups and committees working in that area. The FEB was set up in Paris, subordinate to the Council Deputies.

Development of the integrated military force also proceeded rapidly after the appointment of General Eisenhower as the first SACEUR during the Brussels North Atlantic Council in December 1950. Eisenhower quickly appointed US Lieutenant General Alfred M. Gruenther as his Chief of Staff and delegated to him the primary task of setting up the Supreme Headquarters Allied Powers Europe (SHAPE). General Gruenther in turn handpicked a small cadre of US officers to begin the work in January 1951. Officers from other NATO countries joined the US members of the SHAPE Advance Planning Group shortly thereafter, meeting (in some style) at the Hotel Astoria near the Étoile in Paris. This planning group addressed practical, technical, and often political questions of all sorts in deciding how SHAPE would be organized and staffed, the method through which the SACEUR would command and control the integrated force, and even where the headquarters would be permanently located. Opportunely, these planners were able to capitalize on the efforts of three regional planning groups that had been established during the first Council session in September 1949. Even more enterprising, these planners made use of prior studies undertaken by the Brussels Treaty's so-called Western Union,[84] the use of which not only prevented the NATO officers from having to duplicate the same work but also aided in the development of professional rapport and consensus-making: "Western Union had also created the precedent of an international and inter-service staff, working together in time of peace and using the same two official languages as NATO—French and English. In addition, they had bequeathed to SHAPE not only their many studies of the defence of what was to be the central sector of the SHAPE Command, but, more important, a number of officers of different nationalities with the invaluable experience of working together as an allied team."[85] France donated an area near Versailles to serve as the permanent home of SHAPE, and French Army engineers supervised the construction of prefabricated structures into which the headquarters moved in June 1951, having extended their stay at the Hotel Astoria for as long as possible after SHAPE officially assumed operational control on April 2, 1951.

The early development of the integrated force is less significant for its substance than for the manner in which it occurred. As in the earlier Spofford negotiations, deliberations on the substance of the SHAPE planning occurred at a relatively low level among technical specialists, while the leading figures (i.e., Eisenhower) remained happy to delegate those activities. In fact, Eisenhower was not present in Paris at all for the early activities of the SHAPE planning group but instead embarked on a lengthy tour of NATO capitals to establish (or, in many cases, reestablish) relationships with the important civilian and military leaders in Europe and to discuss the capabilities and intentions of the NATO members. Eisenhower knew that the economic and political will to rearm Western Europe would not be sufficient to meet the threat from the East on its own, and that German troops would ultimately be needed.[86] But he also knew that such a sensitive issue ought not to be discussed prematurely, and that the development of a strong integrated military force under American leadership was the best way to set the conditions for German involvement.[87] Already a well-known international figure in his own right, Eisenhower had also become the leading figure in NATO, which at this point had no secretary-general or other high official of rival stature. Eisenhower's position as SACEUR, combined with his personal reputation stemming from World War II leadership, gave him access and the power that NATO had not previously possessed. At the conclusion of his trip, Eisenhower gave testimony to the US Congress, indicating that he found strong support for the development of NATO with material contributions and leadership from the United States, and a strong commitment to defense, albeit under the economic constraints then prevailing in Europe. Despite the reservations of some American lawmakers who continued to oppose US entanglement in European security, Eisenhower's confidence in the project ultimately carried the day.[88]

The development of SHAPE, like the creation of the international civilian staff under the Council Deputies, institutionalized military staff and planning at the international, NATO level. A future SACEUR, Andrew J. Goodpaster, later reflected: "Among the primary features of the organization [SHAPE], probably the most important was that the headquarters was both international and integrated. The headquarters would not function as a committee made up of a number of national delegations, but rather as a single unified organization in which all officers, regardless of nationality, worked for the common mission assigned to Eisenhower: to develop an integrated, effective force for the defence of Western Europe and to conduct that defence, should hostilities occur."[89] To be sure, national military representatives remained part of the national delegations to NATO, but they acted separately and apart from the integrated, international staff at SHAPE.

The NATO civilian organizations developed in early 1951 lost little time in consolidating the influence of the new structures and in recommending further organizational adaptation to strengthen NATO institutions and strategic capability. The role of key institutional actors within NATO such as Ambassador

Spofford and General Eisenhower continued to grow in significance, while the North Atlantic Council's pattern of delegating sensitive issues to lower-level technocratic bodies carried on as well. The September 1951 Council session in Ottawa, meeting for the first time with both foreign and defense ministers in joint session, debated reports from the Council Deputies, Defence Production Board, the FEB, and the Military Committee. All the committees described shortcomings in the respective military and economic/defense-industrial areas for which they were responsible but struggled to issue comprehensive recommendations. The FEB, in particular, noted that it could not properly evaluate NATO's defense economic performance without detailed military guidance from which costs could be estimated, and that the FEB itself was neither capable of assessing the general trade-offs between military and economic risk (i.e., "guns vs. butter") nor authorized to do so. General Eisenhower agreed, stating that he found his military duties "so closely interlocked with economic, financial and social matters that it was often impractical, and indeed quite unrealistic, to consider one of these fields without giving due attention to the others."[90] Spofford included a separate note to the Council regarding these reports that highlighted the difficulty each NATO agency faced in carrying out its work for want of information from other agencies, suggesting the need for further organizational change.

Not able to fully address the issues that Spofford and Eisenhower had summarized in a single session, the NAC created an ad hoc structure known as the Temporary Council Committee (TCC) to determine the requirements of "fulfilling a militarily acceptable NATO plan for the defence of Western Europe and the realistic political-economic capabilities of the member countries."[91] The TCC was to be composed of one member of each of the twelve NATO countries but in fact delegated its work to an executive board of three: W. Averell Harriman of the United States, Jean Monnet of France, and Sir Edwin Plowden of the United Kingdom. The "Three Wise Men,"[92] as they came to be called, established an international staff from all NATO agencies and from member-state delegations, and requested detailed military and defense economic information from each of the member-states. As information from the member-states flowed in, committees working under the Executive Board analyzed the information. The Screening and Costing Committee of the Executive Board evaluated each country's military plans in consultation with senior military representatives from the country in question, recommending cuts and changes that would maximize efficiency throughout the Alliance. The Executive Board later conducted similar conferences with government representatives of each member-state to discuss recommended changes across all relevant military and economic areas. This clearly demonstrated the new power of the NATO institutions. As Lord Ismay reflected, the TCC "and their staff were not acting as national representatives: they had been commissioned by the Council to do a specific job for NATO as a whole. That sovereign governments submitted to this searching cross-examination by an international staff, parted with some of their most jealously guarded secrets and debated in common measures affecting matters of high policy, was a signal victory for the NATO spirit."[93]

The TCC submitted its final report on December 18, 1951, about two months after the effort had begun. The report gave a summary of each member-state's military and defense economic capabilities, along with recommendations for their improvement. The report emphasized that military strength required firm economic foundations, and in terms of distributing the costs of the common defense recommended that "other things being equal, the greater the level of income or the potential rate of increase in income expected in a country, the higher can be the proportion of national income devoted to defence."[94] Notwithstanding this, some member-states felt that the larger members had not been scrutinized to the same extent as the smaller members. This is perhaps unsurprising, given that the Three Wise Men were from larger countries. Nevertheless, Averell Harriman could not be faulted for accuracy in describing the TCC report as "the first comprehensive review of how the resources of the member countries under peacetime conditions can best be employed in the interest of common security."[95] The specific targets outlined in the TCC report would lead directly to the momentous strategic force goal decisions taken later at the Lisbon Conference in February 1952. Regarding the TCC's impact on the institutions of NATO, the TCC report also recommended the continued strengthening and coordination of NATO agencies. Perhaps taking note of the extraordinary influence that the TCC had exercised with respect to the member-states, the TCC report recommended that similar exercises occur more regularly. This recommendation was the genesis of what in later years became known as the NATO Annual Review, a fairly sweeping series of organizational and strategic assessments.

As NATO pursued its own internal organizational adaptation, it explicitly took note of the alternative institutional arrangements being considered for European defense. In addition to its capitalizing on the prior work of the Western Union, NATO directly engaged with the EDC negotiations as that some kind of agreement or treaty seemed likely to emerge. At the North Atlantic Council meeting of November 24–28, 1951, in Rome, held shortly after the Conference on the European Defence Community earlier that month in Paris, the Council Deputies was instructed to make recommendations on how the relationship between NATO and the EDC should take shape.[96] This report would ultimately lead to the May 1952 EDC protocol to the North Atlantic Treaty, extending the latter's Article 5 collective defense obligations to the members of the EDC (including West Germany) and locating the EDC within the umbrella of NATO's mandate.

The Lisbon Conference, beginning with the North Atlantic Council meeting on February 20, 1952, was one of the signal events in NATO history. All of the adaptive organizational and strategic work of the TCC, as well as NATO's efforts to engage with its institutional rival in the EDC, combined to present a vast agenda of work and sweeping changes in the Alliance, preparing it for the eventual incorporation of the Federal Republic of Germany nearly three years later and bringing closure to the critical juncture touched off by the outbreak of the Korean War. The Council noted that the negotiations among the three occupying powers with Germany that it had sanctioned one year prior had failed to produce any results. In view of the report of the Paris Conference on a European army and internal reports on the EDC delivered by the Council Deputies and the Military Committee, the Council recognized that the EDC negotiations had achieved a breakthrough agreement on the involvement of Germany in the European army project and recommended to member-states that a protocol to the North Atlantic Treaty should be signed granting Article 5 collective defense guarantees to all EDC countries—in effect, extending the North Atlantic Treaty to include Germany by way of the EDC.[97] The EDC Treaty and the Protocol to the North Atlantic Treaty were signed concurrently in Paris on May 27, 1952.

The Lisbon Conference decisions on further institutional changes within NATO were no less significant. Just as previous developments had institutionalized NATO's integrated military force under the leadership of General Eisenhower, Lisbon represented a culminating point in the development of the civilian structure of NATO's institutions. The most noteworthy decision along these lines was the appointment of a secretary-general as the senior-most civilian official in NATO, with responsibilities to direct a strengthened NATO international staff/secretariat and serve as vice chairman of the North Atlantic Council. The Council would thereafter meet in permanent session, and member-states would appoint permanent representatives (i.e., ambassadors) as the heads of national delegations for times during which ministers were not present. The Council would further assume the responsibilities of the FEB, Defence Production Board, and Council Deputies. The international staff/secretariat would assume many of the duties that the Council Deputies had discharged, including the sorts of analysis and planning that would precede the future TCC-like NATO Annual Review. To facilitate all of this, a permanent NATO headquarters

would be established in Paris.[98] On April 4, 1952, having implemented these
Lisbon decisions, Ambassador Spofford concluded the business of the Council
Deputies, and Hastings Ismay, former general and chief military assistant to
Winston Churchill during World War II, then serving as secretary of state for
Commonwealth affairs in Churchill's government, took up the posts of vice
chairman of the North Atlantic Council and secretary-general of NATO.[99]

In order to address the atmosphere of crisis precipitated by the outbreak of
the Korean War, NATO undertook a variety of internal organizational adaptations aimed at bolstering the capacity of the institution to address the perceived
increase in strategic threats. The creation of the integrated military structure
was meant to increase the peacetime preparedness of NATO to carry out the
forward defense strategy to which its members had agreed and also served to
reassure members that the United States would not abandon Europe in turning
its immediate attentions to Asia. Leadership of the integrated force in the person of General Dwight Eisenhower brought credibility and prestige to the new
institutional position of supreme allied commander, and the general successfully advocated the effective early development of SHAPE and the integrated
military structure more generally. The civilian side of NATO also developed
new, international capabilities. Although the North Atlantic Council's substantive remit expanded to include broad political, economic, and defense policy
matters, this council of member-state governments increasingly delegated
much of its detailed work to international staff. The chairman of the Council
Deputies, Ambassador Charles Spofford, was especially influential in these proceedings, from NATO's initial reaction to the Korean War in July 1950 through
the TCC. The Lisbon Conference consolidated these developments with the appointment of a NATO secretary-general, expanded international staff/secretariat,
and establishment of the permanent institutional headquarters in Paris. All the
while, important and complicated issues were delegated to lower-level technocratic
committees in order to foster consensus outside the formal spotlight of the regular intergovernmental Council sessions. Moreover, NATO showed a deft ability
to engage directly with alternative institutions working in the same areas, most
notably in copying the work of the Western Union Command Organization in
developing the initial plans for SHAPE and in co-opting the nascent EDC by
developing a protocol to the North Atlantic Treaty that brought the EDC under
NATO's Article 5 collective defense protection. This latter development in particular was important because all EDC members, including West Germany,
would be party to this protocol, a breakthrough that foreshadowed the ultimate
membership of Germany in NATO after the collapse of the EDC.

NATO Strategic Adaptation, 1951–1954

The Lisbon Conference was important in the development of not only NATO's organization but also its strategy. While the Strategic Concept of December 1949 and Medium Term Defence Plan of April 1950 had articulated the outlines of the ways that NATO would pursue the ends of European defense in a general war, the Lisbon Conference produced a series of force goals that ambitiously set out an agreement on the means required to pursue such a strategy. These goals represented a high point of ambition for NATO strategy, as economic constraints later cooled enthusiasm for the fulfillment of the Lisbon force goals. Just as the institutions of NATO played an important role in developing the recommendations for the Lisbon force goals (through the work of the TCC), so institutional NATO actors would also have a key role in the development of the Alliance's strategy following the abandonment of such an ambitious economic and military buildup. An important part of this strategy would be a willingness to consider enlargement of NATO membership, in the cases first of Greece and Turkey, and later of Germany. Whereas the Council Deputies had been leading internal actors before Lisbon, the new secretary-general and international staff/secretariat played important roles thereafter.

An awareness of the importance of military means motivated some of the earliest strategic appraisals within NATO following the outbreak of the Korean War. The July 1950 meeting of the Council Deputies in the weeks following the initial invasion was one of the first instances in which internal organizational actors took a leading role in fostering NATO-wide cooperation to address the urgency of the times. The efforts of the Council Deputies under Charles Spofford to collect information on the available resources of the member-states, together with their political will for an active response to Korea, set the stage for the North Atlantic Council meetings of September and December 1950, at which the creation of the NATO supreme allied commander and the rearmament of Germany were proposed. Another important development of the same December 1950 North Atlantic Council session was a public commitment by the United States to increase the size of its conventional forces in Europe and to place all US forces in Europe under General Eisenhower's command. France followed suit, pledging that its three divisions stationed in Germany would be placed under NATO command and adding two more divisions in 1951. Canada deployed one brigade and eleven fighter squadrons to Europe during this period as well.[100] The United States committed four additional divisions to join its forces already in Germany during 1952, bringing the total US force presence in Europe to 400,000.[101] At the time SHAPE was activated in April 1951, fewer than fifteen divisions and one thousand combat aircraft were available to NATO. By December of the same year, NATO forces comprised thirty-five divisions, just fewer than three thousand aircraft, and seven hundred naval vessels.[102] Although some of this increase was simply administrative (i.e., the allocation of existing national forces to NATO's integrated military structure), a substantial military buildup was nevertheless under way.

The economic foundations of the military buildup also occupied an early and important place in NATO strategy. The growth of military forces was a potentially expensive undertaking, and Alliance members showed concern over the economic consequences of rapid rearmament, especially given its effects on economic recovery in Europe. Moreover, just as the outbreak of the Korean War had undermined the perception of military stability in Europe, so, too, did the critical juncture disturb the economic situation. Inflation was a chief symptom, as domestic prices for industrial raw materials as much as doubled within six months and the vast expenditures on the Korean War itself (especially by the United States) contributed to scarcity of imports. Various NATO institutions studied the potential economic costs of NATO's Strategic Concept and Medium Term Defence Plan, and one council deputy summarized the inflationary concerns when he said, "the requirements of a specific rearmament programme had been rendered completely inaccurate by the rise in prices, to such an extent that, in certain cases, the very implementation of such programmes might be imperilled."[103] Such concerns fed directly into the logic of NATO's organizational reforms in this period, as competencies in many economic and military matters were consolidated in organizations such as the FEB. These concerns also contributed to the work of the TCC and the subsequent NATO Annual Review process, at which military and economic performances were assessed.

Although the Lisbon force goals of February 1952 ambitiously called for the development of forty-two ready divisions and forty-five (later increased to forty-eight) reserve divisions by 1954, cost concerns ultimately prevented the realization of those goals. The NAC downwardly revised force targets in April 1953 to thirty ready divisions and thirty-six reserve divisions. Although these downward revisions were justified in the name of reprioritizing quality over quantity, it had also become clear by this time that the economic resources and political will of the Alliance members would not support further increases toward the large targets set at Lisbon.[104] Part of this reality was due to the economic imbalances among Alliance member-states, as in 1953 the combined gross national product of all NATO Europe countries, US$113 billion, amounted to less than one-third of the combined US$362 billion GNP of Canada and the United States.[105] As the

Marshall Plan and various forms of economic aid were winding down, North American military aid to Europe nearly quadrupled during 1952 and 1953. The United States and Canada provided weapons, ammunition, and other military equipment under the principle of "mutual aid" outlined in Article 3 of the North Atlantic Treaty. Of the roughly US$30 billion in all kinds of economic and military aid from North America to Europe between 1948 and 1954, more than half was military equipment provided by or paid for by the United States.[106] Although the legal framework for this aid was usually bilateral, the NATO Annual Review processes in these years shaped the substance of what sorts of equipment European members could best use.[107]

But even NATO's North American members increasingly found the political and economic demands of rearmament difficult to sustain. The United States had increased its defense expenditures more than threefold between 1950 and 1952, and at US$47.6 billion, defense spending represented 58 percent of the total US national budget in 1952.[108] Even though much of this spending was due to the Korean War, NATO strategy was unavoidably affected. General Eisenhower stepped down as supreme allied commander in order to pursue the presidency in the United States, and Ismay, the new secretary-general, facilitated the installment of his American replacement General Matthew B. Ridgway in May 1952.[109] As president, Eisenhower effected a significant turn in US defense policy with the "New Look," seeking to reduce costs by placing greater emphasis on the use of nuclear weapons. Although the new policy, set forth in United States National Security Council document NSC 162/2, dealt globally with US interests, it specifically articulated the new emphasis on nuclear deterrence with respect to Europe, reading: "The major deterrent to aggression against Western Europe is the manifest determination of the United States to use its atomic capability and massive retaliatory power if the area is attacked."[110]

The American turn toward reliance on nuclear weapons did not satisfactorily solve NATO's strategic demands, however. The experience of the Korean War continued to show that a wholesale dependence on nuclear deterrence without conventional forces reflected wishful thinking, motivated more by political and economic considerations than strategic logic. In fact, NATO's first attempt to examine how to incorporate nuclear weapons into strategy demonstrated just that: SACEUR Ridgway submitted a report to the Standing Group on July 10, 1953, with the estimated force requirements for a strategy that made more extensive use of nuclear weapons. Ridgway's report, citing the likelihood of increased casualties in a nuclear exchange, actually called for increases rather than decreases to the required conventional force strength of NATO.[111] The report deepened Ridgway's existing unpopularity with the Eisenhower adminis-tration and a number of European audiences, and may have further hastened his replacement as SACEUR later that month.[112] The new SACEUR, General Alfred Gruenther, had been Eisenhower's handpicked deputy when the latter was ap-pointed as the inaugural SACEUR, and Gruenther promptly resumed study on changes to NATO strategy, commencing a familiarly worded "New Approach" at SHAPE in August 1953 that more closely followed the prevailing political attitudes about future NATO strategy. The NAC endorsed this fresh analysis in its Annual Review for 1954.[113] The New Approach would ultimately lead to changes in the overall NATO strategy, notably the Strategic Concept document MC14/2 of May 1957 that enshrined the doctrine of "massive retaliation."[114] In the meantime, however, NATO still had to grapple with the issue of its strength in conventional forces.[115]

The secretary-general emerged as a steadying force in helping to keep the follow-through on conventional force development on the agenda at NATO. Lord Ismay became secretary-general after contentious debate over the roles and responsibilities of the new position.[116] Although some member-states sup-ported the creation of an increasingly strong institutional leadership within the Alliance, others sought to limit the new position's ability independently to set agendas and recommend action. In the document specifying the particular du-ties of the secretary-general and secretariat, none are specified in the areas of political consultation or coordination.[117] Ismay is often remembered as a some-what passive secretary-general, especially in comparison to some of his more vocal successors.[118] But given the concerns about the creation of institutional positions that were too obviously powerful, Ismay's nonaggressive style of lead-ership did much to ensure the influence of the office. Of course, General Ismay had experience in managing statesmen's concerns as Winston Churchill's chief military assistant during World War II. But unlike the Council Deputies, who at once served as both international institutional actors and representatives of their home governments, the secretary-general and reorganized international staff/secretariat represented only NATO as a whole. This development increased the organization's independence, but the new institutional actors were not vested with any decision-making powers (in contrast to, say, the EDC institutions, which would be able to take action with the approval of all its members). Thus, for the NATO secretary-general, too vocal a stance on substantive issues could result in the marginalization of his office by the member-states. To mitigate this, Ismay, shortly after taking office, sought and received approval from the NAC before he established a Political Affairs Division of the secretariat in order to delegate and depoliticize some of the political analysis.[119] But the secretary-general's office grew in stature under Lord Ismay primarily because he withheld his own opinion and refrained from making substantive recommendations. Instead, the secretary-general exercised institutional convening and agenda-setting powers. He was particularly effective at continuing the Council Deputies' practice of holding informal meetings to test the feasibility of new ideas and to build consensus. Whereas normal Council sessions saw four or more staff advisors attending each permanent representative, informal sessions consisted of the secretary-general and permanent representatives only. A third type of meeting, called a restricted session, allowed for one or two advisors to the permanent representatives at most. Lord Ismay convened 118 such informal and restricted sessions from 1952 to 1955, an average of about one every twelve days. He was also in the habit of hosting private luncheons for permanent representatives, which offered further opportunity for informal consultation while also developing personal rapport.[120] Ismay crafted a role as secretary-general of promoting Alliance cooperation and coordination. But if he rarely used the office to enter the fray of political debate, he certainly played a role in keeping NATO's agenda focused on the tough issues. The dossiers of the international staff and secretariat during this period included not merely technical or functional matters but also highly politicized topics, including, inter alia, the EDC, the relationship of NATO to other defense organizations, Korea, and US defense policy.[121] Ismay also played a leading role in encouraging member-states to follow through on their commitments to provide the means to carry out NATO's strategy.

One month before the armistice in Korea, taking note that the feeling of crisis that had characterized the Alliance during the three years of war in Asia was subsiding, Ismay prepared a detailed memorandum on the imperative of continuing NATO's development and keeping the issue of conventional force development on the Council's agenda.[122] In a somewhat extraordinary move, Ismay also traveled to represent the Alliance in a non-NATO institutional context. Although he was not empowered to make any decisions or to commit NATO to any particular course of action, Ismay attended the trilateral meeting of Britain, France, and the United States in Bermuda in December 1953. Although his announced intention was to attend as an observer only, his position and presence allowed him to communicate and advocate the NATO point of view on Korea, Germany, and European defense.[123] Ismay also frequently appeared publicly, taking official trips to Alliance member-states fifteen times between 1952 and 1955. One observer remarked, "Ismay has emerged, even more than [SACEUR]

General Gruenther, as the real successor to Gen. Eisenhower as supreme figure-head and symbol of the Western Alliance."[124]

But with waning political support and economic capacity to fulfill the rear-mament goals set out at Lisbon in 1952, and with the New Look's emphasis on nuclear weapons not wholly satisfactory, changes to NATO membership and the German question in particular became key once again. Although the sensitive issue of German rearmament was still being pursued through the EDC, NATO had established a record of shaping strategy by addressing changes in member-ship, namely through its negotiations with Greece and Turkey to shore up the western position in the Mediterranean and southern Europe. The NAC first con-sidered relations with Greece and Turkey in 1950,[125] but deliberations continued through 1951 on whether the advantages of a strengthened southern flank for NATO were worth the potential risk of extending the Alliance to the Caucasus border of the Soviet Union (as would be the case with Turkey). The Council Deputies, once again, bore primary responsibility for carrying out the internal NATO study on this question, for feeling for possible consensus (Scandinavian countries were initially opposed to Turkish and Greek membership), and for direct negotiations following the Turkish and Greek applications to join NATO in May 1951.[126] The Council Deputies drafted and signed a protocol on the acces-sion of the two countries on October 22, 1951, and Greece and Turkey formally joined NATO on February 18, 1952.[127] Although some opposition to enlarg-ing the membership of NATO did occur during this time, two institutional as-pects of NATO helped overcome those reservations. First, the study of the bene-fits and risks to these new members was done in a manner that kept differences below the high politics of the NAC chamber, as the Council Deputies, Standing Group, and other institutional actors worked on the issue over a period of several months. Second, informal consultations among members and with the NATO staff helped assuage concerns and build consensus before the issues ever came to the point of impasse at formal NAC sessions.

Conclusion: The London Conference and Germany in NATO

After four years of development and deliberation, the EDC initiative suddenly unraveled on August 30, 1954, following the suspension of the treaty debate in the French National Assembly. With this action, the complex arrangement in which Germany would be included in a supranational European army that itself would be incorporated into NATO also failed to materialize. But where the EDC had comprehensively failed to get started, the intervening period had seen dramatic organizational and strategic adaptation in NATO. The formation of the integrated military structure, appointment and succession of supreme allied commanders, consolidation of the NAC's ministerial responsibilities, establishment of a permanent NATO international civilian staff and secretariat, appointment of a secretary-general, and growth of the institution at its permanent headquarters in Paris and subordinate headquarters throughout NATO territory showed impressive institutional change during this period. Strategically, the Alliance had dramatically increased troop strength and defense spending, systematized these efforts in the combining of economic and military analysis in the TCC and NATO Annual Review, and exercised the principles of self-help and mutual aid to effect the resourcing of the evolving NATO strategy. Where nuclear deterrence and the increased efforts of the original treaty members alone could not guarantee the desired outcomes, NATO incorporated Greece and Turkey into its membership in order to strengthen its position in the Mediterranean and southern Europe. If Alliance member-states had failed to achieve any progress in direct consultations with Germany, NATO had accomplished a lot in preparation.

By the time of the EDC's rejection in 1954, some of the urgency of the security situation had subsided with the armistice in Korea in 1953—but the essential parameters of the German question still remained. The preceding years' development had also yielded a fairly obvious understanding as to how the German question might be answered. As Britain had not wanted to participate in any supranational solution, Foreign Minister Anthony Eden took the lead in convening a conference in London on September 28, 1954, with the delegations of the six EDC countries, the United Kingdom, United States, and Canada. The London Conference "Final Act" described the results in six parts. First, France, the United Kingdom, and the United States would end their occupation of Germany, revoking the occupation statute and removing the allied high commissioners. Second, the Brussels Treaty would be revised to form the Western Europe Union, which Germany and Italy would be invited to join as members.[128] The WEU would regulate the quantities and types of weapons possessed by its members, allowing for close European (and especially French) monitoring of German rearmament. Germany agreed not to manufacture atomic, biological, or chemical weapons; missiles or mines; warships or strategic bombers. Third, the United Kingdom undertook to maintain a force of four army divisions and a tactical air force in continental Europe. Together with the forces already pledged by the United States in NATO, these armies would provide material security against a resurgent Germany. Fourth, the next meeting of the NAC should invite the Federal Republic of Germany to join the alliance as a full member.

Fifth, Germany declared that it would conduct its policy within the bounds of the United Nations Charter, the Brussels Treaty, and the North Atlantic Treaty, specifically renouncing the use of force to change its borders or compel reunification. In response, France, the United Kingdom, and the United States would recognize the Federal Republic of Germany as the only German government "freely and legitimately constituted."[129] Part six of the final act dealt with how the previous five sections would be realized through the formal proceedings of the North Atlantic Treaty and other relevant agreements. The agreements reached at the London Conference answered the German question and established the postwar European security system that endured for decades.

The NAC duly invited Germany to join NATO on October 23, 1954. Twelve major treaties were signed the next day, and Germany took up membership of NATO following the ratifications on May 6, 1955.[130] Although the negotiations and decisions of the London and Paris Conferences were taken outside the formal context of the NATO institutions, NATO's organizational and strategic developments had made it the most viable institutional framework for putting a rearmed Germany to use in defending the West during the Cold War. Moreover, NATO's adaptations in addressing its organizational and strategic shortcomings surrounding the German question contributed to a sense of confidence in the capacity of NATO to endure challenges and adapt accordingly. Aside from the agreement that Germany would join NATO as a full member, the other decisions reached at the London Conference essentially constituted caveats and safeguards on the manner of German rearmament so as to provide reassurances to France or the other European members. Satisfied that the German question had been answered in these agreements, this resolution culminated with a famous episode: French Ambassador René Massigli, specifically addressing the United Kingdom's pledge to commit conventional forces in Europe, wept as he pronounced, "for fifty years—ever since 1905—French public opinion has waited for this announcement, and at last we have it!"[131]

The case of NATO in early Cold War Europe illustrates several features of how NATO adapts. Alliance organization and strategy had been "leisurely" or path-dependent in its initial development, and the question of how Germany would be integrated into the postwar Western order remained an open question even after the North Atlantic Treaty's signing. The outbreak of the Korean War was a critical juncture for NATO, exposing weaknesses in its institutional capacity and strategy, and loosening the structural constraints on novel solutions to the German question. The pressures of contingency led both internal NATO actors and states to propose possible and plausible solutions. The supranational

EDC represented an institutional alternative to NATO. But support for the EDC foundered on the high price its institutions would charge in member-state sovereignty, the lack of clear material gains in security commitments or defense resources (especially given the nonparticipation of the United Kingdom and the United States), and the lack of a sufficiently broad or durable coalition of powerful actors to support the EDC treaty through its ratification. The 1954 London and Paris agreements on the return of sovereignty to Germany and its membership of NATO provided the key element in the satisfaction of the German question that would return path-dependent stability to the Alliance.

Internal actors played important roles in NATO's organizational and strategic adaptation. National actors initially generated acrimony and inconclusiveness in their proposals within NATO, as French resistance to the bold Acheson plan to rearm Germany deadlocked the North Atlantic Council and contributed to the counterproposal of the Pleven Plan for an EDC. Taking a different approach, internal NATO actors played key roles in adapting NATO's institutions in order to ultimately find approval among member-states while still plausibly addressing the underlying strategic challenges. The chairman of the Council Deputies, Charles Spofford of the United States, played an early and important role in convening the Council Deputies, setting agendas, and obtaining an early commitment to NATO adaptation and institutional growth. General Eisenhower played a similar, if more public, role in the development of a truly international military organization at SHAPE in his role as the first supreme allied commander of NATO. Later, after the initial urgency of the Korean War had subsided, the new secretary-general, Lord Ismay, continued to maintain pressure within the Alliance in order to finalize an answer to the German question through NATO.

Institutional NATO actors pursued organizational and strategic adaptations through a variety of techniques. Because states maintained ultimate decision-making powers, internal NATO actors employed convening, agenda-setting, and delegating powers to promote adaptation. For example, Spofford's convening of the Council Deputies was the first institutional action NATO took in response to the critical juncture of the Korean War; however, his limited agenda during the summer of 1950 included only a sharing of information and a commitment to consensus-building within a NATO context. These techniques allowed institutional actors to keep explosive or contentious issues from coming to a head too quickly. At the same time, institutional actors promoted the growth of the international organization and kept issues from stagnating by delegating work across various forums until consensus developed. The TCC's recommendations, followed by the creation of an enlarged permanent international staff and secretariat under a secretary-general at Lisbon in 1952, were high points for this technique. Internal NATO actors benefited in their efforts to promote adaptations because they possessed expert information about the technical merits of proposed institutional changes and because they often also had privileged information about the member-states' views on the proposals to guide their agenda-setting. Certain internal actors also benefited from being dual-hatted as national actors. Most notably, Charles Spofford was both chairman of the Council Deputies and US deputy. Dwight Eisenhower was both NATO supreme allied commander and commander of US forces in Europe (not to mention later president of the United States). This dual-hatting allowed these actors to blend powers or to invoke the special credibility, prestige, and power of the United States in the service of their NATO-specific institutional duties. In contrast, Lord Ismay had to play a more cautious and neutral hand as an internal NATO actor only.

For all the organizational and strategic adaptation that occurred within NATO, it is worth emphasizing that these changes were relatively slow and imperfect if effective in promoting institutional endurance. The critical juncture loosened constraints on action but did not eliminate resistance to change or political wrangling. The resistance to change manifested in the need to undertake laborious informal discussions and negotiations before issues could be decided at the North Atlantic Council, and the frequent delegation or buck-passing of contentious issues among various committees or parts of the institution, all with the effect of delaying very swift action. Delays played a positive role, however, in allowing the initially "shocking" new idea of German rearmament to become familiar and more palatable. NATO may undergo significant organizational and strategic adaptation, but that is not the same as saying that the changes are perfectly effective. NATO deliberately weakened its strategy in the downward revision of the Lisbon force goals and complicated the efficiency of its internal process in order to balance requirements for continued institutional endurance. This is not necessarily bad; it simply institutionalizes moderation and compromise, facilitating limited consensus if not making all member-states fully satisfied.

CHAPTER FIVE

Flexible Response and the Future Tasks of the Alliance, 1962–1967

The structure of international relations changed during the late 1950s and early 1960s. Although this change is not as sharply identifiable as the beginning or end of the Cold War, its effects on the Cold War and on NATO were no less important. The military balance between the two superpowers assumed the character of "mutually assured destruction" (MAD), as the lethality of nuclear weapons grew and the Soviet Union narrowed the technological lead that the United States had enjoyed earlier in the Cold War. Meanwhile European recovery had matured out of its early postwar fragility, and European countries began to demonstrate greater clout and confidence. These developments were long in the making but presented a number of challenges for NATO. The most salient was the credibility of NATO strategy and the related issues of extended nuclear deterrence to Europe and control over nuclear weapons in the Alliance. More broad and perhaps more fundamental, however, was the fact that these structural stresses encouraged greater national independence in the conduct of foreign policy. This was true intrabloc, as European countries sought to update their relations with one another and with the United States. And it was also true interbloc, as superpower parity increased the significance of the US-Soviet bilateral relationship, and détente later allowed for greater exchanges among countries on both sides of the Iron Curtain.

The critical juncture that loosened the constraints within NATO on action to address these challenges occurred in the twin shocks of the Second Berlin Crisis and the Cuban Missile Crisis. These events introduced an element of contingency into how the various problems would be addressed but produced no immediate consensus within the existing NATO structures as to how they would be overcome. As in the 1950s, it would take several years between the start of the crises and the momentous decisions that ultimately would follow. Whereas the breakdown of the EDC had been the breakthrough that led to a solution to the question of German membership in NATO during the early Cold War era, the withdrawal of France from NATO's integrated military structure in 1966 was the catalyzing event of the later period. Although the French departure was the most significant rejection of NATO's formal organization in the history of the Alliance, it also allowed further adaptations to both organization and strategy that greatly strengthened NATO and promoted its endurance.

Four important adaptations occurred during this period. First were sweeping organizational changes, including the merging of NATO headquarters in Europe, the creation of a truly international permanent staff for the Military Committee, a strengthening of institutional military authority in the SACEUR and SHAPE following the elimination of the nationally dominated tripartite Standing Group, and the establishment of a two-tiered political structure in which the secretary-general presided over both a North Atlantic Council of all members and a Defense Planning Committee that accommodated French desires for independence. Second, on the nuclear issue, the creation of a permanent Nuclear Planning Group (NPG) fostered confidence in the credibility of nuclear deterrence while preserving independent national nuclear forces and stopping short of an objectionable Multilateral Force (MLF). Third, progress on the nuclear issue helped pave the way for the official change of NATO strategy away from "massive retaliation" and toward a viable version of "flexible response." Finally, just as the critical juncture in the 1950s had led NATO to transform itself from something that more closely resembled a traditional alliance into a highly institutionalized international military organization, the critical juncture in the 1960s led to a broadening of NATO's scope from defense and military coordination to the active promotion of peace through political consultation and détente; these were "The Future Tasks of the Alliance," known as the Harmel Report. Most of these adaptations proved successful and durable enough to last until the end of the Cold War.

National independence was a driving force in all of these NATO developments. Accordingly, state actors played influential roles and constrained NATO. The French president, Charles de Gaulle, was the most dramatic player in these broader international politics. Within the institutions of NATO, US Defense Secretary Robert McNamara, Belgian Foreign Minister Pierre Harmel, and Belgian Permanent Representative André de Staercke played important national roles. Institutional NATO actors during this period relied less on agenda-setting (which national actors were doing in abundance) and instead focused most of their efforts on moderating, convening, and delaying in order to facilitate adaptation. Important institutional actors in these regards included SACEUR General Lyman Lemnitzer and Secretaries-General Dirk Stikker and Manlio Brosio.

The Structural Problems of Nuclear Deterrence in Cold War Europe

Nuclear weapons produced what Soviet theorists first called a "revolution in military affairs."[1] Like previous advances in military technology, nuclear weapons promised to make war more destructive and lethal. But unlike previous technologies, the ability of states realistically to contemplate the use of nuclear weapons decreased even as their number and destructive potential increased. Nuclear war was not to be a Clausewitzian extension of politics by other means but rather the end that politics and military preparedness sought to avoid.[2] This was the goal of deterrence. For Europe, caught between the nuclear superpowers and closely tied to them, credible nuclear deterrence was essential for security.[3] The United States maintained this nuclear deterrent, and its structural foundation was credible in the early Cold War years. But as both the Soviet Union and the United States developed vastly more powerful weapons and the means to deliver them, the evolving superpower parity and expectation of MAD created structural problems for the continued extension of American nuclear deterrence to Europe.

Winston Churchill reflected a widely held confidence that the European allies could benefit from the deterrent effect of America's monopoly on nuclear weapons when he reflected in March 1949: "It is certain that Europe would have been communized and London under bombardment some time ago but for the deterrent of the atomic bomb in the hands of the United States."[4] The United States had the technological means and also the apparent resolve. US National Security Council document NSC 30, "United States Policy on Atomic Warfare" of September 1948, indicated that the United States should be "ready to utilize promptly and effectively all appropriate means available, including atomic weapons, in the interests of national security."[5] President Truman expressed some reservations about nuclear weapons by this time but supported NSC 30 nonetheless.[6] Putting policy into practice, the United States deployed a fleet of sixty nuclear-capable B-29 Superfortress bombers to the United Kingdom in response to the Berlin blockade during the summer of 1948.[7]

The B-29, though developed during World War II, remained the mainstay of the US strategic bomber fleet until the arrival of the transcontinental B-52 in 1955. In the absence of aerial refueling capability for all its bombers, their relatively short range meant that the United States needed bases in Europe. The security of allied bases in Western Europe was therefore vital to the credibility of the US nuclear deterrent, and this fact helped legitimize America's extended nuclear deterrence to Europe. Europeans could rest assured that the United States would defend Europe if for no other reason than to ensure the safety of its forward bases. Moreover, the Soviet Union possessed no similarly proximate bases to America from which it could launch a retaliatory strike. Thus, even when the Soviet Union ended the American monopoly on nuclear weapons on August 29, 1949, the United States remained safe because the USSR lacked the long-range aircraft or forward bases to deliver nuclear weapons against targets in North America.

Although the 1950–1953 Korean War demanded the use of conventional military forces, the incoming administration of US President Dwight Eisenhower was prepared to increase America's reliance on nuclear weapons. The resulting New Look policy, expressed in the NSC 162/2 document of October 30, 1953, articulated the strategic rationale for a strong nuclear deterrent, its fiscal attractiveness when compared with large conventional forces, and the continuing importance of the European allies in supporting the American strategy.[8] The New Look also came to be associated with the doctrine of massive retaliation, a term coined by US Secretary of State John Foster Dulles during a speech to the Council on Foreign Relations in New York on January 12, 1954, in which he said: "There is no local defense which alone will contain the mighty land power of the Communist world. Local defenses must be reinforced by the further deterrent of massive retaliatory power."[9] Although Dulles later came to distance himself from the term and draw a greater continuity with previous policies, massive retaliation caught on as a shorthand description of the essential military doctrine and strategy that would accompany the New Look policy.[10]

The United States was able to pursue this policy because, as Samuel Huntington observed, "[t]he basic military fact of the New Look was the overwhelming American superiority in nuclear weapons and the means of delivering them."[11] The United States had superior technology, greater numbers of bombs, and bases in Europe from which to deliver them. It had the capability to destroy the Soviet Union with nuclear weapons but was not similarly vulnerable. As a result, the extended deterrence of the American nuclear force to protect Europe was viable. America needed European bases to maintain its nuclear posture, and it could risk nuclear war with the Soviet Union over Europe without seriously risking its own national survival in such a conflict.

However, military and technological developments would soon even the odds between the superpowers, putting an end to the American sense of invulnerability and undermining the credibility of extended deterrence to Europe.[12] To preserve its technological lead, the United States initially responded to the loss of its nuclear monopoly by developing vastly more powerful fusion-based weapons. These thermonuclear, or hydrogen, bombs had the potential for almost unimaginable destructive power, even when compared to earlier fission weapons. The United States tested its first thermonuclear device on November 1, 1952, yielding an explosive power nearly five hundred times more powerful than the fission bomb dropped on Nagasaki. But the Soviet Union responded in kind, testing its first fusion device nine months later on August 12, 1953, and its first true thermonuclear bomb on November 23, 1955. The United States maintained a certain technical lead in design and materials during this period, but both superpowers successfully validated and established the new technology.[13]

The combination of more destructive weapons with longer-range, transcontinental delivery systems further upset the military balance. Advances in strategic bomber and missile technologies would allow delivery of nuclear weapons without the need for the kind of forward bases that America had depended on in Europe. The Soviet Union unveiled its new transcontinental Tu-95 Bison bomber, capable of delivering a nuclear payload all the way to the United States, at the 1955 Moscow Air Show. The apparently large number of new strategic bombers available to the Soviet Union gave rise to a perceived "bomber gap" in the United States. But the Soviet Union had placed even greater emphasis on the development of intercontinental ballistic missiles (ICBMs), capable of delivering a nuclear payload that would be impossible to intercept. Though the USSR tested its first ICBM on May 15, 1957, it was the launch of the first artificial satellite, *Sputnik*, on October 5 that led to widespread hysteria in the United States about the new Soviet threat. As the first US ICBM wouldn't be tested until November 1958, *Sputnik* led to the perception of a "missile gap" to replace the bomber gap.[14] New technologies further abolished any remaining illusions that either superpower could somehow remain unscathed in a nuclear war. Intermediate-range ballistic missiles (IRBMs), sophisticated air defense early warning networks, and submarine-launched ballistic missiles (SLBMs) developed in both the United States and the Soviet Union. These varied methods of launching nuclear strikes and for detecting an attack once under way virtually eliminated the possibility that a preventive war or surprise first strike could allow one superpower to destroy the other without risk of reprisal.

The problem for West European security, then, was that the structural basis of Alliance cooperation on nuclear deterrence had broken down. The advent of more powerful, transcontinental nuclear forces and MAD nullified both pillars that underpinned the credibility of America's extended deterrence to Europe. Whereas the United States once needed forward bases in Europe, it now had the power to reach the Soviet Union directly with new technologies that did not require European bases or cooperation. More importantly, whereas America had once been able to extend deterrence to Europe without incurring significant risk to its home territory, the same advances in Soviet weapon and delivery technology meant that the United States could no longer offer massive retaliation in defense of Europe without risking its own assured destruction.

The Problems of NATO Organization and Strategy in the Age of MAD

The structural shift in the nuclear balance between the superpowers also undermined the organization and strategy of NATO, which had developed only incrementally since the sweeping adaptations of the early 1950s. Organizationally, the integrated military command structure had been updated to incorporate Germany in 1955. The boundaries separating regional NATO commands were redrawn under the direction of SACEUR General Lauris Norstad, but their actual structure remained largely unchanged as the German armed forces were developed and incorporated.[15] The secretary-general had assumed the role of nonvoting chairman of the NAC in 1955, but other changes in the civilian organization were relatively minor. Secretary-General Dirk Stikker's personal preference for formal meetings led to a decline of the weekly luncheons and other informal assemblies that Lord Ismay had introduced. But this reflected less of an organizational change than a difference in leadership style.

Strategically, NATO had embraced a reliance on nuclear weapons in its strategy that mirrored the policies that the United States had implemented during the Eisenhower administration. NATO formally adopted its own version of massive retaliation as a result of the "New Approach" studies that SACEUR General Gruenther began at SHAPE during the summer of 1953. As with the Eisenhower administration's New Look, the New Approach in NATO sought to achieve similar political and economic aims by avoiding the large-scale buildup of conventional military forces outlined in NATO's 1952 Lisbon force goals. The incorporation of Greece, Turkey, and, above all, Germany into the Alliance was an important part of that effort, as the resources of those countries would contribute to the overall military balance in NATO's favor.[16] A strategy of massive retaliation in which nuclear weapons would provide deterrence to supplement conventional defense was another part of that effort.

The potential benefits of a turn toward nuclear deterrence initially enjoyed some support in NATO. As the New Approach studies were under way, the NAC lent backing to the reassessment of required military forces in its *Annual Review* completed in December 1953.[17] A coordinated diplomatic effort at the member-state level gave added force and direction to the New Approach, when US Secretary of State John Foster Dulles gave a special address to the NAC in April 1954, encouraging greater reliance on nuclear weapons in NATO strategy.[18] After a full year of work, SHAPE completed the New Approach studies during the summer of 1954, issuing two reports to the Standing Group: the SACEUR's Capabilities Study for 1957 and "The Most Effective Pattern of NATO Military Strength for the Next Few Years."[19] The collapse of the EDC and the subsequent negotiations at the London and Paris conferences over the incorporation of West Germany into the Alliance dominated the NATO agenda during the autumn of 1954. But when the Military Committee met to consider the strategic implications of those events, they had a new ready-made military plan in the form of the SHAPE and Standing Group reports.

The prevailing agreed strategic guidance at the time remained the document MC 14/1 of December 9, 1952, which reflected the conventionally oriented Lisbon force goals of that year and did not factor in the new development of Germany's entry into the Alliance. MC 14/1 had taken a balanced position on nuclear weapons, acknowledging that in a war "all types of weapons, without exception, might be used by either side" while affirming that "as the conventional NATO forces at present in being fall far short of requirements, no relaxation can be allowed in their planned expansion until progress in the development of weapons justifies a reassessment."[20] The New Approach constituted that reassessment, and "The Most Effective Pattern of NATO Military Strength for the Next Few Years," also known as MC 48, plainly said that "superiority in atomic weapons and the capability to deliver them will be *the most important factor* in a major war in the foreseeable future."[21] MC 48 further specified that NATO military planners should "make preparations on the assumption that atomic and thermo-nuclear weapons will be used in defence in the outset," since "NATO would be unable to prevent the rapid overrunning of Europe unless NATO immediately employed these weapons both strategically and tactically."[22] Thus MC 48 not only elevated the importance of nuclear weapons but also explicitly advanced the view that NATO would consider a first-use policy with respect to their employment.

The NAC approved MC 48 in a ministerial session on December 17, 1954. Although the Council clarified that approval "did not involve the delegation of the responsibility of governments" to authorize release of nuclear weapons during a conflict, it had endorsed massive retaliation. Further strategy developed incrementally, starting with a note in the December 1954 *Annual Review* that recommended NATO clarify "how the reassessment in MC 48 of the pattern of military strength should affect national defense programs."[23] The Military Committee fulfilled that request in document MC 48/1 of September 1955, simply titled "The Most Effective Pattern of NATO Military Strength for the Next Few Years—Report No. 2."[24] This report, adopted by the NAC in December 1955, affirmed the centrality of nuclear weapons outlined in MC 48 but noted that the integration of German forces into NATO would not be complete until 1959 at the earliest. In the meantime, starting in the summer of 1956, the Military Committee and Standing Group went about reconciling the substance of the new emphasis on nuclear weapons with the old strategy documents that were still in effect.

The result was a new NATO Strategic Concept and detailed implementation measures, documents MC 14/2 and MC 48/2, respectively, adopted in May 1957. The new Strategic Concept emphasized nuclear weapons while also retaining continuity with the earlier concept of defending as far "forward" to the east as possible:

In preparation for a general war, should one be forced upon us,

a. We must first ensure the ability to carry out an instant and devastating nuclear counter-offensive by all available means and develop the capability to absorb and survive the enemy's onslaught.

b. Concurrently and closely related to the attainment of this aim, we must develop our ability to use our land, sea and air forces for defense of the territories and sea areas of NATO as far forward as possible to maintain the integrity of the NATO area, counting on the use of nuclear weapons from the outset.[25]

As in its earlier qualifications to MC 48 concerning the maintenance of national decision-making on the release of nuclear weapons, the NAC issued political guidance that emphasized the "responsibility of governments to make decisions for putting NATO military plans into action," thus making clear that massive retaliation was a strategy that still left some room for politics and policy.[26]

A number of historians have rightly pointed out that some of the language in MC 14/2 also foreshadows the later move away from massive retaliation.[27] Where MC 48 maintained an exclusive focus on threats requiring a nuclear response, MC 14/2 indicated the emergence of broader considerations: "NATO must also be prepared to react instantly and in appropriate strength to—and therefore maintain the means to deal with—any other aggressions against NATO territory, such as infiltrations, incursions or hostile local actions without necessarily having recourse to nuclear weapons."[28] The differentiation of possible scenarios and the guarding of final decision-making authority suggest that the kinds of thinking that would emerge later in the flexible response strategy had already begun to gain purchase between the adoption of MC 48 in 1953 and MC 14/2 in 1957. But in terms of the official focus of the new Strategic Concept, the overall reliance on nuclear weapons and massive retaliation remained primary.

The acceptance of massive retaliation represented continuity and stability in the development of NATO strategy, notwithstanding the military significance of the shift from conventional defense to nuclear deterrence and its acknowledged limitations even as it was being established. NATO strategic planning after the outbreak of the Korean War and up to the 1952 Lisbon Conference had represented the ascendancy of military considerations over the constraints of political and economic feasibility. But by mid-1953, the economic and political pressures epitomized in the New Look were calling for a reassessment.[29] Especially after Germany joined NATO in 1955, the combination of European economic concerns and the United States' unilateral turn toward nuclear weapons in Eisenhower's New Look constrained NATO to the point that a flawed strategy became the most feasible course for the Alliance to adopt. As in other developments, an institutional actor, namely SACEUR Gruenther, leveraged his position as a NATO actor who also had close official and personal ties to the US president, to co-opt the American strategy for use in NATO.[30] Massive retaliation promised to achieve the ends of defense without costly conventional means, satisfying both European and American political and economic preferences. While the 1957 Strategic Concept had demonstrated NATO's ability to produce an institutional output that was politically and institutionally acceptable, the problematic content of the strategy still left NATO with unsettled risks. The process of NATO's adoption of the strategy had occurred during years when the technological development of thermonuclear weapons, transcontinental delivery mechanisms, and a more general arrival of MAD all served to undermine a strategic rationale that had been tenuous even when the United States and NATO enjoyed more obvious advantages. Thus the problems of credible deterrence, control over nuclear weapons, and strategic flexibility remained unresolved issues even (or perhaps especially) as NATO had officially adopted massive retaliation toward the end of the 1950s.

Critical Juncture: Crises in Cuba and Berlin

Powerful economic, political, and organizational constraints attended NATO's adoption of and adherence to the massive retaliation strategy during the 1950s. While the member-states welcomed the possibility for savings or the avoidance of overinvestment in large conventional military forces, the increasingly institutionalized and powerful organizations of NATO were able to sustain the New Approach studies at SHAPE until they came to be adopted officially in MC 48 and MC 14/2. Shortly, however, events began to expose the limitations of the strategy and of NATO's institutional capacity.

Identifying the critical juncture during this period is not a trivial exercise. A number of significant events occurred that, in their own ways, had long-lasting effects on politics among NATO countries. The Suez Crisis of 1956 and the launch of *Sputnik* in 1957, for example, undoubtedly contributed to an awareness of NATO's limitations; but these crises did not reach the level at which the erstwhile structural constraints on action in NATO were relaxed to allow for a serious reappraisal. Conversely, the combined effect of the Second Berlin Crisis from 1958 to 1962 and the 1962 Cuban Missile Crisis did find enough institutional resonance for NATO to address the organizational and strategic inadequacies that had become apparent.

The 1956 Suez Crisis is rightly considered a key event in the international relations of the period but was not a critical juncture for NATO. The collusion of Britain, France, and Israel in the invasion of Egypt; the failure of the operation; the opposition of the United States to the actions of its Western allies; and the Soviet exploitation of the situation in its concurrent invasion of Hungary all had long-standing effects on the foreign policies of the countries involved. Extraordinarily, the United States and Soviet Union aligned to condemn the actions of Britain and France. The military shortcomings of the operation seemed to underscore how weak the European powers had become. And the memory of the Suez Crisis would figure in future relations between Britain, France, and the United States. But it had almost no effect in destabilizing the development of the 1957 Strategic Concept. The NAC's political directive to the military authorities drafting the new strategy, issued in December 1956, shortly after the Suez Crisis, made only a general statement that "although NATO defence planning is limited to the defence of the treaty area, it is necessary to take account of dangers which may arise for NATO because of developments outside that area," while even then affirming that "NATO military authorities have no responsibility or authority except with respect to incidents which are covered by Articles 5 and 6 of the North Atlantic Treaty."[31] In other words, the Suez Crisis may have been an acrimonious incident among some Alliance members, but that didn't need to disrupt NATO institutions too much.[32]

Similarly, the launch of *Sputnik* contributed to an awareness of the limitations of the New Look and New Approach but essentially reinforced the understanding of known problems without crossing the thresholds of momentousness and contingency required in a critical juncture. *Sputnik*, moreover, was illustrative of a background condition in the bilateral security competition between the United States and the Soviet Union and affected NATO mostly indirectly through the credibility of US-extended nuclear deterrence. Here, the launch of the first artificial satellite into space by the Soviet Union was a political and public morale setback for the United States and the West. The US Congress, Air Force, and political figures, including John F. Kennedy (who coined the *missile gap* term in 1958 and made it a significant issue in the 1960 presidential campaign), all played a role in promoting concern, either out of ignorance or self-interest.[33] But the missile gap's falsehood was known to the Eisenhower administration and almost immediately acknowledged by the Kennedy administration once in office.[34] Its effect was greater on the course of American domestic politics than in any other context.

The Second Berlin Crisis came closer to upsetting the constraints on action in NATO because it more clearly carried the direct risk of war, culminating as it did in an armed standoff between Soviet and American tanks at the renowned Checkpoint Charlie between East and West Berlin. The sixteen-hour confrontation on October 27–28, 1961, began not with an intentional act of state policy but rather with an essentially haphazard dispute over the showing of passports at a zone crossing five days earlier. Tensions escalated rapidly and dangerously, however. In the words of Colonel Jim Atwood of the US military mission in Berlin: "Instructions were given to our tank commander that he was to roll up and confront the Soviet tank. . . . There was live ammunition in both tanks of the Russians and the Americans. It was an unexpected, sudden confrontation that in my opinion was the closest that the Russians and the allies came to going to war in the entire Cold War period."[35]

This escalation reflected a peak of heightened tension over Berlin that had been under way for nearly three years.[36] The Second Berlin Crisis most clearly began with Premier Nikita Khrushchev's declaration in November 1958 that the Soviet Union intended unilaterally to end the postwar agreements on access to the city by turning control over East Berlin to the East German government. After that, the ups and downs of the crisis had included a withdrawal of the Soviet declaration in May 1959, a failed conference of the Big Four foreign ministers over Berlin's status, the suspension of further negotiations following the shooting down of US pilot Gary Powers and his U-2 spy plane over Soviet airspace in May 1960, a renewed pledge by Khrushchev to make a unilateral agreement over Berlin with East Germany in June 1961, and the erection of the Berlin Wall starting on August 13, 1961.

Concerning and problematic as these developments were, wrangling over Berlin was expected. The likelihood that Berlin would be a target of interference by the Soviet Union had been clear at least since the first Berlin blockade of 1948–1949, which the Western allies had successfully overcome with the Berlin Airlift. Tension over Berlin existed, but so did a pattern of predictability with respect to the issues and the stakes that NATO had not satisfactorily incorporated into its official strategy. The delicacy of the situation in Berlin underscored the kind of situation for which massive retaliation did not provide suitably flexible options. This was acknowledged in practice when in early 1959 a tripartite planning staff involving the western occupying powers—Britain, France, and the United States—met under the code name LIVE OAK to develop options for dealing with Soviet escalation. Following the erection of the Berlin Wall, NATO developed its own Berlin contingency plans (BERCONs) that foresaw a much greater range of differentiated responses to provocations in Berlin, including the deployment of up to four conventional army divisions and even demonstrations with tactical nuclear weapons.[37] Thus NATO actions toward the end of the Second Berlin Crisis represented a de facto implementation of a flexible response to Soviet action. But none of that was as yet codified in strategy, nor did the Second Berlin Crisis sufficiently loosen the constraints in NATO for a frank revaluation of the agreed Strategic Concept as written.

Whereas the armed standoff in Berlin arose spontaneously from tensions on the ground, the Cuban Missile Crisis arose out of decisions made at the highest levels of state policy. Where the showdown at Checkpoint Charlie involved tanks, superpower confrontation over Cuba directly involved nuclear weapons. For thirteen days in October 1962, nuclear war seemed possible after the United States discovered that the Soviet Union was secretly installing nuclear missiles in Cuba. The United States implemented a "quarantine" on maritime shipments to Cuba and deliberated military options for destroying the missiles and invading Cuba, until a deal was struck over their removal. Not an academic or hypothetical danger, and not a spontaneous flaring of tension on the ground, the Cuban missile crisis had involved the actual risk of war.

While the Cuban Missile Crisis had been even more dangerous than the Berlin Crisis, NATO's organization and strategy was even less prepared to cope with it. Like the outbreak of the Korean War, the events of the Cuban Missile Crisis took place outside Europe and the international institutions involved in dealing with its immediate aspects were non-NATO. The United Nations Security Council once again played a role, as it had in Korea, and so did the Organization of American States, highlighting the crisis as perhaps a pan-American or hemispheric crisis rather than a transatlantic or Euro-Atlantic one.[38] SACEUR Norstad advised against NATO action generally, writing to President Kennedy at the height of the crisis: "As you probably know, I have not declared a formal NATO alert but have asked all NATO commands and national MODs [Ministries of Defense] to operate in an awareness of the critical international situation. This will be accepted by all the countries whereas the declaration of an alert would cause difficulty without producing any better results."[39] From a military point of view, Norstad perceived NATO's nuclear preparations to be ill-suited for the situation, writing several days later: "At the time of the Berlin Crisis in 1959, we were forced to move our strike fighter squadrons from France to the U.K. and the Federal Republic because of our inability to work out stockpile arrangements with the French government. [This] led to dangerous concentration of aircraft, a situation which continues to exist. . . . This is essentially a NATO problem rather than one of American interest only.[40] Compounding NATO's incapacity to play a greater political or diplomatic role in promoting Alliance solidarity was Secretary-General Stikker's hospitalization the previous month for what was diagnosed as intestinal cancer."[41]

The Cuban Missile Crisis affected NATO in ways comparable to the outbreak of the Korean War, namely by making the prospect of war seem more likely and more urgent in unexpected ways. The NAC reflected that "the recent attempt by the Soviet Union to tilt the balance of force against the West by secretly stationing nuclear missiles in Cuba brought *the world* to the verge of war." But the Council also acknowledged that "the peril was averted by the firmness and restraint of the United States," and only vaguely "supported by the Alliance and other free nations."[42] This outside support was minimal, as Kennedy indicated when he wrote of his "inability to widen the circle of discussion . . . to enlist the support of NATO" during the crisis.[43] Despite NATO's exclusion, or perhaps because of it, the deficiencies in NATO's organization and strategy were brought into high relief.

Moreover, the Cuban Missile Crisis had served as a real test of America's relations with its other NATO allies during a nuclear standoff with the Soviet Union. The credibility of extended nuclear deterrence was no longer speculative, but a tangible concern. British officials approached General Norstad during the crisis to ask whether the United States "would trade [its] missiles in Turkey for missiles in Cuba," a compromise that the United States, in fact, secretly agreed to do.[44] Norstad, when considering this trade, questioned "the effect on Greece and Turkey, both of whom live in a constant fear of being left alone," and asked more generally whether "the threat of missiles pointed at the U.S. can force a weakening of our NATO defenses under Soviet pressure."[45] Concern also existed about whether the crisis in Cuba had increased the danger to Berlin, either as a result of the greater Soviet likelihood of aggressiveness there or diminished American resolve to counter it, which Kennedy acknowledged in instructing the SACEUR to "increase determination in Europe and to prevent or limit any tendency to argue that if trouble comes in Berlin, it will be the result of our action in Cuba."[46] Combined with the events of the Berlin Crisis, the Cuban Missile Crisis finally confronted NATO's organization and strategy with real problems of incontrovertible momentousness and contingency.

Contingency

The structural indeterminism at the critical juncture following the Second Berlin Crisis and the Cuban Missile Crisis led to at least two kinds of alternatives for addressing the challenges raised. One set of eventualities involved specific proposals for directly addressing the credibility of nuclear deterrence. These proposals included further development of European nuclear forces on the one hand and creation of a combined multilateral nuclear force in NATO on the other. Britain and France continued the development of independent national nuclear programs, but Britain increasingly turned toward bilateral nuclear cooperation with the United States, while France remained committed to European solutions. By contrast, the NATO MLF proposals envisaged shared control over nuclear weapons at the NATO level.

Unlike the specific nuclear proposals, the other set of contingencies involved a much broader revaluation of international politics in view of emerging détente. Here, Alliance member-states pursued relatively independent national agendas, few of which were overlapping or even pointed in the same direction, and for which NATO initially seemed to have little relevance.

European Nuclear Forces versus NATO's Multilateral Force

Britain and France had pursued the development of independent nuclear forces before the critical juncture, especially in the case of the British nuclear program's origins in World War II. Britain had a close relationship with the United States during the war years and immediately afterward, in which the two countries cooperated and shared nuclear knowledge and technology.[47] Official collaboration ended shortly after the war with the arrival of Clement Attlee's government in 1945. But Churchill made the development of an independent nuclear force a foreign policy priority when he returned to power in 1951, and Britain entered the nuclear club on its own with a test in 1952. To maintain Britain's global military role without the unmaintainable costs of a large conventional army, nuclear weapons seemed an expedient way to retain power and influence on the cheap.

Britain's further development of an independent nuclear deterrent involved increasing bilateral cooperation with the United States, commencing most notably at a meeting in Bermuda on March 21–24, 1957. Bilateral cooperation was not intended to subordinate Britain to American power and technological prowess but rather to avoid the unnecessary expense of reinventing technology that the United States had already developed.[48] The most important outcome of the Bermuda meeting allowed US-built Thor IRBMs with a range of 1,500 miles to be placed in Britain. Thor would give Britain access to a new class of missile technology, even if the warheads would be retained under US control and launched only with the dual-key concurrence of both countries.[49] Since acceptance of the Thor missiles would be likely to disrupt Britain's own nascent Blue Streak missile programme, this arrangement served an American interest to maintain nuclear primacy by forestalling further development of independent alternatives. In addition, the United States asked Britain for a secret agreement to oppose prospective French plans to develop its own nuclear forces.[50]

France initially sought to establish privileged arrangements for control over nuclear weapons within the Alliance when, in September 1958, de Gaulle suggested to President Eisenhower that decisions in NATO on the use of nuclear weapons should be taken up by a three-power directorate to include the United States, Britain, and France.[51] When the United States rejected this proposal, France pressed ahead with the development of a fully autonomous nuclear deterrent, the force de frappe. Unlike Britain, which sought active assistance from and collaboration with the United States, France opted instead for full autonomy. As far as France was concerned, assistance entailed an unwanted level of American influence and perpetuated an unhealthy dependence on the United States. Moreover, a fully independent nuclear force would place France in the elite club of nuclear powers, giving it greater prestige and defense autonomy in addition to deterrence.[52] France exploded its first nuclear device in the Sahara desert on February 13, 1960.

The development of French and British nuclear forces had not resolved NATO's deterrence dilemmas, however. For one thing, the United States still possessed and would continue to maintain the overwhelming majority of nuclear weapons within the Alliance. More important, however, was the problematic logic of independent nuclear forces in the first place: What value were NATO's defense and deterrence capabilities if member-states needed independent national deterrents? Excepting Britain and France, the logic of developing independent national nuclear forces did not transfer to other NATO allies. For smaller NATO countries, development of such advanced and expensive capabilities was simply impractical. But the real difficulty was Germany, which had felt the vulnerability of its position especially and obviously during the Berlin Crisis but was barred from having its own independent nuclear force under the agreements leading to its membership in NATO in 1955. A uniform recourse to independent national efforts was not a viable option for strengthening deterrence.

Nevertheless, initial efforts to strengthen nuclear deterrence focused on continued intergovernmental cooperation along the lines of the bilateral Anglo-American nuclear cooperation. A key event in this respect was a meeting in Nassau in December 1962, at which the United States offered the Polaris SLBM. The transfer of Polaris missiles to Britain would involve the pairing of American-built Polaris missiles with nuclear warheads built and controlled by the British, thus establishing an interdependent relationship in which Britain had some autonomous control over its nuclear weapons while remaining dependent on the United States for equipment.[53] It was also thought that a similar arrangement might be possible between the United States and France, with the United States counting on the added benefit that France would need to rely on it for warheads as well as Polaris missiles because French warhead design was then incompatible with Polaris.[54] For France, however, the special Anglo-American cooperation served not as reassurance against a potential American decoupling from Europe but rather as a sign of further isolation and abandonment. The outcome of the Nassau meeting therefore saw France not only reject the proposal of nuclear interdependence with the United States but also punish Britain for its special relationship by vetoing British entry into the European Economic Community (EEC) in January 1963.[55]

The French alternative to US-led intergovernmental sharing was to reinforce continental European solidarity. Unlike the EDC proposal, French ideas for maintaining independence did not involve the creation of new supranational defense organizations. The apparent motivation to have autonomous continental European institutional alternatives to a US-dominated NATO was consistent even with the pre–de Gaulle French experiments with European defense cooperation during the 1950s.[56] The civilian European Atomic Energy Community had been established in March 1957, and its executive functions merged with the EEC in 1965.[57] Military arrangements for continental sharing of nuclear technology had been discussed in the EEC and WEU forums as well.[58] After Nassau, France responded to the Anglo-American special relationship by pursuing closer alignment with Germany, typified in the Élysée Treaty of January 22, 1963.[59] Franco-German cooperation was not specifically related to nuclear cooperation, but the relationship provided France with a hedge against isolation in the emerging proposals for a multilateral nuclear force in NATO.[60]

Multilateral proposals involving the United States and NATO, to deal with the deteriorating credibility of America's extended nuclear deterrence and European desire for autonomy, had been made as early as 1960, when SACEUR Norstad proposed the creation of a combined land-based force of medium-range nuclear missiles. The NAC approved a study of the Norstad Plan in December 1960.[61] Between 1960 and 1964, various proposals for a multilateral nuclear force were discussed within the Alliance. Although there was some variation in the proposals, particularly with respect to the weapons systems used, the main idea was a nuclear force to which any NATO member could contribute and share ownership of the weapon, but in which operational command of the weapons would rest with the SACEUR. The intended benefit was that European NATO members could attain nuclear status through their ownership of weapons, while operational control would remain centralized in NATO. This option was designed to be particularly attractive to West Germany. Because the MLF would involve SACEUR's operational control, Germany's assumed nuclear ambitions could be accommodated, while the United States could assume greater centralized control over European nuclear arsenals since the SACEUR would be American. This latter point made the MLF unattractive to Britain and France, which would lose national control over any nuclear forces contributed to a centralized MLF. France was especially vehement in its opposition to the MLF, which led to fears that the proposal might further damage Alliance cohesion rather than help it. Moreover, the Soviet Union strongly opposed the MLF concept on the grounds that it would allow Germany to become a nuclear power. The USSR made abandonment of the MLF a key negotiating objective in discussions leading to the Treaty on the Non-Proliferation of Nuclear Weapons (NPT), the success of which was an important US objective for preventing the spread of nuclear weapons in the Third World.[62] Ultimately, the cool reception in Britain, France, and other European countries, combined with Soviet opposition and the lure of the NPT, led to the abandonment of the MLF in December 1964, leaving the matter of nuclear cooperation in NATO unresolved.[63]

Independent National Foreign Policy in Détente

During this time of increasing concern within the West about the credibility of extended nuclear deterrence and its implications for European security, the overall Cold War context was one of emerging détente. Following the Berlin and Cuban crises, mechanisms were put in place to reduce tensions and limit the potential for hostilities between the superpowers. In 1963, the hotline agreement between the United States and USSR and the Partial Test Ban Treaty showed signs that the superpowers were seeking to limit the possibility of war and learning to coexist peacefully with one another.[64]

With the reduced prospect for war, there was similarly a reduced need for the West to be rigidly united in hard-line opposition to the Soviet Union.[65] On the contrary, several European states felt it was in their interest to cultivate closer relations with the East. Belgium, Italy, and Denmark increased their contacts with Eastern European countries. A "grand coalition" of Christian Democrats and Social Democrats in Germany began to turn away from Adenauer's hard line toward the East; they released a Peace Note in March 1966 that signaled readiness for détente and foreshadowed the *Ostpolitik* of Willi Brandt that would begin in 1969.[66]

Britain, by contrast, seemed uncertain about its place in the new international politics. The retreat from empire and simmering domestic social and economic difficulties diminished rather than emboldened British foreign policy in the era of détente. More fundamental for Britain perhaps than for any other major power was the question of how the island nation would conceive of its place and role in the world, and specifically whether it would be a globally oriented country, with primary ties to the Commonwealth, or a European country engaged in the rapidly developing project of supranational integration.[67]

More than any other country, France seized this structural opportunity to pursue greater autonomy for itself and for Europe within the Western bloc. Desire for autonomy, grandeur, and leadership were core elements of French foreign policy under Charles de Gaulle, who came to lead the newly established French Fifth Republic in 1958. The desire for independence was not limited to the nuclear issue but was rather a broad vision for France's proper place in the world. De Gaulle saw France as a leading world power and pursued policies to maintain or improve French power and influence. Establishing leadership in Europe was essential to this strategy. De Gaulle feared Britain as a potential rival for its leadership in the EEC and was also wary in case the close Anglo-American relationship allowed the United States to use Britain as its "Trojan horse in Europe."[68] According to de Gaulle, Europe needed to be "a political entity distinct from other entities."[69] Europe needed to extricate itself from the bipolar system of international relations dominated by the United States and Soviet Union. France recognized communist China in 1964, and de Gaulle traveled to the Soviet Union (1966), Poland (1967), and Romania (1968) to speak about cooperation from the Atlantic to the Urals (i.e., a Europe without America).[70]

France is often portrayed as a spoiler to Alliance solidarity during this era: difficult and intransigent, if not dangerously destabilizing. Because French criticism and opposition were often directed at Britain and the United States, this view is especially common in the English-language scholarship. Though France was singularly vocal in its criticism and bold in its opposition to British and American influence, the rationale for this behavior was in many ways shrewd and compelling. History had taught France not to be naive about the value of alliances.[71] De Gaulle especially had learned this lesson during World War II, when alliances did not prevent the rapid fall of France in 1940 or the sidelining of French participation in the major allied conferences and decisions of the war thereafter.[72] America's lack of support for French foreign policy in the Suez Crisis demonstrated that, in the Atlantic Alliance as before, military dependence on others was a potential source of weakness. America's refusal to consider nuclear assistance for the French war in Indochina further demonstrated that France could not always rely on other countries for help. If historical circumstances prevented Germany from escaping dependence on others in the postwar era, France did not suffer such constraints. And détente provided an opportunity to pursue greater autonomy.

Economic integration and closer political ties with Germany and other European countries could help reduce European dependence on the superpowers, but de Gaulle believed that Europe could achieve this independence only if it had "personality from the point of view of defence. Defence is always at the base of politics."[73] Independent nuclear forces were an important but incomplete part of this agenda. To make Europe more autonomous from the United States in military affairs, France targeted NATO as the embodiment of unhealthy American hegemony in Europe. France had taken some steps to distance itself from NATO following the rejection of de Gaulle's proposal for tripartite control over nuclear weapons in 1958. In March 1959, de Gaulle removed the French Mediterranean fleet from NATO's control, arguing that NATO's geographic mandate did not extend far enough to defend French national interests in the southern Mediterranean. The following month, de Gaulle forbade the United States from positioning any of its nuclear weapons in France. In 1963, France also refused to sign the American-led Partial Test Ban Treaty. But the coup de grâce came at a press conference in February 1966 when de Gaulle announced France's complete withdrawal from the NATO integrated military command structure, the expulsion of allied military headquarters from Paris, and a demand for all foreign troops to leave French soil.[74] Invoking a nationalistic tone, de Gaulle stated: "There is no longer any actual or possible subordination of our forces to a foreign power. In six months there will be no Allied command, unit, base, or army on our soil. We will restore their wholly national character to our army, navy, and air force in matters of command, operations and training."[75] France therefore met the contingency of the era not primarily with non-NATO institutional alternatives but rather with the most significant rejection of NATO institutions in the Alliance's history.

Adaptation in NATO

De Gaulle, in his first press conference after winning reelection as president of the French Republic, reiterated a pledge to break with the "obsolete forms" of NATO. Although France would go on to withdraw from many of the formal organizations of NATO's integrated military structure, de Gaulle's reference to obsolete forms perfectly captures the distinction at the heart of this study's research question: assuming a foreign policy commitment among states to alignment within the Alliance, how does the institution known as NATO continue to endure as its institutional expression? De Gaulle's declared intention to break with the obsolete forms of NATO did not indicate a commitment to break with the Alliance, or necessarily a desire to abandon the institutions of NATO that were still relevant or could be adapted to a relevant purpose. De Gaulle expressed these views clearly in handwritten letters to President Johnson, Prime Minister Wilson, Chancellor Erhard, and Italian President Saragat, which, in addition to detailing the rationale for breaking with the integrated military command, also expressed a continuing and firm commitment to the Alliance as agreed in the North Atlantic Treaty, saying that France would "be determined to fight on the side of her allies in the event one of them should be the object of an unprovoked aggression."[76]

Nevertheless, France's withdrawal from the integrated military structure remains the most significant rejection of NATO's formal organization as the institutional expression of the Alliance in its history. To be sure, non-NATO institutional alternatives attended other critical junctures in NATO's history, and some of those alternatives were pursued and implemented in concert with adaptations in NATO. Moreover, France did not ultimately withdraw from all of NATO's formal organizations—just those militarily related ones that de Gaulle characterized as obsolete forms in an era of European national assertiveness and détente. But the impact of the French move was sweeping and catalyzed a variety of consequent organizational adaptations in NATO.

In the changes that followed, national actors from other European states as well as the United States played assertive and significant roles. Ultimately, however, the moderating influences of Secretary-General Brosio and SACEUR Lemnitzer also significantly influenced the changes as well as turning what could have been perceived as an unmitigated organizational setback for NATO into an opportunity for beneficial organizational adaptation. The key national figure in the organizational changes was Belgian permanent representative André de Staercke, who stepped in during the most awkward and volatile period to facilitate practical decision-making among the fourteen remaining allies, while institutional actors like Brosio tried to maintain neutrality in what they perceived as an intrabloc dispute. Brosio's conciliation, pragmatism, and moderation contrasted with other figures who took a harder line, including US permanent representative Harlan Cleveland, who arrived at NATO in September 1965 ready to represent the prevailing US view at the time, which was that France should not be allowed to obstruct NATO planning, and that in the worst case NATO should be prepared to defend against the Soviet bloc without France.[77]

The French foreign ministry delivered notes to the governments of the other Alliance members, stating its intention to withdraw from the integrated military structure and to have all commands associated with that structure removed from French territory. Interestingly, as if to underscore that France viewed this decision as an intergovernmental rather than a NATO matter, these notes were delivered to the various states' diplomatic representatives to France, not to their permanent representatives to NATO or to any NATO official. Following a US request for clarification and details, France issued a second note on March 29, 1966, specifying an expected time line for compliance. French military personnel assigned to NATO commands (i.e., those French forces in Germany and staff assigned to various NATO headquarters) would terminate their assignments effective July 1, 1966. NATO headquarters and installations in France were given one year to vacate, by April 1, 1967, with a further request that all US and Canadian forces clear out their own installations by the same date.[78] France indicated that it would consider retaining its forces in Germany according to the Paris Conference agreements of 1954, but on a national basis rather than as part of an integrated NATO command.[79]

Organizational Adaptation and Removal to Belgium

The initial institutional reaction in NATO was muted, as if no one was quite sure who should act and what the right action would be. Secretary-General Brosio in particular did not offer an assertive reaction to the French move, generating some criticism from those who desired more forceful leadership. In retrospect, however, Brosio's initial silence on the matter allowed NATO institutions to retain a certain impartiality. Although Brosio was not pleased with the French withdrawal, he too treated the matter as essentially intergovernmental. The French decision to use national diplomatic channels was helpful to Brosio since it did not compel the secretary-general to take sides. Brosio felt that his duties were to all of the Alliance and that it would be inappropriate to intervene directly in a political dispute among members, regardless of the fact that one member opposed all the others. Brosio accepted only a limited mandate supported by all members, including France, which required him to commence a study of the problems related to the French withdrawal but not (by implication) to attempt their solution. The international staff quickly identified more than fifty.[80] Brosio remitted these challenges directly to the remaining fourteen NATO member-states themselves.

The fourteen, or *les quatorze*, as they quickly became known in Paris, swiftly found leadership in de Staercke, the senior member of the NATO diplomatic corps and, usefully, first alphabetically in the speakers' list during formal NATO meetings, which he attended as Belgium's permanent representative. Many of the initial meetings were informal, however, and even occurred in de Staercke's apartment in the days immediately following the French announcement.[81] Within ten days, les quatorze adopted a resolution based on a British draft that declared their belief in the importance of NATO's military organization and their resolve to continue their participation in it. As with the initial French note, this resolution was agreed and released individually by the fourteen member governments, not through NATO channels.

Notwithstanding the serious logistical, financial, and administrative challenges of compliance with the French demands, some of the more interesting and contingent decisions about the future of the Alliance had to do with adapting the military organization so that it could function without French involvement. The first change, agreed almost immediately, was the dissolution of the Standing Group, the tripartite military staff consisting of France, Britain, and the United States based in Washington. Initially established in the early days after the North Atlantic Treaty but before the sweeping institutional development that had occurred in the 1950s, the Standing Group had become an anachronism. It occupied a place between the military authorities of NATO and the Military Committee but did not serve either and was seen as not performing well. It was eliminated and its functions assigned to the Military Committee itself. Significantly, the Military Committee also gained an independent international staff of its own to deal with its increased responsibility. In the same way that the institutionalization of an international staff had occurred for the

NAC after the creation of the secretary-general post, an international military staff with a chairman was created for the Military Committee, signaling its growing independent institutional power. Moreover, the Military Committee's meetings were moved from North America to Europe, ending the somewhat controversial and inefficient separation of the two bodies and consolidating NATO institutions.[82]

A more vexing question was that of where NATO institutions would consolidate after expulsion from France. There was some question about whether they would need to relocate at all; as the French decision applied only to military structures and implied that locations in Paris would not be affected, NATO's civilian headquarters in particular seemed able to remain. SACEUR Lemnitzer contacted the French chief of staff, General Charles Ailleret, in order to discover France's position on this and to explore the more general question of how France might cooperate with NATO forces in the event of a war.[83] But de Gaulle's political guidance left little room for negotiation. Brosio discreetly supported those among les quatorze, including West Germany and Belgium, who did not want to risk further separating France by unilaterally removing all NATO bodies from Paris. But the United Kingdom and the United States argued that it would not be feasible to maintain any NATO bodies in France if the possibility existed that France might obstruct its work, especially in the event of a war.[84] This, combined with indications that France would not oppose the complete removal of all NATO presence in Paris, led to a search for alternatives.

De Staercke, meanwhile, was providing necessary leadership among the fourteen, but over time the relaying of messages through the Belgian delegation to France and back to les quatorze was beginning to be perceived as inefficient and a possible source of suspicion and diplomatic intrigue, particularly among the Americans and the British. SACEUR Lemnitzer then stepped in to assert greater institutional leadership in the search for a new location for SHAPE. A general consensus existed for a new headquarters somewhere in the Benelux countries, and Lemnitzer preferred a location near Brussels that would have good infrastructure, communications, and a sizable local labor force. De Staercke, though, worried about the impression of several thousand uniforms moving into the capital of historically neutral Belgium and cognizant of the opportunity to promote economic growth in the Belgian countryside closer to France, suggested the site near Mons (where it has remained to this day). Lemnitzer objected to this remote location, but Belgian domestic politics were at issue and NATO was not in a strong bargaining position. The Council approved Mons, and Lemnitzer reluctantly accepted. The movement of other NATO headquarters went more smoothly, however, with the headquarters for Allied Forces Central Europe moving from Fontainebleau to Brunssum in the Netherlands (where the contemporary NATO Joint Forces Command headquarters remains to this day) and the NATO Defense College moving to Rome, where it also remains to this day. Lemnitzer also diplomatically sent a letter to thank President de Gaulle for the French people's hospitality that NATO had enjoyed in Paris, along with an offer to call on the president if that would be agreeable. De Gaulle responded with great gallantry, expressing his high esteem for the supreme allied commander and inviting him to the Élysée Palace. Significantly, de Gaulle had refused audiences with NATO secretaries-general in the past. This prompt invitation to the SACEUR under the circumstances, to say nothing of the lavish honors and entertainments, was distinctive and meaningful. Later, at a grand ceremony at Les Invalides, de Gaulle presented Lemnitzer with the insignia of a Knight, Grand Cross of the Legion of Honor.[85]

Secretary-General Brosio also became more heavily involved in overseeing the organizational adaptations to NATO after the Council gave him unambiguous authority to do so. Once the Council authorized the search for new headquarters locations in Belgium, Brosio stayed abreast of the discussions between Lemnitzer and de Staercke. Brosio also traveled to Brussels in November 1966 to secure facilities for the new civilian headquarters. Most significantly, Brosio stepped back into active leadership once the Council formally authorized the remaining fourteen members to meet as the Defence Planning Committee (DPC). Brosio had not wanted to convene the fourteen informally since that could undermine the impartiality and legitimacy of the secretary-general's post. But once authorized by the Council, he sat as chairman of the DPC. In its last ministerial meeting at the Porte Dauphine in December 1966, the NAC authorized the fourteen members meeting without France to direct the military affairs of NATO while meeting as the DPC.[86]

The DPC had been originally established in Ottawa in 1963, but, like NATO's short-lived Defense Committee of the early 1950s, the DPC had struggled to find an effective role until it became the expedient institutional location for the remaining NATO members to meet without France. All members found satisfaction in this arrangement. France acknowledged that a practical reality would be that the DPC would meet and make decisions in its absence. But, as a NATO committee, France would have full access to its proposed agendas, outcomes, and information, and would be able to raise any issues it had with DPC business at a meeting of the full Council. For the others, meeting at the DPC allowed NATO to carry on without obstruction.[87] Paradoxically, the French withdrawal from the military aspects of NATO actually helped pave the way for solutions to organizational challenges in that area by creating a two-tiered structure for political consultation and decision-making.

Nuclear Planning Group

The problems of nuclear sharing that had been abandoned after the breakdown of the MLF in 1964 remained important. If anything, the American commitment to the NPT heightened the profile of the issue by accentuating the difference in status between the nuclear and nonnuclear members of the Alliance. For those nonnuclear states that had a stake in the MLF, particularly Germany, another solution had to be found. French withdrawal from the parts of the integrated military command allowed other actors to reinvigorate efforts to find a solution.[88]

In 1963, the Labour Party in Britain had proposed some sort of cooperation in nuclear planning as an alternative to sharing actual nuclear hardware. Following their electoral victory and the breakdown of the proposals over the MLF, Harold Wilson's Labour government officially proposed such a plan to President Lyndon Johnson in December 1964. US Defense Secretary McNamara favored the plan and sponsored the creation of a "Special Committee" to evaluate the possibilities at the meeting of NATO defense ministers in the spring of 1965. Brosio found the new proposal constructive but was concerned that McNamara's specification that only four or five leading members of the Alliance be included in the Special Committee might alienate excluded members. However, the plan was initially well received, and both France and West Germany agreed to study it. Although France ultimately declared that it would have no part in any system that might institutionally entrench the privileged position of the United States, it also made clear that it would not object to others continuing to work on further cooperation.[89] With the French explicitly allowing further work to proceed, Brosio assumed nominal chairmanship of the Special Committee of Defence Ministers, established at the ministers' meeting of November 1965.[90]

The Special Committee was organized into three working groups that would deal with communications, intelligence and data exchange, and nuclear planning. Although each working group would consist of only five members, the membership of each committee was slightly different and offered the possibility of fairly broad participation by member-states. Brosio, however, was excluded from any serious substantive role, as were the SACEUR and other key NATO institutional actors. McNamara in particular felt that a small working group was most conducive to progress and was particularly pleased that the NPG would comprise only defense ministers.

The Special Committee working groups met for the first time in February 1966, as France was making its withdrawal from the integrated military system. Both the communications and the intelligence and data-sharing working groups finished their work by May, but the NPG continued to meet into the autumn of 1966. As discussions dragged on, McNamara slowly began to value the participation of the secretary-general. Brosio participated in discussions at the fourth meeting of the NPG in Rome, which dealt largely with organizational questions in which the secretary-general was expert. Following this meeting, McNamara was willing to have Brosio participate in and chair future meetings of the NPG as well as the full Special Committee but reiterated his preference for the efficiency of small groups. Brosio countered that, if the NPG was going to become a more permanent consultative arrangement, then wider participation of member-states would be necessary.[91] An agreement settled on the idea of seven members in the NPG, of which the United States, United Kingdom, West Germany, and Italy would be permanent members and three additional members would be elected on a rotating basis. The larger steering committee would be renamed the Nuclear Defence Affairs Committee (NDAC) and would be open to all NATO members. France opposed this plan as well, but following France's withdrawal from NATO's military organization, the DPC quickly implemented the proposal at its meeting of December 14, 1966, establishing an NDAC and NPG as permanent NATO bodies responsible for the political and military aspects of nuclear planning, respectively.[92]

The purpose of the NPG was to make plans and build trust among the Alliance members. The NPG was a planning organization and had no operational control. Its work would lead up to the beginning of a conflict, at which time the president of the United States would have ultimate authority over whether and when to use nuclear weapons. Yet the NPG was important to Europeans because, whereas the MLF was to have consisted of tactical nuclear forces only, it allowed the European members to have information and influence over NATO's entire arsenal of strategic and tactical nuclear weapons.[93] Although the United States remained the final arbiter of the planning and targeting of its strategic forces, the other NATO allies were privy to information about these forces. With this level of disclosure about nuclear plans and procedures, Europeans were able to understand the circumstances under which America would use strategic nuclear weapons in defense of Europe. Additionally, the NPG established a forum in which the United States and European countries were able to establish protocols for the use of tactical nuclear weapons in Europe.

The NPG institutionalized a pattern of cooperation and conflict resolution among the allies over issues of deterrence. It constituted a process through which the allies could discuss plans for strategic and tactical nuclear forces, antiballistic missiles, nonproliferation, and any new issues that could arise in the future. Europeans were given a voice, and Americans retained overall control of their forces.[94] Furthermore, because the NPG did not involve the actual sharing of nuclear materials and equipment, the NPG solution allowed the United States to continue working with the Soviet Union toward the NPT, which was signed on July 1, 1968. The NPG was also an important enabler for future strategic adaptation in NATO. Through the work of the NPG, a sufficient level of trust and agreement over nuclear plans was established so that European states could have greater confidence about movement toward a strategy of flexible response.

Flexible Response

The Second Berlin Crisis and the Cuban Missile Crisis had shown that, in the actualities of Cold War confrontation, the conceptual ideas surrounding massive retaliation were not working. Flexible response had, in practice, become a reality in NATO's BERCONs and in the response to the Cuban Missile Crisis. But official NATO strategy had not yet adapted or caught up. As US Secretary of Defense Robert McNamara stated in remarks to the NAC in May 1962: "Our great nuclear superiority for general war does not solve all our problems of deterring and dealing with less than all-out direct assault. . . . Recent events concerning Berlin may provide relevant evidence of the utility of limited but decisive action."[95] Drawing similar conclusions before the same audience in December of that year, McNamara continued: "The forces that were on the cutting edge of action [in the Cuban Missile Crisis] were the non-nuclear ones. Nuclear force was not irrelevant but it was in the background. Non-nuclear forces were our sword, our nuclear forces were our shield."[96]

In fact, pressure to adapt NATO strategy to conform to the realities of flexible response had been mounting for some time. As previously noted, the existing Strategic Concept in MC 14/2 had acknowledged the possibility of differentiated threats and the need for differentiated responses, even while outlining massive retaliation.[97] Reflecting the changing political winds, a meeting of NATO ministers in Oslo on May 8–10, 1961, "invited the Council in Permanent Session, in close co-operation with the military authorities, to continue its studies of *all aspects* of the military posture of the Alliance, with a view to improving its deterrent and defensive strength."[98]

The NAC duly took up the subject in December, when McNamara perhaps

first used the term *flexible response* before the Council, but there was no immediate consensus. As in 1950 when Dean Acheson came before the Council with
the intention of demonstrating American leadership on the German question,
France offered the most direct resistance to McNamara's call for a change to
flexible response. France was opposed to any walking back from the clear and
firm guarantees of massive retaliation, and the final communiqué of the session
made no mention of any reconsideration of strategy, focusing mostly on the particulars of the Berlin situation and finding general agreement only on the idea
that "the countries of the Alliance must continue to strengthen their forces and
modernize equipment so as to be able to deal with any form of attack."[99]

Faced with the familiar prospect of disagreement between France and the
United States over the direction of future NATO strategy, Secretary-General
Stikker emerged as a leading actor in promoting consensus. Combining several
issues during a meeting in Athens in April 1962, Stikker presented a special report on NATO defense policy that, while focused on the issue of political control
over nuclear weapons, also ventured into recommendations over the differentiated or flexible circumstances in which nuclear weapons might be authorized
for employment. The report ranged from recommendations on the fairly unambiguous and immediate retaliatory use of nuclear weapons in the event of a
Soviet nuclear strike to suggestions for various consultative procedures in other
scenarios, concluding that any nuclear use would be "on the scale appropriate
to the circumstances."[100] France initially opposed the recommendations of the
report as a potential rejection of massive retaliation. But, as the recommendations were open to fairly wide interpretation, the secretary-general was able to
find a compromise acceptable to France, which became known as the "Athens
Guidelines."[101]

In September 1962, Secretary-General Stikker employed the same tactic of
advancing strategic adaptation in the delivery of another NATO defense policy
report that more explicitly confronted the underlying assumptions and logic
of massive retaliation, arguing that "because the inevitability of escalation of
nuclear warfare is often assumed, the idea is being encouraged that no choice
is open between conventional defence and all-out nuclear warfare."[102] Several
member-states joined France in deeming this language too radical a revision
of the prevailing strategic orthodoxy. Few copies of the paper were retained,
and the recommendations were largely dismissed as the Cuban Missile Crisis
raised more urgent practical questions.

In early 1963, following the Cuban Missile Crisis, Secretary-General Stikker
resumed his efforts at promoting greater flexibility in NATO strategy. He im-

mediately made more headway. Stikker devised a major NATO force planning exercise that was aimed at the practical difficulties of relating the current strategy and force requirements to probable contingencies. To facilitate the exercise, the NAC directed the Military Committee to prepare an "Appreciation of the Military Situation as it Affects NATO up to 1970." Following the pattern of innocuously titled projects disguising rather significant changes for NATO, the resulting document, known as "MC 100/1 (Draft)" and finished in September 1963, called for an extraordinary level of strategic flexibility. Even more than Stikker's April 1962 NATO defense policy paper that envisioned a graduated use of nuclear weapons, "MC 100/1 (Draft)" embraced flexibility in describing the possibility of countering Soviet aggression with conventional means, as well as options for the employment of nuclear forces in either tactical or more general fashions.[103] Such proposals not only clashed with established plans regarding the relative speed and scale with which nuclear weapons might be used but also explicitly suggested that nuclear forces might not be employed at all. Unlike the earlier language in MC 14/2, which suggested that nuclear forces might not be necessary for ambiguous local incursions or infiltrations, here were recommendations on the potential abandonment of massive retaliation even in the event of a more general conflict. This concerned some Europeans who reasoned that, without the detailed information about nuclear posture that the NPG would later facilitate, any move away from massive retaliation could have been construed as merely institutionalizing a diluted American commitment to the defense of Europe.

Stikker did not have to be seen as the sponsor of such radical ideas, as MC 100/1 was a Military Committee document. But France still categorically opposed it. Unlike the "Athens Guidelines," there was no way of cleverly fashioning compromise language to make the ideas in MC 100/1 seem compatible with massive retaliation. Work on the document, and indeed on the broader NATO force planning exercise, stalled over the impasse. The assassination of US president Kennedy in November 1963 and the resulting revaluation of US defense policy under President Johnson further lessened the momentum for continued efforts at flexible response. Despite Stikker's efforts to facilitate adaptation of NATO's strategy, the lack of consensus among the members, and between France and the United States in particular, constrained further action.

Only after France withdrew from the integrated military structure in 1966 was further progress on the adaptation of NATO strategy possible. French nonparticipation in various institutional settings within NATO lifted constraints on action in those settings. A key institutional development in this regard was the convening of the DPC, established incidentally as part of Stikker's NATO force planning exercise in 1963 but given new a function as a forum in which the NAC met without France to deliberate on defense matters after 1966. Because France had been the main opponent to changes to NATO strategy, the DPC offered an institutional setting in which political approval for strategic adaptation could proceed.

Movement toward flexible response proceeded rapidly. The Military Committee met informally on October 7, 1966, to undertake a detailed and region-specific analysis of various contingencies and concluded with a general agreement on the need for flexibility in addressing the most likely foreseeable challenges. Meeting in a chiefs of staff session on December 12–13, the Military Committee formally endorsed the informal recommendation and called for the preparation of a new strategy document to replace MC 14/2. As expected, political approval to undertake the drafting of a new strategy came from the DPC. In its "Decisions of the Defence Planning Committee in Ministerial Session" of May 11, 1967, the political leadership's guidance to NATO military authorities was that "the overall strategic concept for NATO should be revised to allow NATO a greater flexibility and to provide for the employment as appropriate of one or more of direct defence, deliberate escalation and general nuclear response." This political guidance clearly reflected the need for strategic flexibility. However, the guidance also added a significant ordering principle in stating that the aim of a flexible response was in "confronting the enemy with a credible threat of escalation in response to any aggression below the level of a major nuclear attack." Thus the new NATO strategy should be flexible, but it should not be extemporary.

The new Strategic Concept, MC 14/3, and the implementation document, MC 48/3, would further develop the concepts of flexibility structured according to predictable escalation.[104] Regarding flexibility, MC 14/3 explained that

the deterrent concept of the Alliance is based on:

a. A manifest determination to act jointly and defend the North Atlantic Treaty area against all forms of aggression;

b. A recognisable capability of the Alliance to respond effectively, regardless of the level of aggression;

c. A flexibility which will prevent the potential aggressor from predicting with confidence NATO's specific response to aggression, and which will lead him to conclude that an unacceptable degree of risk would be involved regardless of the nature of his attack.

On the specific types of responses called for by the DPC, MC 14/3 defined "direct defence" and "deliberate escalation" in terms of their relationship to "general nuclear response":

a. Direct Defence. Direct defence seeks to defeat the aggression on the level at which the enemy chooses to fight. . . . The direct defence concept includes the use of such available nuclear weapons as may be authorised, either on a pre-planned or case-by-case basis . . .

b. Deliberate Escalation. Deliberate escalation seeks to defend aggression by deliberately raising but where possible controlling, the scope and intensity of combat, making the cost and the risk disproportionate to the aggressor's objectives and the threat of nuclear response progressively more imminent. It does not solely depend on the ability to defeat the enemy's aggression as such; rather, it weakens his will to continue the conflict. Depending on the level at which the aggression starts, the time needed for each escalatory action and reaction and the rate of success, escalatory steps might be selected from among the following examples provided they have not previously been used as part of a direct defensive system: (1) broadening or intensifying a non-nuclear engagement, possibly by opening another front or initiating action at sea in response to low intensity aggression; (2) use of nuclear defence and denial weapons; (3) demonstrative use of nuclear weapons; (4) selective nuclear strikes on interdiction targets; (5) selective nuclear strikes against other suitable military targets.

c. General Nuclear Response. General nuclear response contemplates massive nuclear strikes against the total nuclear threat, other military targets, and urban-industrial targets as required. . . . It is both the ultimate deterrent and, if used, the ultimate military response.[105]

A variety of dates attended the approval and dissemination of the new strategy. The Military Committee in a chiefs of staff session voted on MC 14/3 on September 16, 1967, and disseminated it as a military decision on September 22. The DPC in ministerial session adopted MC 14/3 on December 12, 1967, and issued the final copy on January 16, 1968, with a note that gave primacy on any disputes over interpretation of the new strategy to the ministers' political guidance of May 9, 1967. MC 48/3, representing the detailed and regional analysis of implementing MC 14/3, passed Military Committee approval on May 6, 1969, DPC approval in ministerial session on December 4, 1969, and was issued in final copy on December 8, 1969. Both of these NATO strategy documents, MC 14/3 and MC 48/3, remained in force until the end of the Cold War.

The adoption of the 1967 Strategic Concept was a significant achievement both substantively and procedurally. Substantively, there was a risk that a strategy of flexible response could merely institutionalize a weakened American commitment to European defense, replacing the specific guarantees of massive retaliation with fungible and vague ones. NATO's strategy offered the needed flexibility that was lacking in massive retaliation but preserved the latter's clarity through the principle of deliberate escalation. Especially when combined with the exchanges of information on nuclear deterrence in the NPG, flexible response with deliberate escalation provided strong substance and clear commitments. The procedural use of the DPC to approve the new strategy signaled the workability of the two-tiered political decision-making structure that came about after 1966.

Although flexible response proved durable and the advent of the DPC provided an institutional location for future strategic deliberation and decision-making in NATO, the approval of the new strategy documents did not solve all of NATO's problems. This was partially a result of the fact that the formal adoption of MC 14/3 and MC 48/3 occurred nearly ten years after acknowledgment of the limitations of massive retaliation had begun to take root (as evidenced in the caveating present in MC 14/2) and at least five years after NATO had begun to employ flexible response de facto during the Berlin Crisis. In this sense, NATO was not in the strategic vanguard. Rather than really making strategy, NATO's Strategic Concept was mostly just catching up.[106]

"The Future Tasks of the Alliance"

In as much as the Berlin Crises and the Cuban Missile Crisis had loosened the constraints on action with respect to military strategy, they had also introduced broader political problems that détente and French withdrawal from the integrated military system had underscored.[107] Among the many consequences of the French decision to remain in the Alliance but outside many organizations that had been seen as central to NATO was the implied need to examine NATO's purposes. The French position had raised the question of what it meant to be part of NATO. The larger concern, echoed by others not only during détente but also after the Cold War and during other NATO crises, was that a lack of focus on a tangible purpose like territorial defense would weaken Alliance cohesion and endanger NATO's endurance. Secretary-General Brosio initially expressed a pessimistic view of diversifying NATO's focus, saying: "If we were to conclude that the Soviet threat was not the main problem, we had to ask ourselves what was the meaning of NATO."[108]

Others initially saw opportunity where Brosio saw risks. When NATO moved headquarters from Paris to Brussels, the Belgian government was particularly eager to demonstrate that its commitment to NATO was based on a desire for both military preparedness and stability in Europe through détente. In this context, Belgian foreign minister Pierre Harmel proposed that NATO undertake a study to revitalize the Alliance, articulate its purposes, and strengthen cohesion among its members. To promote this cohesion, it was important to Harmel that all NATO members, including France, participate in the study. The United States and other allies welcomed the Belgian proposal as a possible way to bring France back into the mainstream of the Alliance. France viewed participation as a way to find new directions for NATO favorable to its interests. After a month of discussion and having secured tacit approval from the participants, the NAC approved Harmel's proposal at the important ministerial session of December 15–16, 1966, agreeing "to undertake a broad analysis of international developments since the signing of the North Atlantic Treaty in 1949" in order "to determine the influence of such developments on the Alliance and to identify the tasks which lie before it in order to strength the Alliance as a factor for durable peace."[109]

The preparation of the Harmel Report would take place in four working groups. The first considered East-West relations, détente and its effect on European security, and the potential for a permanent settlement on Germany. The second group considered intra-alliance relations, measures to strengthen cohesion, potential for European cooperation within the Alliance, European integration, and the ideological basis for the Alliance. The third focused on general questions of defense policy, force structure, nuclear arrangements, and arms control. The fourth group considered developments in regions outside the NATO area, particularly with respect to China's status as a nuclear power as of October 1964. The project was intended to be a sweeping reflection on the Alliance's purpose.

If much of the impetus for the study of the future tasks of the Alliance came from national actors, the working groups themselves also involved high-ranking actors outside NATO's formal organization. Former NATO secretary-general Paul-Henri Spaak, who had just retired as Belgian foreign minister, returned to chair one of the working groups. The other key figures in leading the groups and presiding over their interaction were drawn from outside NATO. Klaus Schutz, an undersecretary in the West German Ministry of Foreign Affairs, was overall chairman. John Watson, assistant undersecretary of state in the British Foreign Office, was co-chairman. The other working group chairs included Foy Kohler, a US deputy undersecretary of state, and C. L. Patijn from the Netherlands, member of the Consultative Assembly of the Council of Europe. Secretary-General

Brosio or one of his staff members attended most of the meetings, but the NATO secretariat/international staff did not have a leading role in the working groups, and Brosio expressed some frustration that the process was largely out of his hands.[110]

French commitment to the Harmel project remained a matter of general uncertainty over the course of the next year. Brosio remained concerned that the lack of active French involvement in the contributions to working group sessions reflected poorly on the prospects for agreement. French foreign policy at the time, exemplified in Charles de Gaulle's visits to the Soviet Union and other Eastern bloc countries at the same time as France had disengaged from NATO's integrated military command, offered the potential that even a project as open-ended and flexible as Harmel's might not yield any significant agreement. Working groups forwarded preliminary reports to the NATO Military Committee and to member governments in the summer of 1967. But little consensus emerged in the details, and these reports ultimately failed to influence the final report. In the end, much of the wording in the final draft of the report came down to bilateral consultation between the United States and France. As the undersecretaries haggled over punctuation, many of the institutional actors, including Brosio, were shut out of the process.

Known as the report on "The Future Tasks of the Alliance," the Harmel Report was a concise and general document of only seventeen paragraphs. Whereas the detailed working group reports had sought to find agreement on a range of practical matters, the final report's fundamental assertion was that the Alliance had two functions: to provide for military security and to promote détente. According to the report, NATO's first function is "to maintain adequate military strength and political solidarity to deter aggression and other forms of pressure and to defend the territory of member countries if aggression should occur." This first function essentially affirmed what NATO had been doing all along. The more significant contribution was the report's assertion that NATO's second function is "to pursue the search for progress towards a more stable relationship in which the underlying political issues can be solved." In other words, the report continued, "[m]ilitary security and a policy of détente are not contradictory but complementary."[111]

NATO members adopted the Harmel Report in a ministerial session in December 1967, the first such session at the new headquarters in Belgium. Although the report did not find substantive progress on the detailed issues considered in the working groups, its larger aim—to define the purposes of NATO and to engage all members (France, most of all) in that effort—had been successful.

In this, French desire to cooperate may have been the result of a desire to avoid alienating Germany, France's most important partner in moves toward European integration. Germany and the other allies, for their parts, supported the Harmel Report because it provided a context for rapprochement between France and the United States, then the most important obstacle to Alliance cohesion.[112]

This assertion made NATO's future efforts in security and détente compatible with one another and thus offered a compromise between those NATO members who saw the Alliance as being primarily concerned with deterrence and military preparedness and those members who desired an active policy of détente. The Harmel Report thus expanded NATO's competences to include not only political and military matters of defense but also arms control policy, a multilateral détente policy, and policy concerns outside the North Atlantic area. Although the Harmel Report was criticized for not advocating any specific substantive plans for détente or future military planning, it was easily adopted for this very reason—it was general enough for each country to find it acceptable. In addition, the lack of specific substantive plans created opportunities for NATO's institutional actors, who had not played a significant role in drafting the substantive contents of the Harmel Report. In many ways this makes sense, since the definition of Alliance purposes is a central function of the member-states, while NATO institutions implement organization and strategies to achieve those purposes. Insofar as NATO's institutions were concerned, the fact that Alliance members had agreed to undertake the Harmel project within the auspices of NATO was a positive sign. What remained was for institutional NATO to continue the organization and strategic adaptations for which the states had called. The general, open-ended nature of the report allowed the future tasks it articulated to remain relevant beyond 1967, and indeed the political competences described in the Harmel Report became enduring features of NATO.

Conclusion

This case is exceptionally important in the long history of NATO adaptation and endurance. The critical juncture of the Second Berlin Crisis and Cuban Missile Crisis entailed a real risk that America would decouple from Europe as the structure of international politics changed. The advent of MAD gravely increased the risks to the United States from its commitment to NATO while simultaneously reducing its need for European military cooperation. As European governments and economies emerged from their postwar fragility, the risk of their falling into the communist bloc by domestic political choice or internal subversion decreased, and the United States might have calculated that the continued commitment was not worth the costs. By contrast, the weakening credibility of American extended nuclear deterrence created an impetus in Europe for greater autonomy. These developments were long in the making but were no longer possible to avoid or ignore when the Berlin and Cuban crises demonstrated how real these challenges were.

Moreover, this case is significant for NATO because France's withdrawal from the integrated military structure was such a major rejection of NATO's institutions. Even if France did not contemplate withdrawing from the North Atlantic Treaty and the Alliance overall, its decision was a major blow to the institutions of NATO and entailed a significant challenge to the endurance of those institutions. Insofar as independent national alternatives to security, such as the force de frappe or bilateral efforts at diplomacy and détente, represented an alternative to institutionalized cooperation, the Alliance could have reverted to something that more closely resembled traditional military alliances of the past, in which integrated and institutionalized political and military cooperation was not as significant as it had become in NATO.

In fact, these grave challenges to NATO did not limit its endurance but rather stimulated such sweeping and successful adaptations of organization and strategy that many of the changes made during this period proved durable enough to last until the end of the Cold War. Although some adaptations were arguably incremental or purely transactional, such as the relocation and consolidation of headquarters in Belgium, others were more fundamental. The creation of the NPG and the adoption of the flexible response strategy with deliberate escalation credibly reestablished NATO strategy, facilitated information-sharing on nuclear deterrence, and also allowed for the maintenance of national sovereignty and control over independent nuclear forces. The Harmel Report more broadly expanded the purposes of the Alliance by granting NATO's institutions a role in the future tasks of peace and security promotion through peaceful détente, in addition to military defense and deterrence. The two-tiered political structure that emerged, in which leaders met to discuss defense-related issues in the DPC, from which France abstained participation while all other issues continued to be addressed in the NAC, further reinforced the dual political and military character of NATO's institutions. Thus from what was the greatest setback and rejection of NATO's organization by its member-states came some of its most durable and successful adaptations, increasing NATO's vitality and relevance.

The role of institutional actors themselves in facilitating these adaptations is a mixed record, however. Independent national action was the main alternative to institutionalized cooperation in NATO, and this fact reflected the divergent priorities and interests of many of the member-states. Unlike after the outbreak of the Korean War, when the allies generally agreed on the need for stronger defense but disagreed on the way to implement it, NATO's challenges in this era pitted member-states on different sides of questions of sovereignty that remained within the purview of the states. State actors accordingly set the agenda on many of the adaptations in NATO (e.g., the actions of les quatorze) and often convened their own decision-making venues for important questions concerning the Alliance (e.g., the meetings in Bermuda and Nassau or France's intergovernmental approach to announcing its withdrawal from the integrated military structure).

Alternatively, NATO's institutional actors were often more successful in promoting adaptation when they were concurrently humble about their roles and chose to exercise moderating, information-sharing, and delaying functions. SACEUR Norstad was proactive and forceful about promoting the NATO MLF, but he arguably pushed that agenda too far. Norstad failed to recognize that states were unwilling to give up sovereignty over their nuclear forces, and, as Ridgway had done by opposing the Eisenhower administration's New Look, Norstad hastened his own replacement as SACEUR by opposing the Kennedy administration's view of the MLF and flexible response too vigorously. By contrast, SACEUR Lemnitzer and Secretary-General Brosio deftly avoided embroiling themselves in the highly politicized disputes among members-states and instead served as honest brokers for information-sharing and moderation following the French withdrawal, only taking the lead on the establishment of new structures for NATO when they had unequivocal authority from the member-states to do so. Secretary-General Stikker was bolder about delegating substantive recommendations as to how to move NATO's strategy toward a viable flexible response after 1962. But his most effective promotion of strategic adaptation was probably his convening of the 1963 NATO force planning exercise, which not only co-opted members' interest in flexible response but also incidentally involved the initial creation of the later-important DPC. Thus institutional NATO figures were not always the leading actors in many of the developments during this period, but their role in facilitating adaptation remained imperative.

As with other instances of adaptation in NATO following a critical juncture, changes were long in the making. The Berlin and Cuban crises had finished by the end of 1962, but it was not until 1967 that many of the most important adaptations in NATO had come into force. Moreover, contingency prevailed for the better part of four years while various independent and multilateral alternatives to adaptation were attempted. Only after the French decisions of 1966 forced an urgent reckoning with organizational change did adaptation occur more rapidly. It is possible to draw a strikingly similar comparison with the case of NATO in the 1950s, when four years of contingency followed the outbreak of the Korean War to the final collapse of the EDC in 1954, again the result of decisive French action and which also led to rapid organizational and strategic adaptation within a year.

CHAPTER SIX

NATO and the New World Order, 1992–1997

Studies of NATO often focus on either its history or its post–Cold War activity. Both rightly view the end of the Cold War as a turning point. Unlike previous critical junctures, where important events affecting NATO involved such far-away places as Korea and Cuba, the key events with the end of the Cold War—the fall of the Berlin Wall, democratic revolutions in Eastern Europe, the dissolution of the Warsaw Pact—occurred in Europe. Moreover, NATO's challenge was also of a different character: critical junctures during the Cold War tended to undermine the credibility of NATO's organization and strategy, while the end of the Cold War undermined their relevance. Earlier challenges raised questions about whether NATO could effectively carry out its purposes, while the end of the Cold War raised questions about those purposes themselves. These features make the end of the Cold War easy to identify as an important historical development. Salience notwithstanding, the end of the Cold War was much like any other critical juncture for NATO: it gave rise to contingency within the Alliance and engendered institutional alternatives to NATO. Alternatives were especially plausible because the post–Cold War security environment seemed so different from and more uncertain than the relatively predictable Cold War tensions. Further European integration in the EU and the aspiration of collective security in the Organization for Security and Cooperation in Europe were among the most significant institutional alternatives to NATO in the immediate post–Cold War era.

As in previous cases, NATO adapted its organization and strategy in order to address the challenges to its endurance. The most important strategic adaptations included a new Strategic Concept that greatly expanded NATO's core functions, adding conflict prevention, crisis management, and cooperation with former rivals to the established dual purposes of collective defense and dialogue. Instability in the Balkans prompted further adaptation as NATO applied its strategy in real operations, deploying forces out-of-area and using violence in armed conflict for the first time in Bosnia. Strategic adaptations stimulated organizational changes, such as the downsizing of the integrated military structure and development of more flexible and expeditionary military arrangements such as the Combined Joint Task Force (CJTF). Further organizational and strategic adaptations included the creation of forums for political cooperation, such as the Partnership for Peace (PfP), more institutionalized dialogue in the NATO-Russia Permanent Joint Council (PJC), and enlargement of NATO membership to countries in Central and Eastern Europe.

Institutional actors played leading roles in many of these adaptations. In the absence of strong constraints from member-states, key institutional actors, including Colonel Klaus Wittmann of the International Military Staff (IMS) and Secretary-General Manfred Wörner, made especially strong use of agenda-setting powers to facilitate adaptation. Others, including Assistant Secretary-General Michael Legge and Secretary-General Willy Claes, made robust use of the convening function. Despite little need for institutional actors to employ the delaying function, adaptations nevertheless continued for years as NATO set out to do more in a dynamic post–Cold War security environment.

The Structural Basis of the Cold War's End

Scholars have famously compared the effect of the Cold War's end on the discipline of international relations to that of the *Titanic*'s sinking on the profession of maritime engineering.[1] Both were unexpected and seemed to change everything. Retrospectively, however, several structural elements of the Cold War had been in decline for some time. In terms of direct military confrontation between the superpowers, late Cold War belligerency tended against the high-stakes nuclear brinkmanship of the Cuban Missile Crisis sort and toward proxy conflicts and other more limited, indirect contests.[2] The early 1960s also represented the height of the arms race, after which the revolutionary pace of technological development slowed and various arms control programs reduced the growth in the number and scope of arms.[3] Some historians credit increased US defense spending during the 1980s and programs like the Strategic Defense Initiative (known as Star Wars) with helping to accelerate the demise of an overwhelmed Soviet economic system.[4] But even in economic terms, Western economies had begun irrevocably to outpace the communist bloc as early as the 1950s.[5] Rigid political division in Europe eased through détente in the 1970s, *Ostpolitik* helped normalize relations between Germany and the East, and the pan-European Conference on Security and Cooperation in Europe (CSCE) established a broad agenda for reconciliation and increased interaction.[6] Both sides embraced the Helsinki Final Act of the CSCE in 1975, which offered assurances of territorial stability in Europe desirable to the Soviet Union while affirming a commitment to democracy and individual human rights that were important to the West.[7] Ideological competition had ranged from Nikita Khrushchev's misunderstood but apparently stark "We will bury you" promise in 1956 to Mikhail Gorbachev's abandonment of the class struggle model for peaceful coexistence in his address to the UN General Assembly in December 1988.[8]

Moreover, the Cold War did not end all at once. The Cold War was a useful concept for making sense of international relations, particularly in Europe. But it was a complex period. As Allen Lynch wrote in an aptly titled book in 1992, each successive event in its unraveling prompted observers to conclude "the Cold War is over—again."[9] From the arms control point of view, the unilateral cuts in Soviet conventional forces in 1988 and the 1990 Treaty on Conventional Armed Forces in Europe (CFE) effectively ended the Cold War military confrontation in Europe. The Warsaw Pact disbanded at a meeting in February 1991 and disestablished the Warsaw Treaty in July of that year. Following the transition to world market prices in energy in January 1991, Eastern European states also proclaimed an end to economic cooperation under the Council for Mutual Economic Assistance (known as Comecon). Superpower relations seemed to have entered a new era when the United States and Soviet Union cooperated in support of the 1990 UN Security Council resolution to authorize force against Iraq's invasion of Kuwait and announced a "strategic partnership" and a bilateral Strategic Arms Reduction Treaty (START) in 1991. But the collapse of communist regimes ultimately transformed the political landscape. In all, twenty-eight Eastern European countries and constituent republics of the Soviet Union and Yugoslavia began a transition away from communism between the spring of 1989 and the spring of 1991.[10] Democratic revolutions in Poland, Hungary, East Germany, Czechoslovakia, Bulgaria, and Romania led the way in 1989, during which the fall of the Berlin Wall on November 9 was the most symbolic evidence of change. Finally, following an attempted coup d'état in August 1991, the USSR itself ceased "its existence as a subject of international law and a geopolitical reality" in December 1991.[11]

The Cold War's End as a Critical Juncture for NATO

The structural events leading to the end of the Cold War constituted a critical juncture for NATO. Although previous structural shifts considered in this study involved important global trends or non-European events in critical junctures, such as the Korean War or the Cuban Missile Crisis, the most important developments in this case occurred in Europe. The fact that the Cold War legacy persisted in East Asia, where Korea remained divided and the communist regime in China weathered democratic reform protests in 1989, does not lessen the impact of the changes in Europe on NATO. A loosening of structural constraints on action is the key feature of a critical juncture, and structural changes closer to home are no less significant than those farther away. Moreover, there are more geographic continuities than differences in this case. One such emerging pattern is the central role of Germany, both in general and Berlin in particular, as a setting for moments of crisis. The Berlin crisis of 1948, the second Berlin crisis of 1959–1962, and the fall of the Berlin Wall in 1989 had all visibly demonstrated the emerging effects of significant underlying structural changes. Larger events elsewhere in the international system, including the dissolution of communist regimes in the Soviet Union and throughout the Eastern bloc, contributed to the momentousness of the Zeitgeist in the same way that the Korean War and Cuban Missile Crisis had in earlier times.

As in previous critical junctures, the end of the Cold War challenged the continuing endurance of NATO. These challenges to NATO's organization and strategy as it existed at the Cold War's end were of at least four specific varieties. First and most immediately, the fall of the Berlin Wall gave rise to a resurgence of the familiar German question of how this powerful state in the center of Europe would fit into the new world order.[12] Would reunification occur, and if so how would that affect Germany's place in NATO? The Cold War had kept Germany divided and weak: Soviet domination through the Warsaw Pact kept East Germany down, and West German membership in NATO and the EC had similarly limited the latent danger of German resurgence and revisionism. With the fall of the Berlin Wall and a growing crisis of political legitimacy in the German Democratic Republic (GDR) in late 1989, the issue of German reunification emerged as a real possibility. Although reunification would bring an end to Europe's most symbolic Cold War division, any such move would also involve a potentially dangerous redistribution of power in Europe as well as upsetting NATO's place in the institutional order set up to address the German question since the 1950s. For the Soviet Union, for example, a reunified Germany within NATO would be an unwelcome shift in the balance of power. But for French president Francois Mitterrand, by contrast, a reunified Germany outside NATO and other Western institutions carried the risk that "we will be back in 1913 and we could lose everything."[13] The question of Germany's role in the changing international system was thus the most immediate of the major challenges to arise in the critical juncture of the Cold War's ending. But this was also a question in which independent national political decisions played the most important determining roles. Although reunification was not a foregone conclusion after the fall of the Berlin Wall, the emerging reality of reunification on October 3, 1990, further served to increase the importance of determining institutional arrangements for handling the broader range of post–Cold War challenges.[14]

The second broad challenge to the Alliance in the aftermath of the Cold War resulted from the rapid collapse of Soviet authority in Eastern Europe. If the re-emergence of the German question indicated that NATO's founding purpose of keeping Germany down remained as important as ever, this second challenge reflected the new circumstance that the Soviet Union had indeed been kept out of Western Europe. The end of Soviet power had created the need to build a post–Cold War order in both Western and Eastern Europe. During the Cold War, containment provided security in the West while acknowledging that the influence of the Soviet Union prevailed on the other side of the Iron Curtain. Organizations like the Warsaw Pact and the Council for Mutual Economic Assistance formalized this order, but its real underpinning was in the so-called Brezhnev Doctrine, which defended the Soviet Union's claim to impose its will on other communist states. In successive instances, including Hungary in 1956 and Czechoslovakia in 1968, the West did not interfere as the Soviet Union put down challenges to its hegemony in Eastern Europe. Gorbachev openly repudiated the Brezhnev Doctrine in November 1986, telling Eastern European leaders that the Soviet Union would not use force to keep them in power.[15] When democratic revolutions swept through Eastern Europe in 1989, Gorbachev stayed true to his word.[16] Soviet troops also withdrew from Eastern Europe following demands from Hungary, Poland, and Czechoslovakia after the disbanding of the Warsaw Pact. In sum, the entire system of Soviet-imposed order in Eastern Europe disappeared over the course of approximately eighteen months after 1989, an abrupt ending to a tightly controlled regime that had persisted for more than forty years.[17]

The effect of these changes was uncertainty, confusion, and instability that NATO leaders increasingly viewed as "having a direct effect on the security of the Alliance."[18] The Eastern European states faced political transition from one-party governments, economic transition from communism, and international transition from Soviet satellite status.[19] As Czech leader Václav Havel described, "[O]ur countries are sliding dangerously into a certain political, economic and security vacuum. The old imposed political, economic, and security links have collapsed, but new ones are coming into being slowly and with difficulty, if at all.

At the same time, it is becoming evident that without appropriate external links the very existence of our young democracies is in jeopardy."[20]

Civil war in the breakup of Yugoslavia emerged as the most conspicuous manifestation of this problem. Yugoslavia had been an uneasy multiethnic assemblage, and the post–Cold War power vacuum helped undo it. Following Slovenian and Croatian declarations of independence on June 25, 1991, Bosnia quickly emerged as the main theater of violence after its declaration of independence in March 1992. Serbia and Croatia vied for a greater stake in a post-Yugoslav territorial outcome at Bosnia's expense, and ethnic and sectarian violence erupted between the Bosniak (Muslim) and the minority Serb (Orthodox) and Croat (Catholic) populations in Bosnia. By the end of 1992, more than two-thirds of Bosnia was under Serb control and reports increasingly demonstrated scenes of ethnic cleansing, war crimes, and other atrocities not seen in Europe since World War II.[21] Historical memory compounded the dangers of nationalism, ethnic violence, and instability in the Balkan powder keg and made the risks of post–Cold War instability in Central and Eastern Europe abundantly clear.

A related and third challenge to NATO at the end of the Cold War was that the new Russia remained a significant player in international politics notwithstanding the collapse of the Soviet order. The end of the Cold War did not alter the material fact of Russia's large arsenal of nuclear weapons or the likelihood that a post-Soviet Russia would maintain power and interests with which NATO and other actors would have to contend. Moreover, Russia was also facing the same domestic transitions as the Eastern European countries. The risks of economic depression, political instability, ethnic conflict, and civil war were as real in the former Soviet Union as they were for its former Eastern European client states and their implications for European security similarly relevant. The breakup of the Soviet Union did not involve a full-scale civil war, but it did unleash limited regional conflicts, including those over Nagorno-Karabakh between Armenia and Azerbaijan, the Transnistria region between Moldova and Ukraine, South Ossetia and Abkhazia in Georgia, and Chechnya in Russia's north Caucasus. All of these problems were similar to those in Eastern Europe, but with the added complication that they directly involved a Russian state that remained large and forceful in many ways. As NATO faced challenges from other aspects of the emerging post–Cold War period, the legacy of Russian power would also continue in the new era.

Thus the final challenge to the Alliance in the aftermath of the Cold War was the conceptual issue of NATO's role in the "new world order." Conventional wisdom is that NATO lost its raison d'être with the end of the Cold War.[22] This view is simplistic, since NATO had always served a variety of purposes. NATO's

various adaptations had entailed a variety of other functions as well, most notably the dual purposes of defense and dialogue described in the 1967 report on
the Future Tasks of the Alliance. But, just as the Harmel Report underscored
NATO's need to reconsider its main tasks in light of changes during the 1950s
and '60s, the end of the Cold War also demanded a reconsideration of the most
important tasks in European and transatlantic security. NATO's continued endurance as part of that system was by no means a foregone conclusion. Russian
desires to see NATO disband were more than wishful thinking; they reflected
an understandable logic that saw NATO as the Western analog of the Warsaw
Pact, which had outlived its usefulness and disbanded accordingly. Many observers in the United States also agreed, figuring that costly American defense
support to Europe was no longer needed and could be cut as part of a wider
post–Cold War "peace dividend."

While Charles de Gaulle had once referred to NATO as an obsolete form of the
transatlantic alliance, that charge had intuitively greater and broader resonance
after the Cold War, in part because of how durable NATO's organizational and
strategic adaptations had been in the 1960s. NATO endured at least two critical
junctures and adapted a great deal during its first twenty years after 1949, but
the pace of change slowed during its second twenty years and reflected continuity more than contingency or change. Organizational changes in NATO during
the 1970s and 1980s included the accession of Spain and the establishment of
the NATO Airborne Warning and Control System (AWACS) program. But the
main organizational mechanisms such as political direction in the NAC and
DPC, nuclear consultation in the NPG, and a largely stable integrated military
structure remained mostly invariable. Strategically, flexible response as defined
in MC 14/3 of 1967 remained NATO's official Strategic Concept through the end
of the Cold War. Efforts during the 1970s and 1980s, such as the deployment of
intermediate-range nuclear forces beginning in 1983, represented NATO's application of that strategy more than a rethinking of it. These organizational and
strategic arrangements were well adapted to the demands of the Cold War but
did little to address the emerging challenges of the post–Cold War era.

Contingency and Institutional Alternatives to NATO
in the Post–Cold War Era

The end of the Cold War was a highly contingent historical period. Contingency
is a factor in any critical juncture, but it was especially so in this case not only
because of the sweeping character of the structural shifts occurring but also
because of general optimism about the potential of international institutions

during this time.[23] Unlike previous critical junctures when alternative institutional arrangements to NATO tended to find clear expression in a single institution (e.g., the EDC) or a single organizing principle (e.g., the reassertion of national independence in foreign policy), various institutional alternatives to NATO arose in the early post–Cold War era. Proposals ranged from renewed ambition for the United Nations to the creation of sweeping new arrangements such as a European Confederation, while the EU and the OSCE in Europe further established themselves as more plausible institutional alternatives to NATO also.

The United Nations and the Institutional Bias of Post–Cold War Contingency

The end of the Cold War helped revitalize the United Nations. The prospect of a US or Soviet veto in the Security Council had limited the latter's ability to authorize action during the Cold War. The exception that proved the rule was the UN authorization of peace enforcement action in the Korean War, a decision taken when the Soviet Union declined to attend the Security Council sessions, a situation never again repeated. But following the end of the Cold War, the prospect for better cooperation among former adversaries and a renewed expression of common interests in peace and security led to a greater role for the UN. US and Soviet cooperation on UN authorization to reverse Iraq's invasion of Kuwait in 1990 epitomized the change.

The UN Security Council took action when crisis broke out in the Balkans, first by imposing a weapons embargo on Yugoslavia. In February 1992, it authorized a peacekeeping force, the United Nations Protection Force (UNPROFOR), with the aim of providing stability in support of the diplomatic efforts that the European Communities (EC) in particular continued to pursue. But as negotiations broke down and violence continued, UN efforts in the Balkans appeared increasingly ineffective. This was true even though the size of the UNPROFOR increased to more than thirty-eight thousand troops by November 1994, of whom more than fourteen thousand were from European NATO member countries and Canada.[24] Russia consistently and strongly opposed an expansion of UNPROFOR's mission from peacekeeping to more forceful measures to contain the violence, and several European countries also shared concerns about the risks of becoming embroiled in the conflict. Meanwhile, the security situation continued to deteriorate, culminating in the July 1995 siege of Srebrenica, a UN-designated and UNPROFOR-guarded "safe haven," in which more than seven thousand civilians were massacred.[25]

Although by 1995 the Balkans had cast doubt on the UN's effectiveness as a security actor, the UN still ranked among the more plausible initial alternative institutions for addressing the challenges of the immediate post–Cold War era. Some institutions were proposed and pursued earnestly enough but never realized at all. One example of this genre was François Mitterrand's proposal for a European Confederation. Mitterrand embodied the contingency of the times in his own actions in the immediate post–Cold War period. He had been a leading figure in the proposals for a single currency and greater European integration. He had also expressed a desire to see NATO play a role in managing German reunification. In December 1989, he proposed that the CSCE be convened to affirm the territorial boundaries in a post–Cold War order. And, finally, in remarks on New Year's Eve 1989, Mitterrand proposed a "European Confederation," open to every European state embracing democratic institutions and that "would associate all the States of our continent in a common and permanent organization of exchanges, of peace and of security."[26]

The European Confederation was intended not only to consolidate democratic gains and promote peace but also to realize the Gaullist aspiration of greater independence from the United States. As Mitterrand later explained to Kohl: "I spoke of a possible European confederation, because the countries that have liberated themselves from the Communist yoke should not remain isolated. . . . It is necessary therefore to have an institution to which all democratic countries will have access. People say that the CSCE already exists for that. But it will be very important, for the dignity of these countries, to have a political institution among Europeans alone."[27] Of course, the Eastern European countries did not welcome the idea of including the Soviet Union while excluding the United States. Having just freed themselves from such arrangements, the idea of joining new institutions that might bind them again to the Soviet Union made little sense. Rather, these countries looked instead to Western institutions and to relationships that included the United States especially. As a result, the European Confederation failed to gain any momentum at its intended founding meeting in Prague in June 1991. But the European Confederation proposal serves as an example of the highly contingent institutional circumstances of the early post–Cold War era.

The European Union as an Institutional Alternative to NATO

In contrast to proposals such as the European Confederation, which failed to attract much initial support, deepening efforts at European integration were among the most viable of the institutional alternatives for addressing the challenges of the post–Cold War era. The development of the EC into the EU, further economic integration epitomized by the proposals for a single currency, an agreement on stronger political ties in the Common Foreign and Security Policy (CFSP), and integrated military cooperation in the Eurocorps and WEU all constituted plausible institutional arrangements that were pursued and implemented.

European integration after the Cold War offered the potential to institutionalize cooperation in European foreign policy and defense that had proved elusive ever since the collapse of the EDC. One of the lessons of the EDC's failure was that defense and foreign policy were central to most states' conceptions of national sovereignty, making institutionalized union in those areas difficult to achieve. Subsequent efforts at political integration during the Cold War had reinforced that lesson. The Fouchet Plan of 1961 was ultimately no more successful than the Pléven Plan of 1950.[28] In a remarkable parallel to the French policy toward NATO during de Gaulle's presidency, France also withdrew its representatives from European institutions in 1965, sparking the so-called Empty Chair Crisis. Further efforts to deepen European political integration remained suspended until de Gaulle's departure, after which the 1970 Davignon Report recommended foreign policy coordination be organized on an intergovernmental rather than supranational basis. This informal process would not be established in law or treaties and became known as European Political Cooperation (EPC).[29] EPC had some modest successes during the 1970s, such as a joint EC declaration on Middle East policy in 1970 and common action at the Yaoundé Conventions on aid to developing countries. In 1975, Italian Prime Minister Aldo Moro signed the Helsinki Final Act of the CSCE in the name of the European Community. But EPC involved no new institutions and no binding commitments; it remained a limited, voluntary medium outside the EC.

The end of the Cold War prompted a renewed effort to promote political integration in Europe. Both the revolutions in Eastern Europe and the prospects of Germany's reunification led to a greater need for a common European foreign policy. At a special meeting of the European Council in Dublin in April 1990, European leaders decided on a parallel intergovernmental conference on political union to complement one on economic and monetary union agreed at Strasbourg in 1989.[30] The debate on improving European foreign policy coordination revolved around two proposals. The first, championed by Britain, was for a gradual approach to improving political coordination within the relatively informal EPC while leaving matters of defense to NATO. The second approach, championed by France, Germany, and Italy, was for a more ambitious CFSP.

This latter approach ultimately prevailed in the December 1991 Maastricht Treaty, which established the EU. CFSP was to make up the second of three "pillars" in the new EU (along with the Police and Judicial Cooperation in Criminal Matters pillar, and the existing EC). Although the decision-making process of the CFSP was to remain intergovernmental, CFSP would differ from EPC in that any common positions or joint actions agreed under CFSP would be legally binding on member-states.

The CFSP encompassed an explicit intent to include and develop defense cooperation and integration in the EU. The Maastricht Treaty stipulated that CFSP "shall include all questions related to the security of the Union, including the eventual framing of a common defence policy, which might in time lead to a common defence."[31] Rather than attempting to establish a new supranational institution in the tradition of the EDC, however, the Maastricht Treaty initially signaled intent to revitalize an existing structure for these purposes, namely the WEU. The WEU, created from a modification of the Brussels Treaty in order to help manage German rearmament and inclusion in NATO in 1955, had been alive but politically dormant throughout the Cold War. In 1984, however, the WEU was revived to substitute for a failure to include defense considerations in EPC.[32] The Maastricht Treaty affirmed that the WEU was "an integral part of the development of the [European] Union," and momentum built behind that view. In June 1992, WEU foreign and defense ministers met in Petersberg near Bonn to issue a comprehensive mission statement and list of defense responsibilities known as the Petersberg Tasks. These tasks, largely confined to peacekeeping, humanitarian assistance, rescue, and other operations short of high-intensity conflict, became the basis for Europe's defense autonomy agenda. Meanwhile, France and Germany agreed in 1990 to establish an experimental multinational brigade and expanded the concept in 1992 with the creation of Eurocorps, a multinational headquarters in Strasbourg that would command units contributed from France, Germany, Belgium, Luxembourg, and Spain, and which became operational in 1995.

These efforts toward autonomous European political and defense integration avoided some of the drawbacks that had plagued the EDC and later efforts during the Cold War. Unlike the EDC or the Fouchet Plan, the CFSP abandoned supranational institutional devices and instead embraced intergovernmental cooperation that had seen some potential in the limited successes of the EPC process. In addition, the institutional arrangements set out in the Maastricht Treaty effectively co-opted the WEU, very much in the same way that NATO had co-opted the WEU's earlier Brussels Treaty incarnations for its own purposes during the 1950s.[33] Finally, the efforts to create common military forces in the Eurocorps not only bound Germany in Europe more securely but also generated a small but exclusively European force. Just as NATO had appreciated the need for both organization and capabilities in creating its integrated military structure in the 1950s, so the Eurocorps served a similar logic. Even if it was much smaller in scope and not officially tied to EU institutions in the same way as NATO military authorities, Eurocorps set a remarkable institutional precedent.[34]

But plausible and promising European institutional alternatives quickly proved incomplete and inadequate to address the full range of post–Cold War challenges. On the one hand, this was partially by design, as the efforts at European integration were self-consciously and primarily intended to deepen internal cooperation among EU members, especially with respect to a reunited Germany. On the other hand, the EU was not envisioned to be entirely inward looking, as the CFSP expressly anticipated.[35] Even if the CFSP did not contain a comprehensive plan for managing the decline of the bipolar world order, confidence in the capacity of European institutions to manage instability in Eastern Europe was initially quite strong. Specifically addressing these challenges as they developed in the Balkans, Luxembourg foreign minister Jacques Poos notoriously expressed this view in saying: "This is the hour of Europe. . . . If one problem can be solved by the Europeans, it is the Yugoslav problem. This is a European country and it is not up to the Americans. It is not up to anyone else."[36]

But European efforts to deal with the conflict in the former Yugoslavia did not match this rhetoric. In the first instance, Europe struggled to find a common foreign policy position. While the EC initially worked to oppose a breakup of Yugoslavia, Germany publicly supported Croatian and Slovenian independence.[37] Secondly, EC efforts were ultimately too limited to curtail the violence. Although the EC succeeded in its first effort at mediating a cease-fire of the Ten-Day War (or the Weekend War) in Slovenia, it was the smallest and least complex of the independence movements in the former Yugoslavia.[38] An EC delegation of three foreign ministers—including Jacques Poos—successfully presided at the cease-fire agreement, the Brijuni Declaration, on July 7, 1991. But the relative ease of the Slovenian case may have led to an overestimation of what the EC could achieve in Croatia or Bosnia. As the conflicts worsened, the EC was forced to acknowledge that it lacked the material capability or diplomatic experience to continue efforts to achieve peace and deferred efforts to the UN in July 1992.[39]

Thus European integration was a plausible approach to some European security problems in the post–Cold War era, and it was pursued in the development of institutions such as the EU. The character of these institutional alternatives, including the CFSP of the EU, the revitalization of the WEU, and the creation of integrated military capabilities like the Eurocorps, were noteworthy institutional developments that avoided some of the stumbling blocks that had hampered previous efforts at European political and defense integration during the Cold War. Ultimately, however, these institutional efforts were not complete in addressing the full range of post–Cold War European security challenges. European integration contributed most convincingly to inwardly focused efforts to retain a unified Germany firmly rooted in the Western system. But efforts to address instability in Eastern Europe were beyond reach, foundering in the case of the Balkans both on long-standing difficulties in generating foreign policy consensus among members and on a lack of sufficient institutional capabilities and experience. Moreover, evolving relations with Russia and the challenges attending the former Soviet Union remained outside the focus of these early post–Cold War developments of European institutions.

The OSCE as an Institutional Alternative to NATO

The Organization for Security and Cooperation in Europe emerged as the other main institutional alternative for addressing the challenges of the post–Cold War era. If European integration represented an inwardly focused approach that began with deepening cooperation among Western states but ultimately stopped short of extending stability to Eastern Europe and the former Soviet Union, the OSCE by contrast began with an expansive view of its membership that contributed little to intra-Western cooperation and lacked the political solidarity and material strength to address the most troublesome instances of instability elsewhere.

In the immediate aftermath of the Cold War, however, the ideal of a pan-Euro Atlantic security institution enjoyed a strong measure of support. Such aspirations rested on the view that the former Cold War enemies had no need to maintain adversarial institutional structures and that all states in the region shared a common interest in peace, stability, and security.[40] The success of the CSCE in promoting cooperation on these matters also seemed to offer a model to institutionalize further cooperation. Mikhail Gorbachev advocated this view in June 1990 when he criticized the creation of alliances "on a selective, and in fact discriminatory, basis" and called for an end to "old thinking."[41] Jiri Dienstbier, foreign minister of Czechoslovakia, echoed Gorbachev in calling NATO and the Warsaw Pact "vestiges of the old confrontation" and continued: "We need a new security structure, based on the CSCE, embracing everybody in Europe, and the United States."[42] Both the Warsaw Pact and NATO officially joined in these sentiments. Just as the Harmel Report seemed to offer a consistent basis for such aims in NATO, the final article of the Warsaw Treaty specifically included terms for such an arrangement: "In the event of the organization of a system of collective security in Europe and the conclusion of a general European treaty of collective security to that end, which the contracting parties shall unceasingly seek to bring about, the present treaty shall cease to be effective on the date the general European treaty comes into force."[43] Member-states of NATO and the Warsaw Pact supported this position in a joint statement in 1990 to the effect that "security is indivisible and that the security of each of their countries is inextricably linked to the security of all States participating in the Conference of Security and Cooperation in Europe."[44]

These statements preceded the Charter of Paris for a New Europe, at which members announced the creation of "new structures and institutions of the CSCE process." Among these would be a Council of Foreign Ministers, a Committee of Senior Officials (subordinate to the ministers), a secretariat in Prague, a Conflict Prevention Centre in Vienna, an Office of Free Elections in Warsaw, and a Parliamentary Assembly. The roughly thirty-page Paris document was evenly divided between the charter itself, which reaffirmed the principles of the Helsinki Final Act, and a supplementary appendix with detailed administrative, financial, logistical, procedural, and substantive specifications for the new institutions.[45] In other words, the Charter of Paris not only envisaged greater harmony but mandated new institutional arrangements in considerable detail and specificity.

Further institutional development proceeded in line with the Charter of Paris. In January 1992, the Office for Free Elections became the Office for Democratic Institutions and Human Rights. In March 1992, the Treaty on Open Skies created a regime of unarmed aerial surveillance flights over the territories of CSCE countries, realizing a proposal that President Eisenhower first offered in 1955.[46] A secretary-general's post was established at the CSCE Council of Ministers in December 1992. The CSCE Heads of State Summit in Budapest acknowledged this mounting institutionalization and changed the name to the Organization for Security and Cooperation in Europe (OSCE) in December 1994.[47]

Despite dampened enthusiasm about the CSCE/OSCE's potential to replace other structures as a single, all-encompassing approach to post–Cold War security, it nevertheless engaged with several of the challenges of the day, particularly with respect to instability in the Balkans and the former Soviet Union. On the one hand, the OSCE was the only multilateral institution that played an immediate role in conflict resolution in parts of the former Soviet Union, engaging in Nagorno-Karabakh (from 1992), South Ossetia (also from 1992), Transdini-estria (from 1993), and Chechnya (from 1995). On the other hand, these efforts were generally unsuccessful.[48] Not only were the conflicts deeply entrenched, but Russia continued to play a spoiling role in their resolution within the OSCE.

The OSCE's efforts in the Balkans, meanwhile, included missions in Macedo-nia (from 1992), Kosovo (1992–1993), Bosnia (from 1994), Croatia (from 1996), and Albania (from 1997). Some of these missions, such as conflict prevention in Mace-donia, were ultimately more successful than those in the former Soviet Union. But all of the OSCE's efforts in the Balkans were undertaken in concert with the UN, EU, and NATO, underscoring the limitations of any independent OSCE capacity. Although some observers fairly point out that the OSCE has in the long run played a part in socializing liberal democratic norms in the former communist bloc,[49] these benefits did not offer relief to the most pressing tangible concerns of the immediate post–Cold War era.

Notwithstanding this institutional development, however, the limitations of the CSCE/OSCE for dealing with post–Cold War challenges quickly became ap-parent. More than any other factor, Soviet action during 1991 diminished read-iness to replace the old structures with a pan-European and American approach to security. Using precisely the kind of "selective" or "discriminatory" approach that Gorbachev had derided, the Soviet Union pressed Romania and Hungary for separate treaties that would prevent entry into competing security struc-tures.[50] It blocked the CSCE from taking a role in resolving the independence movements in the Baltic republics. And it worked to undermine the capabilities of the new CSCE institutions generally, particularly with respect to the Con-flict Prevention Centre. Václav Havel summarized evolving thinking in March 1991:

> everything seemed quite clear-cut and simple to us in the first thrilling weeks and
> months of freedom: the Warsaw Pact . . . would dismantle itself in a peaceful fash-
> ion. The North Atlantic Alliance, on the other hand, would begin to transform it-
> self rapidly until it became part of a completely new security structure. . . . [I]t
> seemed to us that the most suitable political ground for the establishment of such
> a security structure might be the Conference on Security and Cooperation in
> Europe. . . . Today we see that the paths of history are more winding, and more
> complicated . . . [than] the ideal of which I have spoken. . . . Certain aspects of the
> development in the Soviet Union give us valid reasons for concern. . . . For us this
> means, first of all, rapidly creating a system of bilateral agreements . . . , cooperation

with the North Atlantic Alliance . . . , association with the European Communities . . . , [and] contacts with the Western European Union.[51]

A number of institutional features limited the OSCE. In the first instance, the OSCE lacked a mandate to enforce matters on its own. Even though the OSCE is recognized as a regional collective security arrangement under the terms of Chapter VIII of the UN charter, the OSCE is institutionally weaker than the UN in many respects. The OSCE lacks a "Security Council" or similar structure that would enable it to take action against any of its members. The only real sanction that the OSCE can offer is suspension from the organization, a course of action that runs counter to its inclusive approach and that has only been attempted once (Serbia and Montenegro on July 8, 1992).[52] Unanimity is the general rule for decision-making in the OSCE, which is difficult to achieve in the best of circumstances due to its large membership. This also allows states that are the subject of OSCE concern effectively to block action against themselves, as Russia did. Moreover, there is no OSCE treaty as such; OSCE founding documents such as the Helsinki Final Act and the Charter of Paris are political commitments but lack the force of treaties in international law.

More concretely, the OSCE lacks hard power. As Alexandra Gheciu observes, "One should not assume that the OSCE was designed as a highly structured, militarily powerful security organization. In fact, the OSCE . . . does not possess military resources to implement its decisions. As a result, to implement its decisions, the OSCE depends on political consensus among its participating states and on the diplomatic skills of its officials and the staff of its field missions."[53] This absence of hard power competences contrasts with NATO's integrated military structure, the nascent European capabilities in the WEU, or the facility to flag military missions in the way that the UN does. Whereas the UNPROFOR mission in the Balkans ultimately consisted of thousands of troops, for example, OSCE missions are of a nonmilitary character and involve far fewer personnel.[54]

There are benefits to the OSCE's low-cost and low-overhead approach, of course, but also limitations. The trade-offs for the OSCE are reflective of the more general, conceptual distinction between collective defense and collective security. Collective defense involves a small number of parties allied against an external threat, while collective security entails internal enforcement of agreed-upon rules among a potentially much larger number of parties. As David Yost argues in characterizing the OSCE, the difference between collective defense and collective security involves a balance between effectiveness and inclusiveness in the design of security institutions: if the EU was effective but not inclusive, the OSCE was inclusive but not effective.[55]

The OSCE and the EU were not the only international institutions proposed during the immediate post–Cold War era, but they receive more detailed attention here because they best fit the criteria for institutional alternatives that were plausible and pursued following a critical juncture. Moreover, the OSCE and the EU were more than just proposals, as both were successfully established and endure to this day. In this respect, it is possible to distinguish these two post–Cold War institutions from proposals in the earlier cases such as the EDC in the 1950s and from contemporaneous proposals such as the European Confederation. The OSCE and the EU were especially viable as institutional alternatives to NATO because they existed and operated to address the challenges of the early post–Cold War era.

Moreover, unlike the EDC or the European Confederation, neither the OSCE nor the EU needed to be created entirely afresh. Some have argued that NATO endures because it was so well established by the end of the Cold War that creating new institutions would be costlier and less practical than relying on old ones.[56] But both the OSCE and the EU had long-standing institutional foundations of their own. If NATO could draw on its historical legacy for strength in adapting to the critical juncture of the Cold War, so, too, could the OSCE and the EU, respectively, draw on decades-old patterns of cooperation in the CSCE and the EC. In other words, any advantage to institutional endurance deriving from the simple fact of longevity was not unique to NATO.

A further factor that contributed to the plausibility of the OSCE and the EU as potential institutional alternatives to NATO is that they were not mutually exclusive. The EU primarily concerned internal integration among a small group of countries and explored capacities as a foreign and defense actor outside its members' territories as a codicil. By contrast, the OSCE was above all a broadly inclusive institution by membership that tested the limits of its capacities to make and enforce difficult resolutions among its members. It is not difficult to imagine these institutions overlapping in a mutually constructive way—as in fact many argue that they have and continue to do.[57] But the overlapping competencies of the OSCE and EU continued to leave some challenges uncovered, as civil war in the Balkans made clear.

NATO Organizational and Strategic Adaptation after the Cold War

NATO adapted a great deal after the Cold War. The main strategic adaptations were in the new Strategic Concept and its implementation in Bosnia. The main organizational adaptations were a revising of the integrated military structure, establishment of partnerships, "interlocking institutions," and, ultimately, enlargement. Institutional mechanisms of agenda-setting and co-opting seemed to be the most important in this case. Institutional actors were key actors in adaptation. Overall, NATO adaptations offered something to all four main challenges inherent in the critical juncture, namely the German question, instability in Eastern Europe, dealing with Russia, and the existential question of roles and purposes.

NATO Strategy after the Cold War

A reexamination of strategy was one of the first adaptations NATO undertook at the end of the Cold War. The 1967 MC 14/3 document had served NATO well for the purpose of collective defense during the Cold War. But both the collapse of the communist order and the nature of the emerging security challenges created obvious reasons to reassess this strategy of flexible response. Post–Cold War security challenges seemed less clear and less certain, as they did not involve the rise of another great power state with a large military to replace the Soviet Union as the principal adversary to the Alliance.

An appreciation of the changing military rather than political situation initially led to calls for a reassessment of NATO strategy. Two weeks after the fall of the Berlin Wall and in view of arms control agreements then in progress, the Military Committee directed NATO military authorities to "carry out a study into Warsaw Pact military capacity after the implementation of the Conventional Forces Europe (CFE) Treaty."[58] The IMS soon conducted such a study under the direction of Klaus Wittmann, a colonel in the German army. The resulting Wittmann Paper somewhat exceeded the limited scope of the Military Committee's request and articulated not merely a report on Warsaw Pact capabilities but rather a sweeping assessment of the emerging strategic environment. Wittmann's paper drew three primary conclusions: (1) the Soviet Union was no longer the principal threat to the Alliance, (2) emerging threats would be much less predictable, and (3) NATO's military capabilities would need to be reorganized in order to become more mobile and more flexible with respect to the sorts of missions that would need to be carried out.[59] The Wittmann Paper had a "catalytic" impact on the need to adapt NATO strategy to the emerging post–Cold War era.[60] High-level support for strategic adaptation followed quickly.

In tracing the adaptation of NATO strategy after the Cold War, a prominent feature was NATO's early resistance to change. Even in recognizing the sweeping transformations occurring in Europe, NATO initially resisted the conclusion that those changes required a reassessment of strategy. Instead, throughout most of 1989 and into 1990, NATO emphasized the continuity of its successful Cold War strategy, which seemed to offer comforting stability in an uncertain time. "As our Alliance celebrates its 40th Anniversary, we measure its achievements with pride," heads of state and government began in their Summit Declaration in May 1989, and they affirmed that "for the foreseeable future, there is no alternative to the Alliance strategy."[61] The NAC reiterated this view the following month, specifying that NATO's strategy remained "a strategy of deterrence based upon an appropriate mix of adequate and effective nuclear and conventional forces which will be kept up-to-date where necessary" and further went on to say this remained true "even after the announced and recently begun unilateral reduction in some of the Warsaw Pact forces."[62] In October 1989, the NPG also "reaffirmed the Alliance strategy of deterrence . . . in the present circumstances and as far as can be foreseen will be needed in Europe."[63] Even after the fall of the Berlin Wall, the NAC in December 1989 maintained that "for the foreseeable future, there is no alternative to the Alliance strategy" and, in contrast to the more inclusive view of security embodied in the later Strategic Concept, asserted instead "the principle of the indivisibility of security *for all member countries.*"[64]

Within six months, NATO's view on the desirability of strategic adaptation had completely reversed. Rather than statements on the lack of strategic alternatives and an emphasis on continuity, NATO's DPC embraced strategic adaption in May 1990, declaring: "[W]e have decided to undertake a review of NATO's military strategy and that we will continue to adapt our defence requirements to ensure that they take full account of the new circumstances now emerging. We will also need to adjust the operational concepts and doctrines which underpin the strategy, so that they continue to meet our security requirements."[65]

A turning point in the political decision-making on strategic adaptation followed directly from the May 1990 DPC meeting, when in June the NAC met at the level of foreign ministers in Turnberry. The Council "noted that the Defence Ministers who participate in the Nuclear Planning Group and the Defence Planning Committee have decided to reconsider their strategy" and took the opportunity to offer broad political guidance for that effort. In so doing, the Council placed strategic reconsideration in the context of a wide-ranging strategic and organizational adaptation: "We must today adapt [NATO] to the enormous changes now taking place. We have already begun this process in the political and defence spheres. . . . [T]he changing European environment now requires of us a broader approach to security based as much on constructive peace-building as on peace-keeping. . . . The modifications in certain aspects of the Alliance's policies and functioning will form part of a broader pattern of adaptation within the Organization."[66] The Council also delegated further work, which was realized extraordinarily quickly in the upcoming summit in July 1990.

The Declaration on a Transformed North Atlantic Alliance, also known as the London Declaration, represented a culmination of initial institutional efforts and included important details on the continuing adaptation of NATO strategy. Two broad concepts that shaped strategic adaptation were the declaration's emphasis on supplementing NATO's military tasks with greater political capability and an expanding geographic conception of NATO's security interests. On the balance between the political and military, the declaration noted that "security and stability do not lie solely in the military dimension, and we intend to enhance the political component of our Alliance." In contrast with its emphasis on the indivisibility of security exclusively among NATO members in 1989, the 1990 London Declaration also shifted to "recognise that, in the new Europe, the security of every state is inseparably linked to the security of its neighbours." Within this more political and more geographically broad conception of security, the London Declaration specifically addressed strategic adaptation, saying: "NATO will prepare a new Allied military strategy moving away from 'forward defence', where appropriate, towards a reduced forward presence and modifying 'flexible response' to reflect a reduced reliance on nuclear weapons." Echoing the Wittmann Paper's analysis of the impacts that a new strategy would have on the organization of NATO forces, the London Declaration also specified that NATO's "integrated force structure and its strategy will change fundamentally" and "will field smaller and restructured active forces. These forces will be highly mobile and versatile so that Allied leaders will have maximum flexibility in deciding how to respond to a crisis."[67]

The Council delegated the actual business of adapting strategy to an "Ad Hoc Group on the Review of NATO's Military Strategy," which was quickly known as the Strategy Review Group (SRG) and which met under the chairmanship of Michael Legge, assistant secretary-general for defense planning and policy. The delegation of this sort of work to the secretariat was a common practice in NATO, but the significant fact of the Council's delegation was that the military authorities and Military Committee had already embarked on studies such as that which led to the Wittmann Paper. Involvement of the secretariat seemed to reflect the Council's desire to increase the standing of NATO's political dimension, though whether this was to be done as part of NATO strategy was not well defined. As Legge observed at the time, alluding to the fact that NATO's defining Cold War strategy as detailed in MC 14/3 was separate from its contemporaneous statement of purposes in the Harmel Report: "What was not so clear at London was how the longstanding, and to some degree separate, political and military components of Alliance policy were to be developed and modified simultaneously in a way that was harmonious and consistent."[68]

Nevertheless, the drafting of the new strategy proceeded remarkably quickly under the secretariat's direction. Following the SRG's establishment in July 1990, an outline of the new Strategic Concept was finished in August, with a first full draft circulated at NATO in October. Reflecting the London Declaration's emphasis on the importance of NATO's political dimension, Legge wrote: "A consensus developed at a very early state in the Group's discussion that the new military strategy would not only have to reflect the present security environment, but also the Alliance's political response to the changed circumstances."[69] The most significant challenge arising at this stage was identifying the correct institutional format in which to continue discussions. As the calls for strategic adaptation originated in the Military Committee and DPC, France's nonparticipation in those forums left it outside the SRG initially. But as it became clear that the SRG would be formulating not just a military strategy but a comprehensive political and military strategic concept, this arrangement appeared increasingly problematic. France voluntarily decided to join the Group in February 1991, relieving the SRG of struggling to encourage participation. As Legge recalled, France's decision to join the SRG "was widely welcomed, and made it possible for the Concept fully to adopt a broad approach to security, integrating both the political and military elements," and noted further that in the final document "France reserved its position on only a few paragraphs which deal with collective defence planning and where France has traditionally maintained a separate approach."[70]

As the political nature of the SRG's work became more prominent, the NAC also stepped in to add detailed political guidance, similar to the way it issued clarifying statements to previous NATO strategies. However, whereas previous Council statements on NATO strategy often read as disclaimers reserving the fundamental rights of states in their sovereign obligations with respect to war and peace, the Council's guidance in June 1991 was to articulate expansive new tasks for NATO, which became known as the "core security functions" and which were copied verbatim into the Strategic Concept. These functions were:

1. To provide one of the indispensable foundations for a stable security environment in Europe, based on the growth of democratic institutions and commitment to the peaceful resolution of disputes . . .

2. To serve, as provided for in Article IV of the North Atlantic Treaty, as a transatlantic forum for Allied consultations on any issues that affect their vital interests . . .

3. To deter and defend against any threat of aggression against the territory of any NATO member state

4. To preserve the strategic balance within Europe.[71]

Further movement toward the new Strategic Concept proceeded rapidly and in line with the Council's guidance.[72] The final draft of the new Strategic Concept was approved and, for the first time, released as an unclassified public document on November 8, 1991.[73]

The new Strategic Concept comprised several noteworthy features. One, as already indicated, was the extent to which it sought explicitly to incorporate NATO's political dimension into strategy. NATO strategy during the Cold War had focused more specifically on the military ways and means of achieving collective defense, as exemplified in MC 14/2 (massive retaliation) and MC 14/3 (flexible response). The Harmel Report had stated that the future tasks of the Alliance would be twofold: defense and détente. But détente (i.e., NATO's externally oriented political and diplomatic dialogue with Cold War adversaries) had not been part of strategy, per se—it was a separate activity. On the one hand, the 1991 Strategic Concept did incorporate both of those long-standing tasks of the Alliance, noting that "the opportunities for achieving Alliance objectives through political means are greater than ever before" and elevating dialogue to coequal status with collective defense. The Strategic Concept also added two new functions: "co-operation with all states in Europe" and "management of crisis and conflict prevention." The inclusion of dialogue, cooperation, crisis management, and conflict prevention with collective defense reflected a "broad approach to security."[74]

On the other hand, NATO also published two other significant political documents on the same day that it released the Strategic Concept. The first, the "Declaration on Peace and Cooperation" (known as the Rome Declaration), was also a declaration of NATO's future political roles. It concerned relations with the Soviet Union and the countries of Central and Eastern Europe, as well as regional security institutions, arms control, and other political challenges. The second document, "Developments in the Soviet Union," established specific but also fundamentally values-driven policies with respect to NATO's most important nonmember country. The publication of two such important political documents at the same time as the new Strategic Concept served to maintain some distinction between NATO policy and NATO strategy. Moreover, about half of the length of the Strategic Concept was reserved for exhaustive "guidelines for defense," which were discussed in far more detail than any of the nonmilitary aspects of the document.[75] Thus, although the Strategic Concept was more political than previous NATO strategy documents, it is perhaps easy to overstate the point. In fact, the pattern of distinguishable NATO documents on policy and strategy set out in the contemporaneous Harmel Report and MC 14/3 strategy of 1967 continued in the 1991 Strategic Concept and separate Rome Declaration.

A second feature of the Strategic Concept was the significant role of institutional actors in its development. The agenda-setting effect of Colonel Klaus Wittmann's paper in the IMS was significant in this regard. Assistant Secretary-General Michael Legge's convening, delegating, and information-sharing roles as the chairman of the SRG helped see the document to rapid completion once the agenda was set. Two points flow from this observation. First, the member-states of the Alliance enjoyed a remarkable harmony of view about the substance of the strategic adaptations that NATO should make. There was almost no substantive opposition to the main ideas set out in the strategy.[76] Even France, which had heavily invested in post–Cold War institutional alternatives in European integration (including the EU and CSCE but also the potential European Confederation proposal), willingly and constructively participated in the SRG without a fundamental difference of view. This fact is all the more significant because France easily could have withheld input on the grounds that strategic adaptation was the responsibility of the DPC or Military Committee, where it did not participate. The prominence of institutional actors in adapting NATO strategy and the particular mechanisms of adaptation they were able to employ reflect the consensus and clear mandate of the states.

The second point about the role of institutional actors is the swiftness with which the new Strategic Concept was written and approved. NATO strategic adaptation often takes a period of years, even after a crisis or other momentous change affecting the Alliance. The Cold War was still ending at the time of NATO's July 1990 London Declaration, and the Soviet Union still existed at the time the new Strategic Concept was approved in November 1991. What distinguishes NATO strategic adaptation after the Cold War is not that the entire process was more rapid, but that it was formalized in a written Strategic Concept so quickly. As Michael Legge observed, "It took the SRG some 16 months to develop the new Strategic Concept . . . , which . . . compares very favourably with the decade of debate which preceded MC 14/3."[77] This rapid conceptualizing was also a reflection of the consensus among the member-states. But it is also a testament to the potential impact that institutional actors can have in discharging their institutional powers and adaptive roles. Recall that there was initially significant resistance to the adaptation of NATO strategy and that momentous events—the unification of Germany, disintegration of the Warsaw Pact, the Gulf War, and the coup attempt in the Soviet Union—occurred during the development of the new Strategic Concept that had almost no disruptive effect on its development once begun.

One event that did result in an appreciable substantive change during the course of the Strategic Concept's development was the increased attention given to crisis management and conflict prevention. As David Yost explains, "The war in Yugoslavia did not begin until 1991, a circumstance that helps to explain why the Alliance's July 1990 London Declaration had nothing to say about the need to be prepared for such crises. [But] [b]y the fall of 1991, the Alliance had adjusted its expectations."[78] In the words of the 1991 Strategic Concept: "Risks to Allied security are less likely to result from calculated aggression against the territory of the Allies, but rather from the adverse consequences of instabilities that may arise from the serious economic, social and political difficulties, including ethnic rivalries and territorial disputes, which are faced by many countries in central and eastern Europe. The tensions . . . could . . . lead to crises inimical to European stability and even to armed conflicts, which could involve outside powers or spill over into NATO countries."[79]

The Strategic Concept's inclusion of crisis management and conflict prevention reflected an appreciation of these developments. But they also presaged some of the difficulties that NATO would encounter in translating the consensus on the general principles of NATO's post–Cold War strategy into an implementable agenda. Nevertheless, the authors of the 1991 Strategic Concept were conscious that their work was only the beginning of strategic adaptation: "The monolithic, massive and potentially immediate threat which was the principal concern of the Alliance in its first forty years has disappeared. On the other hand, a great deal of uncertainty about the future and risks to the security of the Alliance remain. . . . The implementation of the Strategic Concept will thus be kept under review in the light of the evolving security environment. . . . Further adaptation will be made to the extent necessary."[80]

NATO's Post–Cold War Strategy in Practice: Bosnia

Civil war in Bosnia would emerge as the most significant catalyst for NATO's further strategic adaptation. Significantly, therefore, NATO's post–Cold War strategic theory developed before its practice. This was the reverse of the pattern established in previous cases, where changes in NATO's strategic practice preceded a formally agreed change in the Strategic Concept.[81] A partial explanation for this relates to the changing character of conflict after the Cold War. The distinction between strategy in theory and strategy in practice became somewhat confused as a result of nuclear deterrence during the Cold War.[82] Because deterrence concerns the prevention rather than the conduct of war, it involves competition and the potential for conflict more than conflict itself. Because the outbreak of war entails the failure of deterrence by definition, deterrence is fundamentally a peacetime strategy. Strategy-making during peacetime can become a relatively abstract and unilateral exercise, devised according to internal logic among the strategy-makers but detached from the unambiguously reciprocal activity of conflict.

The outbreak of conflicts in Europe after the Cold War, and NATO's prospective involvement in them, altered not only the temporal ordering but also the substantive character of strategic theory and practice. Although the stakes of involvement in a limited civil war failed to exceed those of a potential general nuclear war, strategy even in a limited conflict would have to contend more directly with the courses of events rather than their prevention, and thus the testing of strategic concepts in practice. The inclusion of the out-of-area crisis management and conflict prevention had been among the latest concepts to be included in NATO's new Strategic Concept and they would be applied and tested in the former Yugoslavia.

Secretary-General Manfred Wörner emerged as a leading actor in moving NATO toward involvement in Bosnia. Wörner, the first German to hold the secretary-general's post, entered the position in 1988 after a career in German politics as a leading figure in the Christian Democratic Party, having served as Germany's defense minister, that not only gave him wide-ranging contacts in various NATO countries but also earned him a reputation for being strong on defense through his support for US-led military buildup during the 1980s. A powerful presence with a booming voice who made good use of personal diplomacy through the traditional informal Tuesday luncheons at NATO headquarters (first held during Lord Ismay's time but not always preferred by all secretaries-general), Wörner also made extensive use of modern public diplomacy techniques, traveling widely and taking his messages to member-countries and to the general public. By 1993, he was speaking regularly on the imperative to intervene in Bosnia. Wörner argued that NATO had an imperative to address the conflict, not only in order to guarantee the "coherence of the Alliance even after the Cold War," but also because "violent nationalism in Yugoslavia . . . left to fester . . . can only expand insecurity and instability across Europe."[83] Wörner had also concluded that NATO was the only international institution with the capacity successfully to address the conflict in Bosnia, contending that "[w]hereas in the past it would suffice to deploy a few hundred 'blue helmets' between two parties who had agreed not to fight, today's environment might require far more than such a symbolic presence. . . . [T]he degree of military complexity far exceeds the capabilities of a small, international UN force. Wherever you deal with military operations on a bigger scale you need trained units operating according to agreed procedures and with standardized equipment. In short: you need NATO."[84]

Few other actors within the Alliance shared Wörner's view that "the United Nations are overstretched and underfunded."[85] The UN still claimed competence in the former Yugoslavia, and concerned European countries and Canada were making their principal contributions under the auspices of UNPROFOR. The United States remained only marginally involved and did not actively promote any increased involvement for itself or for NATO. During a visit to NATO headquarters in May 1993, for example, President Bill Clinton's secretary of state Warren Christopher said that he was in "listening mode" and, continuing the previous Bush administration's policy, intended to be "conciliatory" rather than promotional of US or NATO leadership in Bosnia.[86] SACEUR General George Joulwan reinforced this position in emphasizing during congressional testimony that US contributions through 1994 amounted to roughly three hundred personnel or "only about 3 percent" of the peacekeeping forces in the former Yugoslavia.[87]

To be sure, NATO had already demonstrated an awareness that the violence in Bosnia constituted precisely the sort of security challenge in the post–Cold War era that the London Declaration and the new Strategic Concept had set out to counter. In June 1992, NATO had taken note of the "violence and destruction . . . in various areas of the Euro-Atlantic region" and in disintegrating Yugoslavia in particular. But, contrary to NATO's habitual practice of co-opting other institutions, NATO initially subordinated its activities to others, first the CSCE and later the UN. The NAC decided "to support, on a case-by-case basis in accordance with our own procedures, peacekeeping activities under the responsibility of the CSCE, including by making available Alliance resources and experience."[88] The NAC extended this cooperation to include "peacekeeping operations under the authority of the UN Security Council" in December 1992 and agreed to enforce a UN-mandated no-fly zone over Bosnia starting April 12, 1993.[89] On the one hand, these measures were unremarkable since the Strategic Concept envisaged the possibility of such undertakings and NATO's material support was initially quite limited. On the other hand, the articulation of how NATO might actually become involved in a post–Cold War military operation was significant, a fact the NAC noted at the time in announcing: "For the first time in its history, the Alliance is taking part in UN peacekeeping and sanctions enforcement operations."[90] On August 3, 1993, NATO and the UN reached a detailed agreement on how NATO forces would support UNPROFOR efforts. The so-called dual-key approach required that both NATO and the UN would have to authorize any NATO use of force. Although this arrangement was bureaucratically unwieldy and kept NATO subordinate to UN-led operations, it moved NATO one step closer to involvement in Bosnia.

Secretary-General Wörner continued as the leading voice for greater NATO involvement as the UN efforts faltered. Wörner also began directly to criticize the cautious US approach to leadership in the Alliance. Speaking pointedly during remarks at the National Press Club in October 1993, Wörner both criticized and directly appealed to the United States for leadership: "Twice in this century the United States has withdrawn from Europe at its peril. . . . These are lessons which we simply cannot afford to relearn. . . . A superpower simply cannot take a sabbatical from history, not even a vacation. We need [the] United States' leadership. . . . Either you meet crises head-on or they will jump you from behind."[91]

Within the organization, Wörner also exercised tight control over the running NAC sessions. Although most observers described Wörner as exceedingly statesmanlike and respectful in his behavior toward others, he would not hesitate to interrupt or redirect discussion within the NAC to advance further discussion about Bosnia. Wörner leveraged his strong network of contacts with high-level officials from his years in German politics, occasionally threatening to go over or around NATO diplomats to address their home governments directly. Wörner's fluency in English, French, and German allowed him freely and directly to advocate for greater involvement in Bosnia during his personal interactions with NATO officials and member-state diplomats.[92]

In February 1994, the situation in Bosnia appeared to be deteriorating further when Bosnian Serb forces killed sixty-eight people and wounded many more in a mortar attack on the central market in Sarajevo. This attack, part of a larger campaign against Sarajevo, called out for the sort of military response from NATO envisaged in the dual-key agreement with the UN. NATO met the challenge. On February 28, 1994, NATO forces shot down four Bosnian Serb aircraft in an enforcement of the UN no-fly zone over Bosnia. This was NATO's first-ever use of deadly force.[93] Later, on April 10–11, NATO aircraft struck ground targets around Sarajevo in another instance of support to UN operations. Sensing that a turning point was at hand—that the need for greater NATO involvement remained as strong as ever and that a breakthrough in the actual use of NATO force had occurred—Wörner summoned himself for a particularly memorable act of leadership. The secretary-general suffered from terminal illness during his tenure and spent an increasing portion of his time receiving hospital treatment. On April 22, 1994, Wörner removed himself from the hospital against the advice of his doctors and traveled to NATO headquarters to preside over a NAC session on Bosnia, intravenous feeding tubes and other evidence of his declining health clearly visible. This dramatic demonstration of strength and determination paid off, as NAC leaders agreed late in the night to a much-expanded NATO role in the use of air power to protect UN forces and UN-designated safe areas. As Ryan Hendrickson observed in his interviews with those at this meeting: "Wörner's presence at this NAC meeting is recalled by all the participants" and "is regarded by many as his greatest single leadership act while at NATO, and it demonstrated the organizational influence he could exercise once issues reached the NAC."[94]

The events of 1994 set the stage for NATO's further assumption of the leading external role in the Balkan conflicts. As NATO's military credibility grew, that of the UN continued to wane, particularly as Bosnian Serb forces began taking UNPROFOR hostages in the lead-up to the Srebrenica massacre in July 1995. As in 1994, the failure of the UN forces further vindicated Wörner's impression that only NATO had the institutional capacities to intervene effectively.

Although Wörner succumbed to his illness on August 13, 1994, while still in office, NATO involvement continued during the tenure of the succeeding secretary-general Willy Claes and the continuing leadership of SACEUR Joulwan. NATO military action culminated in Operation Deliberate Force, a two-week bombing campaign against the Bosnian Serbs in August and September 1995 that preceded the peace talks in Dayton, Ohio. Initially the result of a dual-key NATO–UN response to another attack on Sarajevo and planned further in a joint NATO–UN planning group, NATO forces and institutional structures were clearly in the lead, with tactical decisions falling to US General Michael Ryan, commander of NATO's Allied Air Forces Southern Europe, and higher-level operational direction from SACEUR Joulwan.[95]

Whereas Secretary-General Wörner had extensively used agenda-setting to push NATO into action in Bosnia, Secretary-General Claes used delaying tactics and deliberately withheld his convening powers in order to allow the military campaign to unfold without further political discussion in the NAC. As US diplomat Richard Holbrooke recalled, Claes's decision *not* to convene a NAC meeting in advance of the initial bombings allowed military action to occur more quickly than it might have otherwise.[96] As Deliberate Force continued, Claes continued to empower military action through decisions not to convene the NAC. The most significant example of this occurred on September 10, 1995, when Claes elected to inform NATO diplomats only after a decision was made to escalate the attacks through the use of Tomahawk cruise missiles.[97] In these cases, Claes himself had been informed of the forthcoming military actions and could have convened NAC meetings before those actions were to occur; the significant decision was that he chose not to, insulating NATO military leaders and taking risk on himself in the event that member-states would object to his withholding.[98]

The General Framework Agreement for Peace in Bosnia and Herzegovina, known as the Dayton Accords, led directly to further NATO involvement in Bosnia through the Implementation Force (IFOR) from December 1995 and later the Stabilization Force (SFOR) from December 1996. These operations put NATO ground forces in peacekeeping roles during the first-ever deployments of NATO troops out-of-area and also involved the first-ever cooperation of NATO forces with non-NATO partner countries.[99] These developments were significant in their own right, but they flowed from the initial decisions on whether and how NATO would implement its post–Cold War strategy in Bosnia.

Although credit for the execution of military operations belongs to the NATO forces that carried them out, the key adaptations in NATO were the result of political figures, namely the two secretaries-general. Wörner, in particular, was a key actor in getting NATO involved in Bosnia, strongly advocating and pushing NATO member-states to act, even to the point of sacrificing his deteriorating health. Wörner's role was revolutionary for NATO in several respects. His agenda-setting was stronger and more direct than any previous secretary-general. Aggressive, independent agenda-setting and direct, public criticism of member-states was unprecedented behavior for a NATO institutional actor. But Wörner publicly and successfully challenged the United States in particular and moved the entire Alliance closer to action. Claes's role was noteworthy for establishing a precedent for post–Cold War civil-military relations in NATO, using his institutional powers to delay and withhold convening of the NAC in order to allow the relatively unencumbered action of NATO military authorities.[100] This too was groundbreaking for a secretary-general. Cold War instances of institutional actors' use of the convening and information-sharing functions had been positive in the sense that secretaries-general would facilitate their occurrence. Claes used the same institutional powers in a negative sense not to convene and to delay the sharing of information. In both cases, the influence of these institutional actors was significant in the first implementation of NATO's post–Cold War strategy.

Adapting NATO's Military Structure

Involvement in Bosnia showed not only how much NATO strategy had adapted to the post–Cold War era but also how much NATO's organization had grappled with the new challenges as well. After decades of defense planning oriented around the prospect of Soviet and Warsaw Pact forces invading through the central region of Germany, the actual circumstances of NATO's first combat operation in Bosnia showed that the integrated military structure was among NATO's organizations that would need to adapt most in order to keep pace with the challenges of the new era and the new NATO strategy.[101]

In fact, institutional actors in NATO's integrated military structure quickly recognized the need for change in view of both the military realities and the political guidance embodied in the 1990 London Declaration. The Wittmann Paper had identified some of the adaptations in the military organization that would logically flow from an appreciation of the changing strategic environment. Following Wittmann's analysis, the key features of the adaptation in NATO's military organizations were that they were intended to become smaller, more flexible with respect to mission, more deployable, and more interoperable with one another.

A review of NATO's military organization ran concurrently with the review of the Strategic Concept and was heavily influenced by it. Two weeks after Assistant Secretary-General Legge met for the first time with what became the SRG (June 21, 1990), the Military Committee decided to establish a Military Strategy Working Group on July 4.[102] Secretary-General Wörner expressed a desire to see both the political and military aspects of NATO's strategy and organizational adaptation developed in tandem, and so it was perhaps not a great surprise that the same Colonel Wittmann of the IMS became the chairman of the Military Strategy Working Group. Accordingly, the work of this group focused a great deal on the potential for crisis management and other new missions that might be called on for NATO forces. The first draft document was completed in June 1991 with the intended document number and title of MC 400, "Directive for Military Implementation of the Alliance Strategic Concept." But this draft foundered on the details of how and when NATO assets might be used for out-of-area missions, despite the agreement in principle in the Strategic Concept that such missions might be undertaken.[103]

Ultimately, the most important early decision on the restructuring of NATO defense organization reflected the easier political consensus on reducing the existing Cold War force structures. Interestingly, SACEUR General John Galvin initially opposed these reductions and argued for maintaining Soviet military power as a key consideration of NATO defense and military planning.[104] In his view, the long-term political future of the Soviet Union was not clear, and the material fact of Soviet armed strength remained the greatest potential threat to the Alliance. But the attractiveness of the peace dividend was overriding. NATO defense ministers announced the restructuring of NATO's conventional forces, as envisaged in the strategy review, in May 1991. Military Committee document MC 317, "NATO Force Structures for the Mid-1990s and Beyond," called for large overall reductions in NATO forces and a slimming of the organizational structure of the integrated military commands. NATO forces would be reduced in size by 25 percent overall and 45 percent in the Central Region compared to 1990 force levels.[105] Nuclear forces would be cut even further, according to an 80 percent reduction of substrategic nuclear weapons announced in October 1991.[106] NATO defense ministers also agreed on a streamlining of headquarters, decreasing the number of major NATO commands from three to two (eliminating the Allied Command Channel but retaining the Supreme Allied Commands for Europe and the Atlantic).[107] These changes were implemented in 1994.

Further organizational changes to the military structure followed from the increasing experience of NATO forces in the Balkans. At the January 1994 Brussels Summit, heads of state declared that "NATO increasingly will be called upon to undertake missions *in addition to* the traditional and fundamental task of collective defence" and that "NATO must continue the adaptation of its command and force structure in line with requirements for flexible and timely responses."[108] In other words, the details of the organizational reform of the integrated military structure would not be dictated by the NAC but rather delegated to the military authorities themselves and subject to later approval. Further, the NAC should act "with the advice of the NATO Military Authorities, to examine how the Alliance's political and military structures and procedures might be developed and adapted."[109] The Military Committee began a long-term study in 1995 to implement these directives, resulting in a series of recommendations for further downsizing the integrated military structure in 1996.[110] The NAC approved recommendations to reduce Allied Command Europe's Major Subordinate Commands from three to two, renaming them Regional Commands in 1997.[111]

Other adaptations of NATO's military structure were more innovative and reflected a more thorough rethinking of military organization than a streamlining of the system of European headquarters. The most important organizational development of this sort was the CJFT concept. The CJTF envisioned an expeditionary force organized from multiple military services (i.e., "joint" ground, air, and/or maritime forces) and multiple countries (i.e., "combined" from two or more participating states), assembled as needed for a specific mission either within NATO territory or out-of-area. Depending on the countries involved, the CJTF could also be a structure that would support the emerging European Security and Defence Identity (ESDI) within the Alliance, thereby offering a solution to many of the emerging political and strategic challenges that NATO was beginning to face in the post–Cold War era.

The CJTF concept was one of the few NATO adaptations of this period that began with a proposal and strong support from member-states. Reflecting a familiar pattern in Alliance history, the United States and France led competing national proposals. The first was that of US Secretary of Defense Les Aspin, who in October 1993 suggested an arrangement in order to promote burden-sharing by encouraging European countries to take a greater role in the provision of NATO capabilities while also allowing for the likelihood that operations falling short of the territorial defense of Alliance members would not obtain unanimous participation and might be better served by "coalitions of the willing."[112] Such coalitions might involve the US and European allies but might also involve operations undertaken by the WEU making use of NATO assets (i.e., those funded by NATO's common infrastructure programs, such as headquarters, logistical depots, airfields, pipelines, radar and air defense capabilities, AWACS aircraft, etc.). This "separable but not separate" organization of assets would offer flexibility without the danger of duplicated effort or the creation of redundant capabilities in European institutions.[113] The United States promoted the CJTF through the DPC, and language was agreed upon in time for inclusion in the Brussels Summit Declaration in January 1994, just three months after Aspin's original proposal: "We endorse the concept of Combined Joint Task Forces as a means to facilitate contingency operations. . . . The Council, with the advice of the NATO Military Authorities, and in coordination with the WEU, will work on implementation in a manner that provides separable but not separate military capabilities that could be employed by NATO or the WEU."[114]

Although endorsement of the CJTF concept had occurred in the Brussels Summit, the working out of its exact details and its implementation were put off until June initially, and ultimately not fully resolved for years. Later in 1994 and 1995, France (with the occasional support of Spain, which was also outside the integrated military structure at this time, and Belgium) championed alternatives. The details based on Aspin's proposal specified that any collective NATO assets made available "for WEU operations undertaken by the European allies in pursuit of their Common Foreign and Security Policy" would be done only "on the basis of consultations in the North Atlantic Council."[115] France viewed this as restrictive but rather than opposing the CJTF instead proposed to limit them only to non-Article 5 tasks and to place them outside the existing integrated military structure.

Ironically, perhaps, the debates actually served to clarify and confirm the parameters of the new CJTF adaptation while also affirming NATO as the member-states' security institution of choice. As David Yost argues, "French terms for CJTF seemed to be calculated to undermine the integrated military structure. Preserving the integrated military structure was a higher priority for most of the Allies than establishing CJTF and pursuing an ESDI on French Terms. Allies within the integrated military structure . . . had invested too much in these command and planning structures to cast them aside in favour of ad hoc CJTF arrangements during a crisis."[116]

Whereas approval of the CJTF concept and NATO's involvement in the Balkans had resulted in a de facto settlement of the question of whether NATO would undertake operations out-of-area, France's proposals on the CJTF importantly reflected the reality that such operations were likely to be politically contentious. The flexibility of the new structures contained a partial solution to this issue, since the CJTF in particular was explicitly designed around the prospect of a "coalition of the willing." But flexibility also created a desire for further organizational adaptation to improve flows of information about the activities of NATO forces and operations.

The June 1996 NATO foreign ministers meeting in Berlin would prove to be the turning point in the long and difficult negotiations on how to implement the 1994 Brussels Summit decisions to adapt NATO's missions and military organization. As with the prominence of national figures in raising proposals for the CJTF, so would decisions of member-state political leadership prove important to their resolution in Berlin. Alliance leaders ultimately retained the requirement for NAC consultations and approval in the use of a CJTF and affirmed that they could be used in both traditional collective defense roles and non-Article 5 roles, all within the integrated military structure: "one system capable of performing multiple functions."[117] Ministers also endorsed the ESDI by making NATO "assets and capabilities" available for military operations led by the WEU, subject to Aspin's conditions that such operations required case-by-case review and consensus approval. But the role of the WEU within NATO would also grow stronger through a multiple-hatting of senior European positions within NATO's integrated military structure as WEU positions also. The deputy supreme allied commander Europe (DSACEUR) in particular would be seen as the potential commander of WEU operations, according to an arrangement originally conceived by American transatlantic relations scholar Stanley R. Sloan in a study for the US Congress.[118] French and British leaders seized on Sloan's proposal as a way to achieve a measure of European autonomy while avoiding duplication of personnel or resources. Somewhat ironically, however, American military leaders in the Joint Chiefs of Staff, as well as SACEUR Joulwan, opposed this strengthening of the WEU because it would, in practice, make some US military capabilities in NATO available to European missions in which the United States may not be an official participant. Consistent with the pattern of a strong NATO member-state conviction carrying the day, however, US president Clinton overruled the SACEUR and approved the deal in the final hours before the Berlin meeting.[119]

On June 13, 1996, NATO announced a number of new organizational features to increase the efficiency of military contingency planning and to establish greater civilian and political control over military activities. These included a Combined Joint Planning Staff at SHAPE to "perform centralised CJTF headquarters planning functions and co-ordination with all relevant headquarters, as well as with forces that might serve under a CJTF headquarters, and as appropriate with the WEU Planning Cell"; a Capabilities Coordination Cell inside the IMS to "provide staff support to the Military Committee on contingency related matters and assist the Military Committee in providing planning guidance to the Major NATO Commanders"; and a Policy Coordination Group at NATO Headquarters to "provide politico-military advice to assist the Council in managing and ensuring timely overall direction of Alliance military operations, particularly crisis management operations . . . and contribute to Council decisions on other topics of a politico-military nature in the adaptation of the Alliance."[120] These organizational adaptations were directly related to the decisions to undertake out-of-area operations and the organizational and strategic developments that had already occurred in the translation of NATO's post–Cold War Strategic Concept into reform of the integrated military structure and action in the Balkans.

Adapting NATO's Institutional Network: Partnerships, Enlargement, and "Interlocking Institutions"

The adaptation of NATO's military organization was most closely connected to the new task of crisis management outlined in the Strategic Concept. The other new task described in the Strategic Concept, cooperation with former adversaries, involved significant organizational adaptations of its own. Whereas the changes to NATO's military structure and other related organizational adaptations were almost purely internal, the adaptations related to cooperation also involved external cooperation with countries and institutions outside the Alliance. NATO's agenda for adapting its institutional network involved three kinds of activities: (1) partnerships with countries outside the Alliance and the creation of new institutional mechanisms to facilitate those partnerships, (2) outright enlargement of NATO's membership, and (3) the notion of "interlocking institutions" in which NATO sought to co-opt or cooperate with other international institutions operating with competencies in European security (e.g., the OSCE and EU). In all these activities, NATO accorded special consideration of Russia and distinguished its activities with that country from those of other Central and Eastern European countries.

Although NATO's 1991 Strategic Concept importantly called for external cooperation of these kinds, the Rome Summit's "Declaration on Peace and Cooperation" was the more important document, laying the foundation for these activities. Issued alongside but separate from the Strategic Concept, the Rome Declaration "defined the future tasks and politics of NATO in relation to the overall institutional framework for Europe's future security and in relation to the evolving partnership and cooperation with the countries of Central and Eastern Europe . . . CSCE . . . European / security identity and defence role."[121] The Rome Declaration envisioned not merely ad hoc or informal cooperation but rather "a more institutional relationship of consultation and cooperation on political and security issues."[122] To this end, NATO established two principal organizations: the North Atlantic Cooperation Council (NACC), which later became the Euro-Atlantic Partnership Council (EAPC), and the Partnership for Peace (PfP).

Although the NACC was a new institution, it was able to build on the initial forays into dialogue and cooperation attempted following the London Declaration of July 1990, which had proposed a series of "military contacts" and "regular diplomatic liaisons" between NATO countries and countries in the Warsaw Pact. The inaugural meeting of the NACC occurred in December 1991 and grew almost immediately to incorporate former constituent republics of the USSR. At the first NACC meeting, states agreed to a wide-ranging agenda of discussions that roughly mirrored the competencies of several NATO committees: "defence planning, conceptual approaches to arms control, democratic concepts of civil-military relations, civil-military coordination of air traffic management, and the conversion of defence production to civilian purposes."[123] At further meetings, the NACC agenda expanded to included topics such as peacekeeping; defense economics and budgeting; military procurement, interoperability, and standardization; and specialized military topics, such as air defense and communications. Although NACC discussions initially included debate over thorny political questions such as the withdraw of Soviet forces from parts of Eastern Europe and Central Asia, the NACC had no institutional competence or capability for taking or enforcing decisions on such matters. As a result, later meetings focused on the aforementioned technical topics rather than political ones. Although the NACC was successful in convening and information-sharing in these regards, it had its limitations. French observers in particular expressed concern that the NACC could be seen as indistinguishable from, and therefore undermine the efforts of, the CSCE.[124] More broadly, it seemed clear that information-sharing symposia on technical aspects of security did not need to be limited only to NATO and former Warsaw Pact members. In May 1997, the NACC was merged into another organization known as the EAPC, which also included members of the PfP.[125]

The PfP ultimately grew to be the more significant NATO organization for cooperation. Open not just to members of the Cold War alliance system but to all members of the CSCE's Euro-Atlantic area, the PfP was both more inclusive than the NACC and also encompassed more substantial practical activities than the discussions characteristic of the NACC. As with the CJTF concept, the PfP was initially proposed by US Secretary of State Les Aspin at an informal NATO defense ministers' meeting in Germany in October 1993, and then subsequently adopted at NATO's Brussels Summit in January 1994.[126] Among the objectives outlined in the PfP framework document were "the development of cooperative military relations with NATO, for the purpose of joint planning, training, and exercises in order to strengthen their ability to undertake missions in the fields of peacekeeping, search and rescue, humanitarian operations," and "the development, over the longer term, of forces that are better able to operate with those of the members of the North Atlantic Alliance."[127] Remarkably, the PfP Framework Document also extends the language of the North Atlantic Treaty's Article 4 on political consultation to PfP members, saying: "NATO will consult with any active participant in the Partnership if that Partner perceives a direct threat to its territorial integrity, political independence, or security."[128]

Unlike the NACC, at which all members met together as individual states, the PfP was organized around "Individual Partnership Programmes" between NATO and the partner country in question. This arrangement allowed for relatively more or less cooperation with certain partners than others as appropriate.

This arrangement also served to increase the institutional position of NATO itself as an actor in the partnership, since partner countries would be interacting directly with NATO institutions rather than in an intergovernmental forum.[129] While the NAC gave primary overall direction to each individual PfP partnership, certain aspects of interoperability and partnership planning were delegated further to a Partnership Coordination Cell located at SHAPE in Mons.[130]

Although NATO invited all CSCE/OSCE states to participate, the PfP arguably came to do more in terms of fostering cooperation in a shorter time than the OSCE. All twenty-two non-NATO NACC countries except Tajikistan joined the PfP, and its membership ultimately came to include thirty-four countries (of which twelve later joined NATO as full members). There is some evidence that institutional NATO actors viewed the PfP as a direct competitor to the OSCE. As Nick Williams of NATO's International Staff argued, the PfP was "the most extensive and intensive programme of military cooperation yet conceived in Europe—quantitatively and qualitatively beyond anything achieved within the OSCE."[131] Moreover, the PfP came to be such a visible and fruitful part of NATO's activities that, even as early as 1996, NATO insiders noted that it was "difficult to imagine a NATO without Partners or indeed a real Partnership without the detailed mechanisms of cooperation that PfP introduced."[132] Additionally, NATO's Mediterranean Dialogue, also created in 1994, established a precedent for institutionalized cooperation with non-NATO countries outside the traditional Euro-Atlantic area.[133] Later NATO initiatives such as the Istanbul Cooperation Initiative with Gulf Cooperation Council members and NATO's bilateral global partnerships can trace their conceptual origins to these early post–Cold War initiatives.

The NACC, PfP, and later the EAPC were significant organizational adaptations that operationalized the decisions made in the Strategic Concept and Rome Declaration to promote cooperation with former adversaries. Institutionalized cooperation was one part of NATO's effort to address the key post–Cold War challenge of instability in Eastern Europe. NATO embarked on partnerships as an extension of the dialogue task originally described in the 1967 Harmel Report but adapted to the new era with a recognition of the continuing need to have links with Russia and the new need to have some kind of contact with peripheral states in the Mediterranean and former Soviet Union. What distinguishes these patterns of cooperation from NATO's task of dialogue expressed in the Harmel Report is not the ambition of greater security through peaceful relations but rather the institutionalization of these initiatives through organizational and strategic adaptation following the Cold War.

Actual enlargement of the Alliance's membership was a second part of NATO's effort to address instability in Eastern Europe. Enlargement was a more revolutionary and contested idea than dialogue or the new cooperation initiatives. Inclusion in the EC seemed like the more natural first step for Eastern European countries that aspired to join the Western system. But it became increasingly clear that the EC/EU countries were not thrilled about enlargement and that enlargement might happen only after aspirant countries had adapted to EU standards. Conversely, NATO adopted the approach of inviting new members *before* they had adjusted to NATO standards.[134]

Although several observers initially read the creation of the PfP as a mechanism for forestalling NATO enlargement, the possibility of extending membership invitations to Central and Eastern European countries was explicit in the PfP's stated aims. At the same Brussels Summit in January 1994 at which NATO announced the PfP, it also affirmed a willingness to consider enlargement. As NATO heads of state and government concluded in Brussels: "We reaffirm that the Alliance, as provided for in Article 10 of the Washington Treaty, remains open to membership of other European states."[135] Four European states had joined the original twelve members during the Cold War, and the founding treaty left the possibility of further enlargement unambiguously open ended, saying that Alliance members "may, by unanimous agreement, invite any other European State in a position to further the principles of this treaty and to contribute to the security of the North Atlantic area to accede to this treaty."[136] The PfP invitation, moreover, invoked these provisions of the treaty and specifically stated: "We expect and would welcome NATO expansion that would reach to democratic states to our East."[137]

Following the 1994 Brussels Summit, NATO released the "Study on Enlargement" in September 1995, which described the goals, aims, and modalities for enlargement. The study calls for "an improved security architecture [to] provide increased stability and security for all in the Euro-Atlantic area" while also affirming that "the Alliance has played and will play a strong, active and essential role as one of the cornerstones of stability and security in Europe."[138] This meant that NATO envisioned enlargement as a way to make itself an essential part of a broader pan-Euro-Atlantic security architecture. The study stated that one of the purposes of enlargement was to "strengthen the Alliance's effectiveness and cohesion; and preserve the Alliance's political and military capability to perform its core functions of common defence as well as to undertake peacekeeping and other new missions."[139] Thus the study articulated clearly the view that enlargement would give force to NATO's new tasks of cooperation while also making clear the desired effect of enlargement on strengthening the cohesion and effectiveness of NATO as an institution. It was from this perspective that NATO embarked on its first round of post–Cold War enlargement. On July 8, 1997, at its Madrid Summit, NATO invited the Czech Republic, Hungary, and Poland to start accession talks with the Alliance.[140]

NATO's institutionalized cooperation and enlargement was not only meant to address the problems of instability in post–Cold War Eastern Europe but also to manage relations with Russia. Although enlargement to include Russian membership in NATO has occasionally been a subject of academic debate, there is no indication that such a radical proposal was the subject of serious consideration within the Alliance. Conversely, continued dialogue and institutionalized cooperation were important parts of NATO's efforts. NATO-Russia relations have not always been harmonious, but NATO's efforts to convene and institutionalize dialogue with Russia did occur. It is possible to draw some comparisons with Russian relations with the West in the OSCE in this regard: differences of view and outright disagreements notwithstanding, participation in institutionalized dialogue was a desirable end unto itself.

Russia participated in the NACC and initially responded favorably to the PfP as well. There is some evidence that Russian support for the PfP derived from the perception that it was a method of putting off enlargement of NATO's membership. For example, Chairman of the Foreign Affairs Committee of the Russian Duma Vladimir Lukin said of the PfP: "If the intention of this formula is to defer the Eastern European countries' affiliation to NATO, 'Partnership' should be welcomed."[141] But as it became increasingly clear that NATO was prepared to consider enlargement, Russian attitudes toward the PfP cooled. Russia signed the PfP framework document in June 1994 but declined to approve either its Individual Partnership Programme (IPP) or any additional measures for enhanced NATO-Russia cooperation at a ministerial meeting with the NAC in December 1994. Although Russia ultimately did sign up to an IPP in May 1995, its participation remained minimal, as the NAC evinced in December 1996: "We welcome Russia's participation in Partnership for Peace and encourage it to take full advantage of the opportunities which the Partnership offers."[142]

At the same time, Russian participation in NATO's IFOR in Bosnia lent optimism to the possibility of cooperation notwithstanding Russia's relative non-participation in the PfP. As the NAC noted, "We value the close and effective cooperation between Russia and NATO in IFOR. This cooperation demonstrates that NATO and Russia can collaborate effectively in the construction of cooperative security structures in Europe."[143] While Russia did not seek greater involvement in the PfP, NATO sought to develop different mechanisms for further cooperation with Russia, stating in particular: "We aim to reach agreement with the Russian Federation on arrangements that can deepen and widen the scope of our current relationship and provide a framework for its future development."[144] These efforts ultimately led to the creation of the NATO-Russia PJC in 1997, which established a program of monthly meetings at NATO headquarters at the level of ambassadors and semiannual meetings at the level of defense ministers.[145] NATO also adopted this same special format in relations with Ukraine, the next largest former Soviet republic by population, establishing the NATO-Ukraine Commission later in 1997.[146]

A third and final way in which NATO adapted its external organization was in its relations with other international institutions. From the earliest days of the Alliance, when NATO made arrangements to supersede or otherwise co-opt the Western Union and the proposed EDC, NATO demonstrated a pattern of direct engagement with alternative European security institutions. But growth and development of so many new such institutions after the Cold War made NATO's efforts in this regard that much more prominent. In earlier periods of contingency following a critical juncture in the Alliance, it was possible to identify a dominant institutional alternative to NATO, such as the EDC or the renationalization of defense policy in the 1960s. But, as previously described, the post–Cold War period gave rise to several plausible institutional alternatives, including the OSCE and the EU most prominently. Moreover, not only were the UN and other international institutions also becoming more active, but NATO's own new partnership initiatives, such as the PfP, also added to the mix of new institutional arrangements in European security. NATO's response to all this was to embrace the idea that multiple institutions with similar goals of peace and security in Europe could be mutually reinforcing of one another. NATO recognized that it was not going to be the only institution involved in the post–Cold War European security architecture. It did, however, embrace the concept of interlocking institutions more than any other. In some cases, NATO co-opted other institutions for its purposes; in others, it simply sought to own the discourse referring to itself as the preeminent security organization to which other institutions might play contributing but ultimately secondary roles.

Manfred Wörner neatly expressed these principles of NATO leadership among European security institutions in 1992, writing: "The building blocks for a new and lasting European order of peace and security are there. It is our historic task to link them together. The concept of interlocking institutions,

which NATO developed, is founded on this basic idea." Wörner outlined NATO's
intention to cooperate with all the other institutions but also foreshadowed
the importance of hard capabilities that NATO possessed uniquely, writing:
"A future European security system is not something that will just happen. . . .
A system of interlocking institutions, even if it can be perfected, will not be
a panacea that acts automatically to prevent and manage crises." In terms of
the relative importance of various institutions in addressing such challenges,
he acknowledges the potential benefits of others but affirms: "Of all existing
international organizations, NATO is best equipped not only with the necessary military means for the defence of its member countries but also with the
politico-military instruments of crisis management."[147]

Some have criticized the effectiveness of this approach, mocking the "interlocking" aspiration with predictions of "interblocking" reality. Others have
pointed to the ill-defined division of labor among various institutions. As Yost
summarizes this criticism: "It is almost as if NATO, after having defeated attempts in 1990–91 to create an all-European collective security organization
under CSCE auspices, is gradually transforming itself into an entity comparable
to such a body."[148] But viewed through the lens of institutional adaptation, efforts
to adapt to new circumstances by creating new organizational capacities and
co-opting other institutions help facilitate NATO's endurance.

Conclusion

The end of the Cold War in Europe was a seismic shift in the structure of international politics and fashioned important challenges to NATO's continuing
endurance. In addition to upsetting the relevance of NATO's organization and
strategy, which were relatively unchanged since the late 1960s, this critical
juncture also entailed the proposal of several viable institutional alternatives to
address the problems of the post–Cold War era. But NATO's own adaptations
were no less sweeping than the changes in the wider world, implementing organizational and strategic changes that addressed all four of its major post–Cold
War challenges: the question of Germany's status and role, instability in Eastern Europe, relations with post-Soviet Russia, and conceptual uncertainty about
NATO's purposes. To be sure, NATO did not solve all of these problems. But to
the extent that there were solutions, NATO was part of them, and NATO's adaptations directly and deliberately addressed them. On the question of German
reunification, for example, the most important events and decisions occurred
among statesmen outside of a NATO context, but NATO's adaptation to include
a reunified Germany was a key provision of that consensus on reunification.

NATO's role as an autonomous actor in setting the terms of adaptation to address the other three challenges is clearer.

Although alternative institutions also played a role in addressing several of these issues, none of the other international institutions engaged in the full range of activity comprising NATO's adaptation, and none duplicated NATO's activity in any one area. Again, NATO's adaptations in incorporating a reunified Germany are comparatively less fundamental than the creation of the EU, the single currency, and other efforts at European integration devised to reinforce Germany's links in Europe. But NATO did more to address instability in Eastern Europe and the Balkans and made institutional overtures toward Russia and the former Soviet Union that fell outside the EU's focus. Equally, the OSCE engaged in the former Soviet Union but could do little to enforce solutions in the Balkans or facilitate intra-Western cooperation, all of which NATO did. Moreover, NATO also embraced the concept of interlocking institutions more than any other, seeking to co-opt or exert leadership in a web of institutions of which it had comfortably unique standing and capability.

Institutional actors in NATO played strikingly influential roles in the wide-ranging organizational and strategic adaptations of the period. In contrast to previous cases, during which institutional actors made use of the more subtle techniques of delaying and moderating in order to promote adaptation, a remarkable characteristic of post–Cold War NATO adaptation was the extent to which institutional actors set the agenda. Colonel Klaus Wittmann was a key actor in the adaptation of NATO strategy, his influential paper helping to overcome initial resistance to change at the member-state level. The influence of the Wittmann Paper's ideas about NATO strategy made their way in a direct fashion from the International Staff to the DPC, the NAC foreign ministers meeting at Turnberry, and ultimately to the London Declaration and the new Strategic Concept. Wittmann's appointment to lead the International Staff's Military Strategy Working Group further privileged his influence in articulating the details of the organizational changes that would accompany the new strategy. In a similar respect, Assistant Secretary-General Michael Legge played an important role as head of the SRG, rapidly transforming the political guidance from the London Declaration and the NAC into the language of the new Strategic Concept despite the swiftly changing international situation in 1990–1991.

The influence of Secretaries-General Wörner and Claes is perhaps even more remarkable. Wörner especially was noteworthy for his use of public diplomacy, in effect an extension of the institutional information-sharing function, with the modification that Wörner shared information outside of NATO channels by speaking with influential groups and leaders in order to promote his views. Although secretaries-general had certainly acted to facilitate adaptation in the past, none had done so by risking direct opposition from the member-states in the ways Wörner and Claes did. As Ryan Hendrickson observed in analyzing the secretary-general during the Cold War: "[S]uccessful independent policy entrepreneurship is not the legacy of NATO's political leadership."[149] Spaak had attempted it, for example, but found himself shut out by the states. Wörner was more successful, not only in setting the agenda with respect to Bosnia but also in directly challenging the member-states—the United States in particular. To be sure, Wörner did not oppose a strong US position with a countervailing one so much as he noted that the United States did not have a strong position and implored the adoption of his own strong views. Likewise, when Claes set precedent by allowing NATO military authorities to carry out operations in Bosnia without convening the NAC, he was not so much contesting an established member-state preference as he was taking a calculated risk in the absence of any state directives. The independent agenda-setting of NATO's institutional actors may not have been possible had states imposed stronger constraints or disagreed among themselves. During instances where states did disagree or mount strong preferences, such as French objections to the NACC and to the details of US Secretary of Defense Les Aspin's proposal for the CJTF concept or in the case of President Clinton's overruling SACEUR Joulwan's reservations about potential strengthening of the DSACEUR position and WEU claims to NATO assets, more typical patterns of NATO's institutional actors' limitations vis-à-vis member-states obtained. NATO institutional actors were able to set the agenda for adaptation when relatively few state constraints permitted their initiative.

Although institutional actors promoted adaptation fairly rapidly, especially with respect to the new Strategic Concept, actual implementation of the new strategy and all the attendant organizational adaptation occurred along a time line spanning several years. Although the most important adaptations of the post–Cold War period were established by 1996 or 1997, the pace of further change in NATO did not slow. Path-dependent institutional stability was never really restored after this critical juncture, as the persistence of conflict and instability would require further adaptations to NATO organization and strategy in practice.

PART THREE

NATO ENDURANCE AND
IMPLICATIONS FOR THE FUTURE

CHAPTER SEVEN

NATO Adaptation into the Twenty-First Century, 1999–2012

The pattern of how NATO has adapted to endure historical challenges also offers insight into explaining the institution's early twenty-first-century trials. The framework of critical junctures can account for the sense of crisis and contingency after the Kosovo air campaign and the terrorist attacks of September 11, 2001, as well as the search for institutional alternatives that followed. Involvement in Afghanistan dramatically demonstrated the adaptation of NATO's organization and strategy in response to the new challenges. Though the outcome of the International Security Assistance Force (ISAF) mission was once thought to be a signal test for NATO's continuing endurance, changes including the adoption of a new Strategic Concept in 2010, intervention in the 2011 Libyan civil war, and the readiness measures following the Russian aggression against Ukraine in 2014 indicate that NATO has moved beyond Afghanistan, even as its involvement there continues well into a second decade.

This chapter considers the applicability of the overall argument on how NATO adapts for explaining contemporary challenges. While this "congruence" test does not offer a full process-tracing analysis of historical and documentary evidence as in previous chapters, it demonstrates the plausibility that institutional actors played consequential roles in facilitating NATO's more recent organizational and strategic adaptation.[1] Although NATO's future remains a topic of important debate, the consistency of NATO's contemporary experience with previous challenges suggests cause for optimism about NATO's continuing endurance as well as for further analysis of how NATO adapts.

Critical Juncture: Kosovo and September 11

NATO's early twenty-first-century challenges fit the pattern of the other cases in this study, particularly the form of a two-stage critical juncture in which events

in Europe combined with events elsewhere to upset prevailing institutional stability. Kosovo's war for independence fits in the larger story of the breakup of the
former Yugoslavia, but NATO's participation in the conflict exceeded the forceful-
ness of its previous Balkan interventions. The Alliance's support of the Kosovars
involved NATO in sustained air combat operations that strained the functioning
of its institutions in a way that previous operations had not. NATO's intervention
began a year after it first threatened to become involved, lasted seventy-eight
days in contrast to the three once predicted by the supreme allied commander,
and included such high-profile internal disputes as General Sir Michael Jackson's refusal of SACEUR General Wesley Clark's order forcibly to prevent Russian seizure of a key airfield.[2]

If involvement in Bosnia had demonstrated that NATO was adapting to the
post–Cold War European security environment by changing its organization
and strategy, the difficulties of sustaining operations in Kosovo left many with
the sense that these adaptations were inadequate. The air campaign exposed the
widening disparity in military capabilities between the United States and the
European members of the Alliance, and also devolved into onerous political
wrangling and charges of bureaucratic micromanagement of military operations.[3] Since NATO had been involved in virtually continuous organizational
adaptation and implementation of its new Strategic Concept during the 1990s,
it was difficult to imagine that further institutional dynamism would be sufficient to overcome these problems. Moreover, diagnoses of NATO's difficulties
in Kosovo compounded broader structural trends and policy preferences within
the Alliance at the turn of the twenty-first century. This was the "unipolar moment" when American power seemed historically unprecedented and transatlantic policy differences had already emerged over issues ranging from the
proposed International Criminal Court to the banana trade.[4]

As NATO reflected on its fiftieth anniversary at the Washington Summit
in 1999, the mood was less triumphal than a decade earlier when pronounce-
ments of the Alliance's success in the Cold War had dominated the sentiment.
Although NATO had adapted to the post–Cold War world, its suitability for undertaking sustained military operations was put into question as a result of the
experience in Kosovo. As the NAC acknowledged at the time: "Kosovo represents
a fundamental challenge."[5] To be sure, Kosovar independence itself was not a
significant enough issue that any of the Alliance members felt compelled to seek
immediate change. But the experience raised questions about NATO's efficacy
in a potential future case where a member faced direct national security concerns calling for sustained expeditionary military operations.

Thus the terrorist attack of September 11, 2001, on the United States was a pivotal moment for NATO too. Cold War challenges to NATO most often undermined the institution's credibility, as when the first Berlin crisis and the outbreak of the Korean War underscored its lack of preparedness for a conventional war in Europe or when the second Berlin crisis and Cuban Missile Crisis exposed the flaws of nuclear deterrence and the strategy of massive retaliation. Post–Cold War challenges to NATO had undermined the institution's relevance by introducing a structure of international politics and new security challenges that were outside anything NATO had conceived during the Cold War. Kosovo and September 11 undermined both credibility and relevance, as the air campaign underscored shortcomings in NATO's institutional warfighting capacities and the terrorist attacks raised the prospect that the Alliance's largest and most powerful member-state might see little utility in turning to NATO after an attack.

Contingency: Article 5 versus Coalitions of the Willing and European Autonomy

Despite differences over other issues, Alliance members initially demonstrated unequivocal solidarity in the aftermath of the September 11 attacks. French support for the United States was particularly noteworthy insofar as the two countries have so often been at odds on the particular details of institutional arrangements for the Alliance. French president Jacques Chirac was the first foreign leader to visit New York City, just days after the attacks on the World Trade Center. And the September 12 headline in *Le Monde*, "We Are All Americans," became a news item in its own right as others embraced the sentiment.[6] Beyond this outpouring of support, however, the attacks gave rise to contingency over how to respond.

At first, the September 11 attacks offered an opportunity for NATO to assert its institutional preeminence. The collective defense provisions of Article 5 of the North Atlantic Treaty—an attack on any one NATO member would be considered an attack on all—remained the bedrock of the Alliance, even with all the adaptation of the institution, including the increasing scope of its functions and breadth of its membership after the Cold War. The senior NATO diplomat, Canadian ambassador David Wright, took note and advised George Robertson, Baron Robertson of Port Ellen, the secretary-general, that conditions might be right for the NAC to invoke Article 5. Lord Robertson seized on the idea and, employing the agenda-setting and convening powers of his office, pressed to make it happen.[7] US permanent representative to NATO R. Nicholas Burns consulted with Washington about the proposal and reported that the United States would consent to a NAC decision on these lines. With European members eager to demonstrate solidarity with the United States, the members of the North Atlantic Treaty decided to invoke the collective defense provisions of Article 5 for the first and only time in history in a NAC decision on September 12, 2001.[8]

But it quickly became apparent that this historic decision did not translate to much serious consideration of a NATO role in the US response to the attack. In the first instance, the circumstances of the NAC decision highlighted NATO's marginality to American decision-making. The United States had not called for the support of the Alliance. Rather, NATO's secretary-general and non-US diplomats had orchestrated the Article 5 decision. Moreover, US approval for the decision seemed to be worked out during a discussion between Ambassador Burns and National Security Advisor Condoleezza Rice, indicating that the matter was not a priority that rated the direct involvement of President Bush.[9] In the days after the attack, discussions among the principal American foreign policy decision-makers at Camp David focused on the coordination of a US response, not a NATO one.[10]

The United States ultimately decided to pursue international cooperation on an ad hoc basis rather than through established alliances or institutions such as NATO. As secretary of defense, Donald Rumsfeld famously articulated the formula: "The mission must determine the coalition; the coalition must not determine the mission."[11] As if specifically to rule out the utility of NATO, he continued to say that if established alliances became involved, "the mission will be dumbed down to the lowest common denominator, and we can't afford that."[12] US intervention in Afghanistan in the autumn of 2001 thus proceeded under the banner of Operation Enduring Freedom, a US-led operation that made use of the CJTF concept for organizing military forces in theater but included no role for NATO. NATO's attempt to make good on its invocation of Article 5 further underscored its marginalization, as it provided only a few AWACS early warning aircraft to patrol American skies, while the main effort of US response to the September 11 attacks went ahead in Afghanistan. Later, the United States reaffirmed its commitment to ad hoc coalitions as it turned its attention toward Iraq in 2002 and 2003. The lead-up to the war in Iraq presented different challenges for NATO, since by that time deep differences had appeared among member-states, with the United Kingdom standing firmly with the United States in support of invasion while France and Germany led an equally determined European opposition to the war.[13]

In many ways, the dynamic of US independence or unilateralism represented a similar logic to European desires for greater national autonomy in defense during the 1960s. In both cases, countries viewed their most basic national security interests to be at risk and lacked confidence in the capacity of NATO to do much about it. Where France was most strident in pursuing its own independent course in the 1960s, the United States played that role in the post–September 11 environment. Where President de Gaulle had made the case for strong, independent military forces and unobstructed foreign policy decision-making in his time, President Bush made similar arguments in laying out the post–September 11 policy of the United States.[14]

Meanwhile, contingency reflected more than a binary choice between NATO and national independence in the post–September 11 era. As in every other case in this study of critical junctures in NATO, moves toward greater European autonomy also gained momentum in the search for institutional alternatives. While the United States was pursuing greater independence, Europeans turned once again to integration. Aspirations for a more coherent and capable European security and defense identity had emerged in the aftermath of the Cold War, but Europe's unsuccessful effort to broker peace in Bosnia had dampened expectations about the potential for the new CFSP of the EU and had particularly underscored the lack of autonomous European capabilities. In fact, the same recognition of the feebleness of European capabilities that frustrated the United States and discouraged it from acting through NATO after September 11 also motivated Europeans to consider new initiatives. The beginnings of a renewed effort occurred in the 1998 St. Malo Declaration, in which British and French leaders committed to the development of greater European defense capabilities.[15] This decision built momentum for the 1999 Helsinki European Council meeting, which established the so-called Headline Goal for the European Union to create by 2003 a rapid reaction force of sixty thousand troops capable of deployment in sixty days. This force would be developed in order to accomplish the tasks set out at the Petersberg conference in June 1992, which included peacekeeping, humanitarian assistance, rescue, and other operations short of high-intensity conflict.[16] EU representatives announced in December 2001 that the nascent EU Rapid Reaction Force was officially ready to undertake limited missions.[17] Further movement toward autonomous European capabilities in defense came in 2003 with the publication of the *European Security Strategy*, which aimed to address the familiar problems of achieving foreign policy consensus among European countries in their integrated defense and security efforts.[18] But the contemporaneous disagreements among European countries over whether to support the US-led invasion of Iraq and the lack of follow-through on the allocation of resources to develop new capabilities dampened these efforts as well.

These differences exacerbated the search for institutional alternatives to defense cooperation, but political consensus grew as the inflammatory rhetoric subsided. Strained relations among the allies had made the various alternatives especially stark, as the American-led coalitions and the European initiatives acquired a rival, mutually exclusive character. Britain and "new Europe" lined up behind the United States' call of "either you are with us or you are with the terrorists," while "old Europe" bristled at the hubris of the *hyperpuissance*.[19] But obstinacy was not long lived as events encouraged renewed cooperation.[20] In Europe, the March 11, 2004, Madrid train bombing (known as 11–M) and the July 7, 2005, London bus bombing (known as 7/7) promoted transatlantic solidarity insofar as Europeans confronted the threat of terrorism in common with the US experience of 9/11.[21] America, for its part, had to confront the limitations of its power as the initially rapid toppling of Saddam Hussein's regime in Iraq led to instability and insurgency for which it was unprepared.[22] Moreover, momentum for European integration suffered a serious blow when referendums on a proposed European constitution failed in 2005. These events by no means pointed the way to any transatlantic consensus about what to do, but they reinforced a sense that the allies were on the same side of pressing security challenges and could benefit from cooperation in NATO. These catalyzing circumstances compare with the 1960s and 1950s cases of critical junctures in NATO, when further actions of member-states (European states, particularly) constrained the viability of institutional alternatives to NATO. These events also conform to the experience of the 1990s when developments in the external security environment spurred organizational and strategic adaptation that NATO member-states could find acceptable.

Organizational Adaptation: Transforming NATO's Integrated Military Structure

NATO undertook substantial organizational adaptation in response to the experience of the Kosovo air campaign and accelerated those changes after September 11. Most organizational adaptations initially concerned the integrated military structure, though enlargement of the Alliance's membership also continued at a remarkable pace. As a result of the difficulties managing air space in its Kosovo campaign, Operation Allied Force, NATO adopted the Combined Air Operations Centre (CAOC) concept to streamline and coordinate air operations.

While a CAOC could provide these functions for the air space of fixed Alliance territory, the concept was also designed to be able to operate in an expeditionary theater of operations. In this way, the CAOC served an airpower-specific purpose analogous to that of the CJTF concept during the early post–Cold War era.

The impetus for further "transformation" of NATO's integrated military structure accelerated after September 11. Though considerable reform during the 1990s had already reduced many Cold War layers of command and control, NATO embarked on a further sweeping overhaul that resulted in the elimination of approximately half of the remaining headquarters, including those at the top level of the integrated military structure. The Supreme Allied Commander Atlantic position based in Norfolk, Virginia, was jettisoned, and all remaining operational command functions were centralized under the Supreme Allied Commander Europe.[23] Because many European members of the Alliance preferred to see an important NATO headquarters retained in the United States, however, a new Allied Command Transformation (ACT) replaced the old Atlantic headquarters. The purpose of the ACT would be to promote the continued development of relevant, expeditionary military capabilities.

NATO's 2002 Prague Summit was a key event in the articulation of several organizational adaptations, as well as political commitments to increased capabilities. In addition to the creation of the new headquarters, NATO agreed to the development of an expeditionary NATO Response Force (NRF). The Prague Capabilities Commitment pledged member-states to maintain levels of defense spending and investment that would allow for realization of the NRF and the transformed capabilities envisioned. Finally, at Prague—the first NATO summit in a former Warsaw Pact country—NATO announced invitations to its largest round of membership enlargement yet, naming seven countries as future members while also further institutionalizing dialogue with the creation of the NATO-Russia Council. Although media headlines emphasized enlarged membership and the new format of relations with Russia, NATO insiders viewed the focus on capabilities as the more transformational. In many ways, the new members were about to join a "new NATO."[24]

Addressing European Institutional Alternatives to Strategic Adaptation

An important prerequisite to twenty-first-century strategic adaptation in NATO was the disambiguation of its roles from the developing aspirations of the EU. Although strained relations among the allies in the run-up to the Iraq war contributed to a perception that EU capabilities could duplicate or otherwise render NATO redundant, NATO persevered in differentiating its institutional roles and responsibilities from the EU. Although this involved the drawing of more clear lines than the co-opting of earlier European initiatives, such as the proposed EDC and WEU during the 1950s, NATO's institutional effort explicitly and directly to engage with potentially rival institutional alternatives is consistent with its historical pattern of engagement with other institutions.

The framework of the NATO-EU agreement on roles and responsibilities came to be known as Berlin Plus, in reference to the June 1996 NATO foreign ministers meeting in Berlin that sought to improve European defense capabilities through the development of the ESDI within NATO. Commitment to Berlin Plus occurred in the context of NATO's April 1999 Washington Summit and was one of the few significant developments in a summit otherwise largely overshadowed by events in the Balkans. NATO updated its Strategic Concept at the 1999 summit, for example, but the new document was only incrementally distinguishable from the 1991 version. In contrast, the statement that NATO would consider "making available its assets and capabilities" for European-led operations was a significant development.[25] NATO began limited institutionalized meetings with the EU in January 2001 and affirmed at the Prague Summit its willingness to share access to common assets and capabilities with the EU in cases where NATO itself was not engaged. These developments led to the signing of a formal agreement on a framework for NATO-EU cooperation and the transition of NATO-led Operation Allied Harmony, in Macedonia, to the EU in March 2003 (at the very height of tensions over the Iraq war). An October 2005 agreement on "permanent military arrangements" established a NATO Liaison Team at the EU Military Staff and a corresponding EU Cell at SHAPE, which became active in March 2006.[26] None of this suggested that NATO-EU relations were seamless or even all that well developed. But, at the very least, in codifying the principle that NATO had the "right of first refusal" over the use of common military assets, it had safeguarded its institutional turf. Moreover, insofar as EU efforts focused on the development of capabilities necessary to carry out the Petersberg tasks, NATO's substantive scope in higher-end defense capabilities remained institutionally unchallenged.

NATO's Strategic Adaptation in Afghanistan

NATO's involvement in Afghanistan proceeded directly from the aftermath of Kosovo and September 11, its initial organizational adaptations and disambiguation of roles with the EU. There is little evidence that NATO independently considered strategy in Afghanistan before becoming involved, however. NATO strategy documents during the Cold War significantly included functional and geographic qualifications in their titles, such as MC 14/3, "Strategic Concept for the Defense of the North Atlantic Treaty Organization Area." From the end of the Cold War, such qualifications disappeared and NATO instead adopted the more generally phrased the "Alliance's Strategic Concept."[27] These changes reflected the broadened substantive and geographic scope of NATO's tasks and purposes. But such breadth also increased the potential for the detachment of NATO strategy from strategy as conceived by others, particularly if NATO were to become involved in activities where it was not the only or the leading strategic actor. Such was the case in Afghanistan.

NATO's involvement in Afghanistan began with strikingly little discussion of the ends desired on the ground or of the ways and means applied to achieve them. Rather, participation reflected the adaptation of NATO to serve as the institutional mechanism of choice for Alliance cooperation on a given problem in which other actors, namely the United States, had set the strategic agenda. Involvement in Afghanistan was politically less polarizing than Iraq and thus imposed lower member-state constraints on NATO action. Even those European countries that most stridently opposed the Iraq war considered military action in Afghanistan justifiable, and many sought ways to contribute. The UN-authorized ISAF offered a way to do that without necessarily becoming entangled in the US-led Operation Enduring Freedom coalition.[28] Before 2003, executive responsibility for the ISAF mission went to a rotation of countries that all happened to be NATO members. When Germany and the Netherlands faced the prospect of shared command of the ISAF in 2003, the possibility of shifting responsibility to NATO offered the potential benefits of reducing both the costs and the likelihood of involvement in combat operations (a thorny constitutional issue for Germany) while at the same time increasing continuity and stability to a mission that had been organized six months at a time. For the United States, organizing European contributions in NATO offered the advantages of potentially sharing more of the burden in Afghanistan with others, thus freeing US resources for Iraq and decreasing the momentum for autonomous European defense initiatives by channeling European energies back into NATO. Moreover, the costs to the US would be low since its own Operation Enduring Freedom coalition would continue to operate independently of the ISAF, and hence the United States wouldn't be constrained by NATO or ISAF organization or procedures.

Secretary-General Lord Robertson once again jumped at the chance to put NATO in the lead. Even if member-states, notably the United States, had not followed through on the invocation of Article 5 after September 11 for NATO-led action, Robertson had demonstrated the ability to obtain a consensus in the NAC on a momentous decision. Involving NATO in the ISAF offered a second opportunity to exercise influential institutional leadership. The secretary-general was the most likely institutional actor to promote action in this regard as well. The SACEUR's dual-hatted responsibility as the commander of US European Command complicated his position. Although this dual-hatting has been an advantage for the SACEUR in other instances, the specific case of Afghanistan entailed potentially awkward organizational considerations for the US military chain of command, in which Afghanistan falls under the US Central Command area of responsibility. Moreover, any lessons learned from Kosovo would also suggest cautiousness for the US military officer serving as SACEUR, as General Wesley Clark prematurely retired from the position after Kosovo due in part to poor relations with other senior US military officers that the air campaign exacerbated.[29]

Thus NATO took command of the ISAF in 2003 for reasons that had more to do with Alliance politics and the promotion of institutional endurance rather than strategic rationale. There is some evidence to suggest that several actors explicitly doubted the cause in Afghanistan, even while committing NATO to it for the good of Alliance solidarity.[30] At the very least, it is clear that no consensus existed on the mission or purposes of the ISAF. Even under NATO's nominal leadership, the various ISAF contributing countries mounted practically independent campaigns in different areas of the country.[31]

Nevertheless, the geographic and functional scope of the ISAF increased dramatically following NATO's assumption of its command. UN Security Council Resolution 1510 extended ISAF's mandate from its limited presence around Kabul to covering the whole of Afghanistan. The NAC authorized a multistage plan for the expansion of the ISAF under NATO's direction, beginning with a December 2003 direction to the supreme allied commander, General James Jones, to begin by assuming command of the German-led Provincial Reconstruction Team (PRT) in Kunduz, northern Afghanistan. At the Istanbul Summit in June 2004, the NAC announced it would establish four new PRTs in northern Afghanistan. And in early 2005, NATO began expansion of the ISAF into western Afghanistan with the assumption of command for PRTs in Herat and Farah provinces.[32]

As preparations began for the third stage of the ISAF expansion into the southern part of the country, there was no avoiding the reality that NATO troops would be increasingly involved in the full spectrum of ground combat operations. Although the northern and western parts of the country were not entirely free of violence, they enjoyed much more stability than the southern and eastern regions that comprised the Taliban's homeland and shared a mountainous and porous border with other Pashtun tribal areas in northwest Pakistan. Nevertheless, ISAF expansion continued into the south in the summer of 2006 and into the east by the end of the year. Although the US-led Operation Enduring Freedom continued for the purposes of organizing some special operations missions, the NATO-led ISAF had displaced the coalition's responsibility for conventional operations and the majority of US troops in Afghanistan were reflagged under the NATO mission.

The expansion of the ISAF mission in Afghanistan inspired two sorts of conclusions about NATO. On the one hand, it indicated the culmination of extraordinary adaptation. Afghanistan represented the first major land combat operation that NATO had ever undertaken. It brought new scale to the out-of-area issue, as central Asia was not only outside the territory of NATO's member-states but entirely outside the Euro-Atlantic region. In addition, many non-NATO member-countries participated in ISAF operations under NATO command. Forty eight countries were participating in the ISAF by 2010 (compared with twenty-eight members of NATO), with non-NATO countries such as Australia providing some of the most significant military contributions.[33]

On the other hand, the situation in Afghanistan did not appear to be going very well. Levels of insurgent violence skyrocketed after 2006. NATO commanders and external commentators pointed to a lack of resources as an overriding problem. Though the ultimate decision on troop levels and other capabilities rested with the member-states, NATO's institutional efforts to convene and set the agenda for greater troop contributions did not meet with great success. Moreover, the ISAF chain of command remained poorly integrated, with many troop-contributing countries asserting so-called national caveats on the implementation of their forces. Countries continued to maintain different ideas about what kind of mission the ISAF was supposed to be. Canada, for example, fought a more or less conventional war against Taliban forces in Kandahar province and shouldered a disproportionate share of the combat casualties. By contrast, German leaders deliberately and seriously avoided the use of the term *Krieg* for years in order to avoid the legal and political consequences of acknowledging that German troops were fighting in a "war" overseas. All of this reflected poorly on NATO and gave rise to questions about whether it would survive Afghanistan.[34]

Ultimately, Americanization brought an end to questions over what Afghanistan would mean for NATO. Remaining challenges for the future of Afghanistan notwithstanding, NATO's organizational and strategic adaptation had proved sufficient to ensure its institutional endurance. When the new administration of US president Barack Obama decided substantially to increase US involvement in Afghanistan, it did so through NATO and the ISAF. On his appointment as the commander of US and NATO forces in Afghanistan, General Stanley McChrystal reorganized and strengthened the ISAF headquarters structure to impose greater unity of command and aligned the efforts of the participants through the promulgation and enforcement of operational guidance based on the new US counterinsurgency doctrine. The NAC also approved a plan to combine efforts for the training of Afghan security forces—a significant aspect of the counterinsurgency campaign—through the creation of a NATO Training Mission-Afghanistan (NTM-A), the commander of which would also be dual-hatted as the commander of the US-led training command and subordinate to the ISAF commander.[35]

Subsequent developments in NATO further demonstrated that the institution had moved on even as its involvement in Afghanistan continued. At its Lisbon Summit in 2010, NATO leaders adopted a new Strategic Concept that reaffirmed the core tasks of collective defense, crisis management, and cooperative security while also perhaps refocusing on "the Defence and Security *of the Members*."[36] At Chicago in 2012, NATO leaders announced a winding down of the ISAF mission by 2014 while also addressing wide-ranging regional and global security concerns in a sixty-five-point statement.[37] NATO confirmed its willingness to act and its primacy as the institution of choice for organizing the military intervention in Libya from February to October 2011.[38] NATO has also pursued naval and counterpiracy operations off the Horn of Africa and the Gulf of Aden, a training mission in Iraq, and advisory assistance to the African Union, among others. The Afghanistan mission continued under the new name of "Resolute Support."

NATO Adaptation into the Twenty-First Century

The patterns of challenges to and adaptations of NATO in the early twenty-first century are broadly consistent with other critical junctures in its history and yield fertile ground for future analysis of the processes for how these adaptations occurred.

The framework of critical junctures seems particularly well suited to explaining NATO's early twenty-first-century challenges, which fit the pattern of earlier cases of a two-stage critical juncture in which events in Europe combined with events elsewhere to upset NATO's prevailing institutional stability. A decade after the end of the Cold War, Kosovo and September 11 undermined both NATO's credibility and relevance, as the air campaign underscored short-comings in NATO's institutional capacities and the terrorist attacks raised the prospect that the Alliance's largest and most powerful member-state might see little utility in turning to NATO after an attack.

These twin shocks gave rise to contingency that pit the prospect of NATO's first-ever invocation of the Washington Treaty's Article 5 against the United States' early preference for ad hoc coalitions and Europe's ambitious efforts at autonomy. These choices represented familiar alternatives to NATO, which faltered for familiar reasons.

The renewal of consensus around adaptations to NATO compares with the 1960s and 1950s cases of critical junctures in NATO when member-states began to view non-NATO institutional alternatives as problematic, as well as with the experience of the 1990s when developments in the external security environment encouraged expediency.

The range of NATO's organizational and strategic adaptations in the early twenty-first century was dramatic but also open-ended. Adaptations included the expeditionary transformation of the integrated military structure, readiness to conduct operations on a global scale, and willingness to cooperate closely with non-NATO "partner" countries. All of these NATO implemented in Afghanistan, where for the first time it became involved in the full spectrum of military operations on the ground in a conflict that has demanded relatively constant further organizational and strategic refinements.

CHAPTER EIGHT

How NATO Adapts

Today's NATO, with nearly thirty members and global reach, differs strikingly from the regional alliance of twelve created in 1949 to "keep the Americans in, the Russians out, and the Germans down." These differences are not simply the effects of the Cold War's end or twenty-first-century exigencies but reflect a more general pattern of adaptability first seen in the incorporation of Germany as a full member of the Alliance in the early 1950s. Unlike other enduring post–World War II institutions that continue to reflect the international politics of their founding era, NATO stands out both for the boldness of its transformations as well as their frequency over a period of nearly seventy years.

This book examines how NATO adapts, using a framework of critical junctures from the literature on historical institutionalism to explain changes in NATO's organization and strategy throughout its history. This approach recognizes NATO not only as an alliance among states but also as a highly organized international institution. The key finding is that NATO's own bureaucratic actors played important and often overlooked roles in its adaptations. This conclusion has implications for knowledge of both NATO and institutional change generally.

After a quarter century of post–Cold War rapprochement and more than a decade of expeditionary effort in Afghanistan, renewed confrontation between Russia and the West has reinvigorated the debate about the relevance of the Atlantic Alliance once again. Crises from Ukraine to North Africa and the Middle East underscore NATO's continuing capacity for adaptation as a defining aspect of European and international security.

Critical Junctures and NATO

Constraints on NATO's organization and strategy derive principally from two sources: the external strategic context of international security and the policies of Alliance member-states. How are these constraints on NATO loosened in a critical juncture? The structural underpinning of institutional stability is usually weak before a critical juncture, but this potential instability is not always recognized within the institution at the time. For example, although Alliance leaders acknowledged the declining credibility of NATO's nuclear strategy in the years before the second Berlin crisis and Cuban Missile Crisis, the end of the Cold War came as a surprise to Alliance leaders, who generally overestimated the strength and durability of the Soviet system.

Thus the weakening structural basis of institutional stability is important for retrospectively understanding how critical junctures were able to occur, but it is not possible to explain the institutional processes of critical junctures in terms of long-term trends alone. Although actors may draw on general structural instability in the contingent after-effects of a critical juncture, relatively short-term shocks were responsible for the actual loosening of constraints on actors in each of these case studies of NATO. This finding is consistent with the theory of critical junctures in institutional analysis.

Although critical junctures do by definition involve a relatively short period of structural indeterminacy, very little else about what makes a critical juncture is required a priori. This is useful for preserving the flexibility and applicability of critical junctures in many different institutional analyses but runs a concurrent risk of vagueness. In order to add greater specificity at least in terms of critical junctures affecting NATO, it is worth noting the twofold nature of events giving rise to the critical junctures in this study. In each case, a local European and a global shock compounded each other to produce a critical juncture: the 1948 Berlin Crisis and the Korean War, the 1959–1962 Berlin Crisis and the Cuban Missile Crisis, the fall of the Berlin Wall and the collapse of the Soviet Union, and the Kosovo air campaign and September 11, 2001, terrorist attacks.

This observation may matter less for the number of shocks needed to produce a critical juncture but rather more for the effects they produce. The first and second Berlin crises seemed to indicate the increased risks of war in Europe but were in themselves less harmful than the actual war in Korea and less dangerous than the nuclear superpower showdown of the Cuban Missile Crisis. The September 11 attacks were clearly more damaging to at least one NATO member than NATO's own strikes against others in Kosovo. But in each case, the combined shocks demonstrated both the likelihood that a security challenge could affect NATO's core area and the fearsome degree of consequence that would come to pass if it did.[1]

Contingency in NATO's Critical Junctures

Critical juncture analysis expects contingency but does not require real-world institutional alternatives. For example, counterfactual analysis can be used to demonstrate the plausibility of alternatives to the course of action taken. Such hypothetical or counterfactual analysis was not necessary in this study, however. In fact, a significant finding of this study is that real-world institutional alternatives to NATO accompanied every critical juncture examined in the case studies. States did not necessarily show any indication of wanting to leave the Alliance (and no state ever has left it), but the real possibility of institutionalizing cooperation in organizations other than NATO was an important aspect of each case examined here. The EDC, the EU, the OSCE, a European Confederation, national independence in nuclear deterrence and foreign policy, and expeditionary ad hoc coalitions of the willing were among the various institutional alternatives to NATO that were genuinely pursued following critical junctures. Some of these alternatives failed, such as the EDC and the European Confederation proposals. But others succeeded in their own right, in many cases contributing to NATO's goals and aims though never actually displacing NATO or duplicating the full range of its institutional capacities. Contingency and institutional alternatives in critical junctures are not always either-or, zero-sum propositions.

A related observation is that most institutional alternatives to NATO embodied proposals for European as opposed to transatlantic arrangements. Whether through European integration in the EDC or the EU or through a greater assertion of national independence in foreign policy or deterrent capabilities, the institutional alternatives to NATO share a common theme of promoting European autonomy. This is more than just the effect of French foreign policy. Although France played a leading role in proposing many of the institutional alternatives to NATO, these alternatives reflected more general balance between the two sides of the Atlantic. On the one hand, the power of the United States gave NATO a significant advantage over exclusively European institutional arrangements. But American power alone did not explain NATO's institutional endurance or adaptation. NATO was not a vehicle for American domination of Western Europe. The consistent proposals for autonomous European alternatives to NATO reflect the independence of NATO's member-states. As John Lewis Gaddis observed, "What is striking about the sphere of influence the United States established in Europe is that its existence and fundamental design reflected as frequently pressures that came *from those incorporated within it* as from the Americans themselves."[2] NATO's ability to co-opt or accommodate the more successful of these proposals is a reflection of its adaptability.

A further aspect of the highly contingent nature of NATO's critical junctures is the relatively long period of time taken to resolve them. In each case studied here, a remarkably consistent period of about five years transpired between the loosening of structural constraints on action in a critical juncture and the ultimate reestablishment of organizational and strategic path-dependence or stability thereafter: from the outbreak of the Korean War in 1950 to West Germany's entry in NATO in 1955, the Cuban Missile Crisis in 1962 to the MC 14/3 Strategic Concept and the Harmel Report in 1967, the end of the Cold War in 1989–1991 to the implementation of NATO's post–Cold War Strategic Concept and military reforms in Bosnia by 1994–1997, and the September 11 attacks in 2001 to the ISAF expansion in Afghanistan in 2006. This observation indicates that NATO may adapt, but that the process of adaptation is not necessarily smooth or swift.

A related observation about the time needed for NATO's organizational and strategic adaptation following a critical juncture is the uncannily consistent tendency for an event to bring closure to contingency and lead to the relatively rapid consolidation of adaptive decisions in about the fourth year following a critical juncture. The collapse of the EDC proposal in 1954, the withdrawal of France from NATO's integrated military structure in 1966, the apparent failure of UN peacekeeping in Bosnia by 1994: each of these events occurred several years after the initial opening of a critical juncture and led directly to significant NATO organizational and strategic adaptations within a year. One may be able to point to NATO's initial assumption of the limited ISAF mandate in 2003 or to the deterioration of the US-led war effort in Iraq and increase in terrorist attacks in Europe during 2004 and 2005 as playing a similar role, but neither the causal effect on further adaptation nor the consistency with timing is as clear. Nevertheless, and especially in the first three case studies, momentous events played an important role in curtailing contingency, facilitating action, and reestablishing stability after a critical juncture. This observation has implications not only for NATO but also for the concept of critical junctures insofar as momentous events may be required not only to create the contingency characteristic of a critical juncture but also to end it.

Organizational and Strategic Adaptation in NATO

NATO adapted following each critical juncture studied here. Although institutional stability often carried the possibility that change for NATO would be considered but not pursued, this did not happen. Often far-reaching changes in NATO's internal organization and external strategy attest to this.

In some cases, organizational and strategic adaptations were highly intertwined. This was true of any decision involving membership, as new member-countries affected both the organizational structure of NATO and its strategy. The addition of Greece, Turkey, and Germany to NATO in the early 1950s not only increased the number of seats at the table in NATO committees and affected the design of the integrated military structure but also directly affected NATO's Cold War strategic concepts such as flexible response and forward defense. After the Cold War, changing membership organization was part of the strategy for consolidating peace and security in Europe. Other organizational changes, such as the development of the NPG and the CJTF concept, also involved both organizational and strategic adaptation.

The tendency in organizational adaptation was not merely toward greater or more institutionalization. Although this was often the case, especially in NATO's early history and after the Cold War, organizational adaptation was not always synonymous with organizational growth. NATO eliminated its Defence Committee, Council Deputies, Standing Group, and other bodies during the 1950s and 1960s, while the integrated military command structure and the nuclear forces available to NATO declined precipitously after the Cold War, for example.

NATO strategy generally reflects policy fairly well. NATO strategy is not always without flaws or developed swiftly, but it does tend to interact well with political guidance from the NAC. In the NATO strategy-making process, the Council consciously provided definitive policy guidance to NATO strategy, ranging from the fairly hands-off caveating of nuclear strategies during the 1960s to the issuing of comprehensive guidance about Germany in the 1950s and after the Cold War. At the same time, policy was not a tyrant in the process, and input from the military authorities in particular has played an important role in the adaptation of NATO strategies, particularly in the case of the Wittmann Paper and the implementation of NATO strategies in operations since the end of the Cold War.

NATO strategy has tended to maintain a distinction between traditional notions of defense-oriented military strategy and a broader conception of politico-military (or "grand") strategy. This has been less true of NATO after the Cold War, as its 1991, 1999, and 2010 Strategic Concepts included broad approaches to security writ-large. But NATO has continued to distinguish between defense and security within these documents.

NATO strategy since the end of the Cold War is distinguishable in that it has encountered actual fighting, whereas NATO strategy during the Cold War relied on deterrence and prevention of war rather than the actual conduct of wartime military operations. NATO's first use of lethal force occurred in the 1994 downing of aircraft in the no-fly zone over Bosnia, and its first full-spectrum ground combat operations occurred in Afghanistan. These cases of actual fighting brought NATO's strategic concepts and plans into practice, while the distinction between the theory and practice of NATO strategy was blurred in the two Cold War case studies. This fact helps explain why NATO's MC 14/3 Strategic Concept remained in effect for more than twenty years between 1967 and 1991. NATO strategy has had to adapt more rapidly in the context of actual military operations. As a result, the conception of strategy as a plan or a product is better for making sense of NATO's strategy and strategic adaptations in peacetime than in war, when it might be more usefully conceived as a process.

Key Actors, Mechanisms, and Units of Analysis in NATO Institutional Adaptation

Institutional actors in NATO were constrained by states in each of the case studies, but they still played consequential, if not always leading, roles in facilitating NATO's adaptation.

The character of state constraints on action tended to affect the kinds of mechanisms that institutional actors employed to facilitate adaptation. When states disagreed with one another or assertively pursued certain courses of action, institutional actors were more likely to employ delaying and moderating tactics. Eisenhower, Ismay, Lemnitzer, and Brosio employed these effectively. When states generally agreed with one another or showed uncertainty and openness about the future, institutional actors were more likely to facilitate adaptation through convening, agenda-setting, and information-sharing. Spofford, Wittmann, Legge, Wörner, and Robertson employed these effectively.

Not all institutional actors employ adaptation mechanisms effectively. Supreme Allied Commanders Ridgway and Norstad both tried unsuccessfully to agenda-set on organizational adaptations (increased conventional forces and the MLF, respectively). But member-states had already committed to different policies (the New Look/massive retaliation and flexible response), putting competing efforts by NATO institutional actors in direct confrontation with member-states' agendas.

It should be said that the general willingness of states to allow institutional actors to set the agenda may have increased over time. For example, the question of whether the secretary-general would have the power to propose initiatives was a hotly debated topic when the post was created, and several countries (notably the United Kingdom) argued vigorously against the establishment of such institutional powers. Secretary-General Wörner's ability to set the agenda on NATO intervention in Bosnia, and to criticize and hector the United States directly in doing so, was a remarkable change from earlier periods of NATO history. Some contemporary evidence also shows that independent agenda-setting is now seen as a relatively uncontroversial part of the secretary-general's job. For example, at the 2012 Chicago Summit, Secretary-General Anders Fogh Rasmussen said at the end of an introductory speech outlining *his* agenda for the summit that *he* would be taking those proposals to the member-states.[3] Such statements about his own role were casually delivered and ordinarily received in 2012 in a way that states would not have tolerated in the 1950s or 1960s.[4] It is not possible in this study to generalize about whether this trend has been consistent throughout the full range of NATO history, but movement toward an increasingly empowered secretary-general is perceptible across the cases evaluated here.

The cases in this study reveal few discernible patterns about who the key institutional actors in NATO adaptation are likely to be. Cases have featured key roles for high-level figures such as the secretary-general and SACEUR, but also for relatively low-level institutional actors in the secretariat, international civilian and military staffs, and the integrated military structure. These results are consistent with thinking about critical junctures, which does not specify theoretically who key actors are likely to be. Empirical, process-tracing analysis remains important for the identification of key actors in critical juncture analysis.

Nevertheless, theory may still guide the identification of key actors. This study's theoretical emphases on power and the role of institutional actors do suggest some likely characteristics. As described in the theoretical chapters, the powers of institutional actors derive ultimately from legitimacy and expertise. The key institutional actors identified in these cases had legitimacy and expertise with respect to NATO's organization and strategy and were able to play a role in adapting those features of the institution. By contrast, few significant actors emerged in these case studies from the various NATO agencies. This is likely to be a reflection of the units of analysis selected for institutional adaptation (namely organization and strategy), which may not play to the power of the NATO agencies as much as to other parts of the institution. A focus on the adaptation of NATO's logistics, economic cooperation, civil emergency planning, common infrastructure, scientific and environmental cooperation, or any other activities in which NATO agencies have a more prominent role and body of expertise may also reveal their capacity to facilitate adaptation as well. Further research would be necessary to test this proposition. But the evidence in this study suggests that considerations of power may be useful not only for explaining how actors facilitate adaptation but also for predicting who key actors might be.

Directions for the Future

Further application of critical junctures could be explored in institutional analyses of NATO. Selection of cases for this study was done on the basis of those critical junctures that presented the greatest challenges to NATO endurance as the institutional embodiment of the transatlantic alliance. Examining other cases when members may have considered or actually did turn away from NATO institutions, such as the Greek withdrawal from the integrated military command structure between 1974 and 1980, may further contribute to an understanding of how NATO adapts.

Further study of NATO could also usefully explore the question of why some historical crises meet the threshold for critical junctures while others do not. For example, the 1956 Suez Crisis was a seminal event in transatlantic relations but did not interrupt the path-dependent stability of NATO's organization or strategy.[5] It is not entirely clear why. Other prominent events that have garnered the title "NATO crisis," such as the "Euromissiles" debate of the 1980s, the Soviet invasion of Afghanistan in 1979, or the Libya campaign of 2011, might be useful for refining the understanding of critical junctures and of when they are likely to find institutional resonance in NATO.

Equally, an application of the critical juncture framework and this study's model of adaptation could also be applied to other international institutions. A particularly interesting assessment might be made of critical junctures in other security institutions, such as the contemporary Russian-led Collective Security Treaty Organization or the Shanghai Cooperation Organization, and especially those that did not endure, such as SEATO or CENTO. A useful contribution to further research on European security might result from an application of the critical juncture framework and this study's model of institutional adaptation to a more thorough investigation of the WEU or the EU.

Examination of the institutional mechanisms of adaptation would benefit most interestingly from further exploration of the co-opting function. The co-opting function of NATO institutional actors also played a role in the development of the mutually reinforcing or interlocking nature of the institutional security arrangements in Europe, which are the most dense of any region in the world. Specific attention could be paid to how or whether NATO is able to co-opt an alternative institution or merely accommodate it while safeguarding its own endurance. The role of NATO's institutional actors in co-opting national actors or other institutions is especially important in this regard, as is any dual-hatting of national actors as NATO institutional actors.

There is room for further systematic study of important NATO institutions and institutional offices. There are no comprehensive histories of the offices of NATO secretary-general or supreme allied commander, for example. The work of Robert S. Jordan on NATO's Cold War political and military leadership is a model for the sort of further research that could be done, and Ryan Hendrickson's study of the secretary-general's role in post–Cold War crises is a welcome contribution. Notwithstanding these, the overall scope of literature on the institution and its key offices is remarkably thin. Further empirical and historical study of NATO institutions would improve knowledge about the role of institutional actors in NATO's adaptation while also expanding the range of data available for comparative institutional analysis.

Finally, contemporary developments suggest some likely directions for the future of NATO organization and strategy. Emerging evidence on NATO's responses to Russia's 2014 aggression against Ukraine points to adaptation, the implementation and implications of which will be years in the making. Decisions to establish eight new headquarters in Eastern Europe reverse a decades-long trend of consolidation in the integrated military structure. Development of new "graduated response plans" implies the revival of the Cold War concepts of deliberate escalation and flexible response. The invitation to Montenegro to become the twenty-ninth NATO member points to the enduring attractiveness and expectations of Alliance membership, while the increasing invocation (often by Turkey) of the North Atlantic Treaty's lesser-known Article 4 on political consultation raises questions about what the character of that membership will mean. Considering the long term in remarks at the sixtieth anniversary of one NATO institution, Secretary-General Jens Stoltenberg concluded: "[O]ur Alliance must also adapt to the long term."[6] How it will do so remains of enduring importance.

Chapter 1 · Introduction

1. See, for example, Jaap de Hoop Scheffer, "A Transforming Alliance," speech by the secretary-general of NATO, the Cambridge Union Society, Cambridge, February 2, 2005. This phrase, well known among NATO historians, appears in many different forms without a reliable primary source. I am grateful to Stanley Sloan for offering this version as perhaps the most accurate version of what Lord Ismay might have said.

2. Ronald Steel, *The End of Alliance: America and the Future of Europe* (New York: Viking, 1964); Wallace J. Thies, *Why NATO Endures* (Cambridge: Cambridge University Press, 2009).

3. Jordan was especially explicit in his focus on "individuals and the impact of their personalities on international events" rather than general theory. Robert S. Jordan, *Political Leadership in NATO: A Study in Multinational Diplomacy* (Boulder, CO: Westview Press, 1979), iii; see also Jordan, ed., *Generals in International Politics: NATO's Supreme Allied Commander, Europe* (Lexington: University Press of Kentucky, 1987); Jordan, *The NATO International Staff/Secretariat, 1952–1957: A Study in International Administration* (London: Oxford University Press, 1967); and Jordan, "A Study of the Role of the International Staff/Secretariat of the North Atlantic Treaty Organization during the Tenure of Lord Ismay as Secretary General," DPhil thesis, Oxford University, 1959.

4. David S. Yost, *NATO Transformed: The Alliance's New Roles in International Security* (Washington, DC: United States Institute of Peace Press, 1998); Rebecca R. Moore, *NATO's New Mission: Projecting Stability in a Post–Cold War World* (Westport, CT: Praeger Security International, 2007).

5. Alexander L. George and Andrew Bennett, *Case Studies and Theory Development in the Social Sciences* (Cambridge, MA: MIT Press, 2005), 205–32.

6. NATO texts do not employ a consistent written style, and both British and American standards are common for English-language documents. This study defers to conventions and spellings according to the *Oxford English Dictionary* but does not impose these where the original is different.

7. East Asia and South America stand out among the few regions of the world in which NATO has not conducted significant military operations since the beginning of the twenty-first century. See Seth A. Johnston, "NATO Is a Global Organization in All but Name," *Yale Journal of International Affairs* 8, no. 2 (Summer 2013): 131–32.

8. Note that this is not the same as selecting cases on the basis of institutional adaptation. Whether or how NATO adapts is borne out in the case study analysis and is not a criterion of the case selection itself.

9. See, for example, James R. Golden, Daniel J. Kaufman, Asa A. Clark IV, and David H. Petraeus, eds., *NATO at Forty: Change, Continuity and Prospects* (London: Westview, 1989); Lawrence S. Kaplan, *The Long Entanglement: NATO's First Fifty Years* (London: Praeger, 1999); Gustav Schmidt, *A History of NATO: The First Fifty Years* (Basingstoke: Palgrave, 2001); Kaplan, *NATO Divided, NATO United: The Evolution of an Alliance* (London: Praeger, 2004).

10. George and Bennett, *Case Studies and Theory Development*, 181–85.

11. On the appropriateness of these conditions for research design, see Stephen Van Evera, *Guide to Methods for Students of Political Science* (Ithaca, NY: Cornell University Press, 1997), 46–47.

12. The logic here is similar to that of the comparative method of agreement: institutional consistency across cases raises the possibility of its causal significance, decreasing the likely causal significance of other factors. The "method of agreement" refers to John Stuart Mill, "Of the Four Methods of Experimental Inquiry," in *A System of Logic*, 9th ed. (London: Longmans, Green, Reader, and Dyer, 1875), 448–71. Problems with Mill's methods have been noted in a variety of publications; see Charles C. Ragin, *The Comparative Method: Moving beyond Qualitative and Quantitative Strategies* (Berkeley: University of California Press, 1987); Morris C. Cohen and Ernest Nagel, *An Introduction to Logic and Scientific Method* (New York: Harcourt, Brace, 1934); George and Bennett, *Case Studies and Theory Development*, 153–60. To be clear, this study does not seek to rule out all noninstitutional variables as having causal significance. It is not feasible to identify all such variables or to investigate all possible causal paths—conditions that would have to be satisfied for the method of agreement to be effective.

Chapter 2 · Historical Institutionalism and the Framework of "Critical Junctures"

1. Dan Reiter, "Learning, Realism, and Alliances: The Weight of the Shadow of the Past," *World Politics* 46, no. 4 (July 1994): 490.

2. For comparison, see Edward Vose Gulick, *Europe's Classical Balance of Power: A Case History of Theory and Practice of One of the Great Concepts of European Statecraft* (Ithaca, NY: Cornell University Press, 1955); William L. Langer, *European Alliances and Alignments: 1871–1890*, 2nd ed. (New York: Alfred A. Knopf, 1962); and A. J. P. Taylor, *The Struggle for Mastery in Europe, 1858–1918* (Oxford: Oxford University Press, 1954).

3. Kenneth W. Abbott and Duncan Snidal, "Why States Act through Formal International Organizations," *Journal of Conflict Resolution* 42, no. 1 (February 1998): 3–32.

4. Tamar Gutner and Alexander Thompson, "The Politics of IO Performance: A Framework," *Review of International Organizations* 5, no. 3 (September 2010): 231.

5. *Oxford English Dictionary*, 2nd ed., s.v. "institution."

6. A sociological approach to defining informal institutions focuses on practices as "recognized patterns of behavior or practice around which expectations converge." Oran Young, "Regime Dynamics: The Rise and Fall of International Regimes," in *International Regimes*, ed. Stephen D. Krasner (Ithaca, NY: Cornell University Press, 1983), 93. Rule-based definitions of informal institutions borrow from rational choice theory and see rules as structuring the expectations of costs and benefits that rational actors pursue

in maximizing utility. Normative definitions of informal institutions, closely associated with constructivism, emphasize the "intersubjective" meanings of identity and action: norms shape ideas about the appropriateness of action or provide a constitutive function in defining identity, interests, and preferences. John Duffield, "What Are International Institutions?," *International Studies Review* 9, no. 1 (Spring 2007): 1–22.

7. As Peter Michael Blau and W. Richard Scott explain in their seminal work on the subject: "In every formal organization there arise informal organizations [institutions]. The constituent groups of the organization, like all groups, develop their own practices, values, norms, and social relations as their members live and work together. The roots of these informal systems are embedded in the formal organization itself and nurtured by the very formality of its arrangements." Peter Michael Blau and W. Richard Scott, *Formal Organizations: A Comparative Approach* (San Francisco: Chandler Publishing Company, 1962; Stanford, CA: Stanford University Press, 2003), 6.

8. Karl Wolfgang Deutsch, *Political Community and the North Atlantic Area: International Organization in the Light of Historical Experience* (Princeton, NJ: Princeton University Press, 1957); see also Emanuel Adler and Michael N. Barnett, *Security Communities* (Cambridge: Cambridge University Press, 1998).

9. This is also how NATO views itself. According to the *NATO Handbook* (Brussels: NATO Office of Information and Press, 1991), 11–13,

NATO is the Organisation which serves the Alliance. It is an inter-governmental organisation in which member countries retain their full sovereignty and independence. The Organisation provides the forum in which they consult together on any issues they may choose to raise and take decision on political and military matters affecting their security. It provides the structures needed to facilitate consultation and cooperation between them, not only in political fields but also in many other areas where policies can be coordinated in order to fulfil the goals of the North Atlantic Treaty. . . . Underpinning these activities is a complex civilian and military structure involving administrative, budgetary and planning staffs, as well as agencies which have been established by the member countries of the Alliance in order to coordinate work in specialized fields—for example, the communications needed to facilitate political consultations and command and control of military forces and the logistics support needed to sustain military forces.

10. Indeed, this is a central part of the argument in Wallace J. Thies, *Why NATO Endures* (Cambridge: Cambridge University Press, 2009).

11. For further explanation of how institutionalism in this context differs from neoliberal international relations theory, see Abbott and Snidal, "Why States Act."

12. The institutional approach may also offer a way to overcome some of the limitations of traditional state-centric theory. See, for example, Zoltan Barany and Robert Rauchhaus, "Explaining NATO's Resilience: Is International Relations Theory Useful?," *Contemporary Security Policy* 32, no. 2 (August 2011): 286–307.

13. Robert B. McCalla, "NATO's Persistence after the Cold War," *International Organization* 50, no. 3 (Summer 1996): 463.

14. Graham T. Allison and Philip Zelikow, *Essence of Decision: Explaining the Cuban Missile Crisis*, 2nd ed. (New York: Longman, 1999), 5–7.

15. James Q. Wilson, *Bureaucracy: What Government Agencies Do and Why They Do It* (New York: Basic Books, 1989), 115.

16. Michael N. Barnett and Martha Finnemore, *Rules for the World: International Organizations in Global Politics* (Ithaca, NY: Cornell University Press, 2004).

17. Barry Posen, *The Sources of Military Doctrine: France, Britain, and Germany between the World Wars* (Ithaca, NY: Cornell University Press, 1984), 39; see also Kurt Lang, "Military Organizations," in *Handbook of Organizations*, ed. James G. March (Chicago: Rand McNally, 1965), 838.

18. Stephen Peter Rosen, "New Ways of War: Understanding Military Innovation," *International Security* 13, no. 1 (Summer 1988): 140.

19. See, for example, Helga Haftendorn, Robert O. Keohane, and Celeste Wallander, eds., *Imperfect Unions: Security Institutions over Time and Space* (Oxford: Oxford University Press, 1999).

20. Anand Menon and Jennifer Welsh, "Understanding NATO's Sustainability: The Limits of Institutionalist Theory," *Global Governance* 17, no. 1 (January–March 2011), 81–94.

21. Celeste A. Wallander, "Institutional Assets and Adaptability: NATO after the Cold War," *International Organization* 54, no. 4 (Autumn 2000): 709.

22. Ibid., 712.

23. Ibid., 709.

24. Menon and Welsh, "Understanding NATO's Sustainability," 84.

25. See, for example, G. John Ikenberry, *After Victory: Institutions, Strategic Restraint, and the Rebuilding of Order after Major Wars* (Princeton, NJ: Princeton University Press, 2001), 17.

26. Conflict in this sense refers to nonviolent disagreement rather than, say, war. Kathleen Thelen, "Historical Institutionalism in Comparative Politics," *Annual Review of Political Science* 2, no. 1 (1999): 369–404.

27. Menon and Welsh, "Understanding NATO's Sustainability," 82, 85.

28. Orfeo Fioretos, "Historical Institutionalism in International Relations," *International Organization* 65, no. 2 (April 2011): 367–99. For the characteristics of historical institutionalism as distinct from other approaches, see Peter A. Hall and Rosemary C. R. Taylor, "Political Science and the Three New Institutionalisms," *Political Studies* 44, no. 5 (1996): 944–45.

29. Paul Pierson, "Increasing Returns, Path Dependence, and the Study of Politics," *American Political Science Review* 92, no. 4 (2000): 251–67; Paul Pierson, *Politics in Time: History, Institutions, and Social Analysis* (Princeton, NJ: Princeton University Press, 2003); and B. Guy Peters, *Institutional Theory in Political Science: The "New Institutionalism,"* 2nd ed. (London: Continuum, 2005).

30. Giovanni Capoccia and R. Daniel Kelemen, "The Study of Critical Junctures: Theory, Narrative, and Counterfactuals in Historical Institutionalism," *World Politics* 59, no. 3 (April 2007): 343.

31. James Mahoney, *The Legacies of Liberalism: Path Dependence and Political Regimes in Central America* (Baltimore: Johns Hopkins University Press, 2002), 7.

32. See, for example, Barrington Moore, *Social Origins of Dictatorship and Democracy: Lord and Peasant in the Making of the Modern World* (Boston: Beacon Press, 1966); Seymour M. Lipset and Stein Rokkan, "Cleavage Structures, Party Systems and Voter Alignments: An Introduction," in *Party Systems and Voter Alignments: Cross-National*

Perspectives, ed. Lipset and Rokkan (New York: Free Press, 1967); Niels Eldredge and Stephen Jay Gould, "Punctuated Equilibria: An Alternative to Phyletic Gradualism," in *Models in Paleobiology*, ed. Thomas J. M. Schopf (San Francisco: Freeman, Cooper, 1972); Peter Gourevitch, *Politics in Hard Times: Comparative Responses to International Economic Crises* (Ithaca, NY: Cornell University Press, 1986), 239; James True, Bryan Jones, and Frank Baumgartner, "Punctuated Equilibrium Theory," in *Theories of the Policy Process*, ed. Paul Sabatier (Boulder, CO: Westview Press, 1999), 175–202; Richard Herrmann and Richard Ned Lebow, eds., *Ending the Cold War: Interpretations, Causation, and the Study of International Relations* (New York: Palgrave Macmillan, 2004), 10; Jack Levy and Gary Goertz, eds., "Causal Explanations, Necessary Conditions, and Case Studies: World War I and the End of the Cold War," unpublished manuscript, 2005, 26–27; and Capoccia and Kelemen, "The Study of Critical Junctures," 346–48.

33. For example, one of the most noteworthy works that generated sustained attention to methodological development of "critical junctures" as such was Ruth Berins Collier and David Collier, *Shaping the Political Arena: Critical Junctures, the Labor Movement, and Regime Dynamics in Latin America* (Princeton, NJ: Princeton University Press, 1991), 29. Notwithstanding the significance of this work in generating research interest in critical junctures, Collier and Collier defined critical junctures in terms requiring institutional change, an unnecessary and methodologically problematic assumption that the Capoccia and Kelemen definition explicitly resolves.

34. Capoccia and Kelemen, "The Study of Critical Junctures," 349–50.

35. Mahoney, *The Legacies of Liberalism*, 7.

36. Capoccia and Kelemen, "The Study of Critical Junctures," 355. Note that this conception does not deny agency (or structure) during times of normal institutional operation. Rather, critical junctures merely account for the particular characteristics of agency under certain structural conditions.

37. Ibid., 353–54.

38. See, for example, the analysis of the lasting effect of the typewriter keyboard in Paul David, "Clio and the Economics of QWERTY," *American Economic Review* 75 (May 1985). For more general accounts, see W. Brian Arthur, "Competing Technologies, Increasing Returns, and Lock-in by Historical Events," *Economic Journal* 99 (March 1989); and W. Brian Arthur, *Increasing Returns and Path Dependence in the Economy* (Ann Arbor: University of Michigan Press, 1994).

39. Kathleen Thelen and Sven Steinmo, "Historical Institutionalism in Comparative Politics," in *Structuring Politics: Historical Institutionalism in Comparative Analysis*, ed. Sven Steinmo, Kathleen Thelen, and Frank Longstreth (Cambridge: Cambridge University Press, 1992), 17.

40. Alexander L. George and Andrew Bennett, *Case Studies and Theory Development in the Social Sciences* (Cambridge, MA: MIT Press, 2005), 206. Capoccia and Kelemen, "The Study of Critical Junctures," 343, 355.

41. Capoccia and Kelemen, "The Study of Critical Junctures," 357.

42. As Capoccia and Kelemen explain, "Contingency implies that wide-ranging change is possible and even likely but also that re-equilibration is not excluded. If an institution enters a critical juncture, in which several options are possible, the outcome may involve the restoration of the pre-critical juncture status quo. Hence, change is not a necessary element of a critical juncture. If a change was possible and plausible, consid-

ered, and ultimately rejected in a situation of high uncertainty, then there is no reason to discard these cases as 'non-critical' junctures" (352).

43. This is a reason why other theories of institutional change, such as incrementalism, functionalist accounts of "spillover," convergence or "isomorphism," and others are not employed in this study. For examples of others, see James Mahoney and Kathleen Thelen, eds., *Explaining Institutional Change: Ambiguity, Agency, and Power* (Cambridge: Cambridge University Press, 2010); Kathleen Thelen, *How Institutions Evolve* (Cambridge: Cambridge University Press 2004); Thelen and Steinmo, "Historical Institutionalism in Comparative Politics"; David Mitrany, "The Functional Approach to World Organisation," *International Affairs* 24, no. 3 (July 1948): 350–63; Ernst B. Haas, *The Uniting of Europe: Political, Social, and Economical Forces, 1950–1957,* 2nd ed. (Stanford, CA: Stanford University Press, 1968); and Paul J. DiMaggio and Walter W. Powell, "The Iron Cage Revisited: Institutional Isomorphism and Collective Rationality in Organizational Fields," *American Sociological Review* 28 (April 1983), 147–60; Walter W. Powell and Paul J. DiMaggio, eds., *The New Institutionalism in Organizational Analysis* (Chicago: University of Chicago Press, 1991).

44. The selection of cases based on critical junctures represents an alternative to the selection of cases on the basis of institutional change. See, for example, Pierson, "Increasing Returns, Path Dependence, and the Study of Politics," 251–67.

Chapter 3 · Institutional Actors and the Mechanisms of NATO Adaptation

1. Change is a general phenomenon. Adaptation is change effected by actors, in other words, "the action of applying one thing to another or of bringing two things together so as to effect a change in the nature of the objects, . . . the action or process of adapting one thing to fit with another, or suit specified conditions, esp. a new or changed environment, etc." *Oxford English Dictionary,* 2nd ed., s.v. "adaptation."

2. Consider, for example, NATO's Allied Command Transformation. See also James Q. Wilson, *Bureaucracy* (New York: Basic Books, 1989), 91.

3. Peter A. Hall, "Historical Institutionalism in Rationalist and Sociological Perspective," in *Explaining Institutional Change: Ambiguity, Agency, and Power,* ed. James Mahoney and Kathleen Thelen (Cambridge: Cambridge University Press, 2010), 207.

4. Duncan Snidal, "Rational Choice and International Relations," in *Handbook of International Relations,* ed. Walter Carlsnaes, Thomas Risse, and Beth A. Simmons (London: Sage, 2002), 73–94; Barbara Koremenos, Charles Lipson, and Duncan Snidal, eds., *The Rational Design of International Institutions* (Cambridge: Cambridge University Press, 2003); and Avner Greif and David Laitin, "A Theory of Endogenous Institutional Change," *American Political Science Review* 98, no. 4 (2004): 633–52.

5. Peter A. Hall and Rosemary C. R. Taylor, "Political Science and the Three New Institutionalisms," *Political Studies* 44, no. 5 (1996): 944–45; and Jon Elster and Aanund Hylland, eds., *Foundations of Social Choice Theory* (Cambridge: Cambridge University Press, 1986).

6. Hall, "Historical Institutionalism in Rationalist and Sociological Perspective," 207; Kenneth Shepsle, "Institutional Equilibrium and Equilibrium Institutions," in *Political Science: The Science of Politics,* ed. Herbert Weisberg (New York: Agathon, 1986), 51–81.

7. James D. Thompson, *Organizations in Action: Social Science Bases of Administrative Theory* (London: McGraw-Hill, 1967).

8. Graham T. Allison and Philip Zelikow, *Essence of Decision: Explaining the Cuban Missile Crisis*, 2nd ed. (New York: Longman, 1999), 7. This second edition actually employs the term *organizational behavior model*, while *organizational process model* is the term used in the original edition: Graham T. Allison, *Essence of Decision: Explaining the Cuban Missile Crisis* (Boston: Little, Brown, 1971).

9. Graham T. Allison, "Conceptual Models and the Cuban Missile Crisis," *The American Political Science Review* 63, no. 3 (September 1969): 689–718.

10. Allison and Zelikow, *Essence of Decision*, 169.

11. As previously shown, formal institutions create embedded informal institutions: just as formal institutions generate explicit rules and routines, their members also develop informal patterns of social relations, practices, values, and norms by living and working together. Peter Michael Blau and W. Richard Scott, *Formal Organizations: A Comparative Approach* (San Francisco: Chandler Publishing, 1962), 1–8.

12. Walter W. Powell and Paul J. DiMaggio, eds., *The New Institutionalism in Organizational Analysis* (Chicago: University of Chicago Press, 1991).

13. Hall, "Historical Institutionalism in Rationalist and Sociological Perspective," 214–15.

14. Orfeo Fioretos, "Historical Institutionalism in International Relations," *International Organization* 65, no. 2 (April 2011): 367–99.

15. Hall and Taylor, "Political Science and the Three New Institutionalisms," 954. Marc Trachtenberg makes a similar point about apolitical character of "rational choice" literature on strategy, which has resonance for other parts of this study. Marc Trachtenberg, *History and Strategy* (Princeton, NJ: Princeton University Press, 1991), vii–x and chapter 1.

16. Joseph S. Nye Jr., "Power and Foreign Policy," *Journal of Political Power* 4, no. 1 (April 2011): 9–24.

17. Hall and Taylor, "Political Science and the Three New Institutionalisms," 941.

18. Rules are not the only relevant source of power, of course. For example, it is sometimes said in NATO circles that "votes are weighed, not counted" in the alliance. The reason is that in most cases the member-states with the resources essential to implementation of a decision naturally have greater influence over the shaping of a consensus. I am grateful to Stanley Sloan for this point.

19. The silence procedure also features in the rules of the Organization for Security and Cooperation in Europe, the Council of the European Union, and other institutions. Geoff R. Berridge, *Diplomacy: Theory and Practice*, 4th ed. (Basingstoke: Palgrave Macmillan, 2010), 158.

20. Jack Knight, *Institutions and Social Conflict* (Cambridge: Cambridge University Press, 1992).

21. Mancur Olson, *The Logic of Collective Action* (Cambridge, MA: Harvard University Press, 1965); Philip M. Burgess and James A. Robinson, "Alliances and the Theory of Collective Action: A Simulation of Coalition Processes," *Midwest Journal of Political Science* 13, no. 2 (May 1969): 194–218; and Nella Van Dyke and Holly J. McCammon, *Strategic Alliances: Coalition Building and Social Movements* (Minneapolis: University of Minnesota Press, 2010).

22. Terry Moe, "Power and Political Institutions," *Perspectives on Politics* 3, no. 2 (June 2005): 215–34.

23. Peter A. Hall, "Preference Formation as a Political Process: The Case of Monetary Union in Europe," in *Preferences and Situations*, ed. Ira Katznelson and Barry Weingast (New York: Russell Sage Foundation, 2005), 129–60.

24. Hall, "Historical Institutionalism in Rationalist and Sociological Perspective," 210–11.

25. For example, Jaap de Hoop Scheffer, "Towards Fairer Burden-Sharing in NATO," *Europe's World* 9 (Summer 2008): 68–73; Simon Lunn, *Burden Sharing in NATO* (London: Royal Institute for International Affairs, 1983); and John R. O'Neal and Mark A. Elrod, "NATO Burden Sharing and the Forces of Change," *International Studies Quarterly* 33, no. 4 (December 1989): 435–56.

26. For example, Stephen D. Krasner, "Structural Causes and Regime Consequences: Regimes as Intervening Variables," *International Organization* 36, no. 2 (Spring 1982): 185.

27. The institutional approach adopted in the present volume also differs from principal-agent theory, which recognizes the potential for institutional independence but discounts the importance of politics and power discussed previously. See, for example, Sanford J. Grossman and Oliver D. Hart, "An Analysis of the Principal-Agent Problem," *Econometrica* 51, no. 1 (January 1983): 7–45; and Jean-Jacques Laffont and David Martimort, *The Theory of Incentives: The Principal-Agent Model* (Princeton, NJ: Princeton University Press, 2002).

28. Michael N. Barnett and Martha Finnemore, "The Politics, Power, and Pathologies of International Organizations," *International Organization* 53, no. 4 (Autumn 1999): 705.

29. For the classic, realist articulation of the elements of national power, see Hans J. Morgenthau, *Politics among Nations: The Struggle for Power and Peace* (New York: Knopf, 1949).

30. Barnett and Finnemore, "The Politics, Power, and Pathologies of International Organizations," 707.

31. Max Weber, *From Max Weber: Essays in Sociology*, ed. and trans. H. H. Gerth and C. Wright Mills (Oxford: Routledge, 1948), 78–79.

32. Ibid., 299; emphasis original.

33. Ibid., 214–16, 240.

34. Barnett and Finnemore, "The Politics, Power, and Pathologies of International Organizations," 708; Weber, *From Max Weber*, 230–35.

35. Kenneth W. Abbott and Duncan Snidal, "Why States Act through Formal International Organizations," *The Journal of Conflict Resolution* 42, no. 1 (February 1998): 9.

36. Barnett and Finnemore, "The Politics, Power, and Pathologies of International Organizations," 708.

37. As Abbott and Snidal further clarify, "IO independence is highly constrained: member states, especially the powerful, can limit the autonomy of IOs, interfere with their operations, ignore their dictates, or restructure and dissolve them. But as in many private transactions, participation by even a partially autonomous, neutral actor can increase efficiency and affect the legitimacy of individual and collective actions. This provides even powerful states with incentives to grant IOs substantial independence." Abbott and Snidal, "Why States Act through Formal International Organizations," 5.

38. Philip Selznick, *TVA and the Grass Roots: A Study in the Sociology of Formal Organization* (Berkeley: University of California Press, 1949), 13–15.

39. For an example of dual-hatting, the Supreme Allied Commander Europe (SACEUR),

the senior military figure in NATO's integrated military structure, has also historically filled a national role as the commander of United States forces in Europe. Dual-hatting of this nature is relatively common in NATO.

40. Tamar Gutner and Alexander Thompson, "The Politics of IO Performance: A Framework," *Review of International Organizations* 5, no. 3 (September 2010): 232.

41. Peter M. Haas, Robert O. Keohane, and Marc A. Levy, eds., *Institutions for the Earth: Sources of Effective International Environmental Protection* (Cambridge, MA: MIT Press, 1993); and Gutner and Thompson, "The Politics of IO Performance," 235.

42. Lawrence Freedman, "Creating Power," remarks delivered at the Oxford Programme on the Changing Character of War Annual Lecture, Oxford, November 29, 2010; and Hew Strachan, "The Lost Meaning of Strategy," *Survival* 47, no. 3 (Autumn 2005): 33–54.

43. J. C. Wylie, *Military Strategy: A General Theory of Power Control* (New Brunswick, NJ: Rutgers University Press, 1967), 14.

44. Carl von Clausewitz, *On War*, ed. and trans. Michael Howard and Peter Paret (Princeton, NJ: Princeton University Press, 1976), 128; see also 177 and 227. Wylie's book is by one account considered "the best book of . . . general strategic theory published in the twentieth century." Colin S. Gray, *The Strategy Bridge: Theory for Practice* (Oxford: Oxford University Press, 2010), 6.

45. Hew Strachan, "Strategy and Contingency," *International Affairs* 87, no. 6 (2011): 1281–96; Peter G. Tsouras, ed., *The Greenhill Dictionary of Military Quotations* (London: Greenhill, 2000), 363–64; and Helmuth Graf von Moltke (the elder), *Militarische Werke*, Vol. 2, Part 2 (Berlin: E. S. Mittler, 1892–1912), 33–40.

46. Sun Tzu's sixth-century B.C. work *The Art of War* is in league with Clausewitz's *On War* among the great works of military strategy. The contemporary literature in business strategy is a separate genre.

47. Wylie, *Military Strategy*, 92; J. C. Wylie, "On Maritime Strategy," *Proceedings* 79, no. 5 (May 1953): 467–77.

48. For example, Colin S. Gray, *Modern Strategy* (Oxford: Oxford University Press, 1999).

49. Richard K. Betts, "Is Strategy an Illusion?," *International Security* 25, no. 2 (Fall 2000): 7–8.

Chapter 4 · *The West German Question in the Early Cold War, 1950–1955*

1. *Public Papers of the Presidents: Harry S. Truman, 1945–1947* (Washington, DC: US Government Printing Office, 1961), 178–79. While Truman's speech to Congress on March 17, 1948, outlined his doctrine, its intellectual justification famously derived from George Kennan, then a US State Department official in Moscow. See George Kennan to George Marshall ["Long Telegram"], February 22, 1946, Harry S. Truman Administration File, Elsey Papers, Harry S. Truman Library and Museum, Independence, Missouri; and George F. Kennan [X], "The Sources of Soviet Conduct," *Foreign Affairs* 25, no. 4 (July 1947): 566–82.

2. For the containment policy's lasting effect on Western strategy throughout the Cold War, see John Lewis Gaddis, *Strategies of Containment: A Critical Appraisal of Postwar American National Security Policy* (New York: Oxford University Press, 1982). A history of the patterns of East-West tension that led to the Cold War may be found in John

Lewis Gaddis, *The United States and the Origins of the Cold War, 1941–1947* (New York: Columbia University Press, 1972).

3. For background on Soviet nonparticipation and the polarizing effect of the Marshall Plan, see Scott D. Parrish and Mikhail M. Narinsky, "New Evidence on the Soviet Rejection of the Marshall Plan, 1947: Two Reports," Cold War International History Project, Working Paper No. 9 (Washington, DC: Woodrow Wilson International Center for Scholars, 1994).

4. Scott Jackson, "Prologue to the Marshall Plan: The Origins of the American Commitment for a European Recovery Program," *Journal of American History* 65, no. 4 (March 1979): 1044.

5. See Michael Hogan, *Marshall Plan: America, Britain, and the Reconstruction of Western Europe, 1947–52* (New York: Cambridge University Press, 1987). Also Melvyn Leffler, "The United States and the Strategic Dimensions of the Marshall Plan," *Diplomatic History* 12 (Summer 1988): 277–306.

6. The five Brussels Treaty signatories were Belgium, France, Luxembourg, the Netherlands, and the United Kingdom. The North Atlantic Treaty signatories included all Brussels Treaty signatories plus Canada, Denmark, Iceland, Italy, Norway, Portugal, and the United States. All three treaties contained mutual defense clauses, though the Dunkirk treaty is specifically directed against aggression from Germany. A. W. DePorte, *Europe between the Superpowers: The Enduring Balance*, 2nd ed. (London: Yale University Press, 1986), 138–41; Olaf Riste, *Western Security—The Formative Years: European and Atlantic Defence, 1947–1953* (New York: Columbia University Press, 1985).

7. The British Embassy to the Department of State, Aide-Mémoire, March 11, 1948, in *Foreign Relations of the United States*, vol. 3, *Western Europe* (Washington, DC: US Government Printing Office, 1974), 46–48.

8. The "German question" involves aspects of unification that transcend the historical scope of this study. During the Cold War, Germany's East-West division emerged as a partial answer to the question during that time. This chapter is primarily concerned with the remaining issues of how the nascent West Germany would be integrated into this order. See, for example, Wilhelm Röpke, *Die Deutsche Frage* (Erlenbach-Zürich: E. Rentsch, 1945); and David Calleo, *The German Problem Reconsidered: Germany and the World Order, 1870 to the Present* (New York: Cambridge University Press, 1978).

9. Memorandum by the Chief of the Division of Central European Affairs, United States Department of State, "Suggested Recommendations on Treatment of Germany from the Cabinet Committee for the President," September 4, 1944, in *Foreign Relations of the United States: The Conference at Quebec* (Washington, DC: US Government Printing Office, 1972), 86–101.

10. "French Economic Recovery: The Monnet Plan," *The World Today* 3, no. 3 (March 1947): 132–41. See also Frances M. B. Lynch, "Resolving the Paradox of the Monnet Plan: National and International Planning in French Reconstruction," *The Economic History Review* 37, no. 2 (May 1984): 229–43.

11. Treaty of Alliance and Mutual Assistance between His Majesty in Respect of the United Kingdom of Great Britain and Northern Ireland and the President of the French Republic [Dunkirk Treaty], Dunkirk, March 4, 1947, in *Treaties and International Agreements Registered or Filed and Recorded with the Secretariat of the United Nations* (New York: United Nations, 1947).

12. Brussels Treaty powers included Belgium, France, Luxembourg, the Netherlands, and the United Kingdom. The Treaty of Economic, Social and Cultural Collaboration and Collective Self-Defence [Brussels Treaty], Brussels, March 17, 1948, Ministère des Affaires Étrangères—Traités et Conventions (1732–1998), AE TC 365, Archives Nationales du Luxembourg.

13. After months of negotiations between the Brussels Treaty powers, the United States, and Canada, the North Atlantic Treaty's remaining original signatory states (Denmark, Iceland, Italy, Norway, and Portugal) were brought into the negotiations just three days before the public release of the treaty text, with Germany excepted entirely, of course. Seth A. Johnston, "Safeguarding the Freedom, Common Heritage, and Civilization of the Peoples: President Truman and the North Atlantic Treaty," in *A Dialogue on the Presidency with a New Generation of Leaders,* ed. Robert E. Henderson (Washington, DC: Center for the Study of the Presidency, 2003), 25–34. See also Cees Wiebes and Bert Zeeman, "Pentagon Negotiations March 1948: The Launching of the North Atlantic Treaty," *International Affairs* 59, no. 3 (Summer 1983): 351–63; and Stanley R. Sloan, *NATO's Future: Toward a New Transatlantic Bargain* (Washington, DC: National Defense University Press, 1985), 3–11.

14. On the shifting impressions over the balance of threat between Germany and the Soviet Union, see Beatrice Heuser, "Stalin as Hitler's Successor: Western Interpretations of the Soviet Threat," in *Securing Peace in Europe, 1945–62,* ed. Beatrice Heuser and Robert O'Neill (London: Macmillan, 1992), 18–23.

15. North Atlantic Treaty [Washington Treaty], Washington, DC, April 4, 1949. Article 3 regards the development of "individual and collective capacities to resist armed attack" by means of "self-help and mutual aid." Article 5 is the collective defense clause stating that an armed attack against any member shall be considered an attack against all.

16. North Atlantic Treaty, Washington, DC, April 4, 1949, Article 9.

17. North Atlantic Council, Document D-4/1, "Report of the International Working Group on Review of Progress in Implementing the North Atlantic Treaty in the Year since Its Signature," London, May 15, 1950.

18. North Atlantic Defense Committee, Document DC 6/1, "The Strategic Concept for the Defense of the North Atlantic Area," December 1, 1949.

19. North Atlantic Defense Committee, Document DC 13, "North Atlantic Treaty Organization Medium Term Plan," March 28, 1950, p. 13; emphasis added.

20. Such a strategy was not only militarily expedient but probably also vital to the political solidarity of the Alliance. As US General Omar Bradley explained: "We cannot count on friends in Western Europe if our strategy in the event of war dictates that we shall first abandon them to the enemy with a promise of later liberation." Marc Trachtenberg, *A Constructed Peace* (Princeton, NJ: Princeton University Press, 1999), 157–58.

21. North Atlantic Defense Committee, "North Atlantic Treaty Organization Medium Term Plan," 66.

22. Congressional Budget Office, "Assessing the NATO/Warsaw Pact Military Balance," Budget Issue Paper for Fiscal Year 1979 (Washington, DC: US Government Printing Office, December 1977); and David R. Stone, *A Military History of Russia: From Ivan the Terrible to the War in Chechnya* (Westport, CT: Praeger Security International, 2006).

23. Bernard Montgomery (Field Marshal), 1st Viscount Montgomery of Alamein, Report to Brussels Treaty Powers on the Military Situation in Germany, June 15, 1950,

Archives of the Western European Union, Public Record Office, Kew, Richmond, Surrey, England.

24. North Atlantic Council, Fourth Session, "Final Communiqué," London, May 15–18, 1950.

25. Hastings (Lord) Ismay, *NATO: The First Five Years* (Paris: North Atlantic Treaty Organization, 1955), 29.

26. Phillip A. Karber and Jerald A. Combs, "The United States, NATO, and the Soviet Threat to Western Europe: Military Estimates and Policy Options, 1945–1963," *Diplomatic History* 22, no. 3 (Summer 1998): 413–14.

27. Edward Fursdon, *The European Defence Community: A History* (London: Macmillan, 1980), 68.

28. Ismay, *NATO*, 31.

29. The Soviet Union was absent from the Security Council deliberations, and the People's Republic of China was at that time not recognized. United Nations Security Council, Resolution 82, June 25, 1950; United Nations Security Council, Resolution 83, June 27, 1950.

30. Roy K. Flint, "Task Force Smith and the 24th Division: Delay and Withdraw, 5–19 July 1950," in *America's First Battles, 1776–1965*, ed. Charles E. Heller and William A Stofft (Lawrence: University Press of Kansas, 1986), 266–99.

31. This, in fact, was the plan before the Korean War. See Operation OFFTACKLE in Kenneth W. Condit, *History of the Joint Chiefs of Staff: The Joint Chiefs of Staff and National Policy*, vol. 2 (Washington, DC: US Government Printing Office, 1986), 301–303. See also David Alan Rosenberg, "The Origins of Overkill: Nuclear Weapons and American Strategy, 1945–1960," *International Security* 7, no. 4 (Spring 1983): 3–71.

32. If Truman's rejection of calls from General MacArthur and others to use atomic weapons was not universally popular, President Eisenhower's equal measure of prudence in denying nuclear weapons to support the French position in 1954 at Dien Bien Phu in Indochina confirmed the risks of assuming the availability of nuclear weapons.

33. The United States not only sent forces to Korea but also deployed forces and increased military aid to Formosa, Indochina, the Philippines, and Japan.

34. See, for example, the "falling domino" principle, "The President's News Conference of April 7, 1954," in *Public Papers of the Presidents: Dwight D. Eisenhower, 1954* (Washington, DC: Government Printing Office, 1960), 381–90. Similar to the domino theory, journalist and political analyst Stewart Alsop invokes a ten-pin bowling analogy in which China was the first of the Asian countries to fall to communism. Stewart Alsop, "We Are Losing Asia Fast," *Saturday Evening Post* 222, no. 37 (March 11, 1950).

35. John W. Dower, *Embracing Defeat: Japan in the Wake of World War II* (London: Allen Lane, 1999).

36. In effect, US diplomacy allowed for the UN flag to be placed on a command that the United States militarily dominated anyway. United Nations Security Council, Resolution 84, July 7, 1950.

37. Pierre Guillen, "Les chefs militaires français, le réarmement de l'Allemagne, et la CED (1950–1954)," *Revue d'histoire de la Deuxième Guerre mondiale et des conflits contemporains* 33, no. 129 (January 1983): 3–33.

38. Georges-Henri Soutou, "France," in *The Origins of the Cold War in Europe: International Perspectives*, ed. David Reynolds (New Haven, CT: Yale University Press, 1994),

109. See also George-Henri Soutou, *L'Alliance incertaine—Les rapports politico-stratégiques franco-allemands (1954–1996)* (Paris: Fayard, 1996).

39. Winston Churchill, Address to the Council of Europe, August 11, 1950, Reports, Council of Europe Consultative Assembly, 2nd Session, August 7–28, 1950, Strasbourg, France.

40. Ibid.

41. Council of Europe Parliamentary Assembly, Document AS(2)52, "Recommendation 5 Relative to the Creation of a European Army, adopted 11th August 1950, on the Conclusion of the Debate on the Report and Message from the Committee of Ministers to the Assembly," Strasbourg, France.

42. Declaration by Robert Schuman, Paris, May 9, 1950, *Histoire de l'Union européenne* / Robert Schuman, Médiathèque centrale de la Commission européenne, Berlaymont 4/363, Brussels.

43. Winston Churchill, Speech to the Academic Youth, Zurich, September 19, 1946, Council of Europe Digital Archive, Strasbourg, France, http://www.coe.int/t/dgal/dit /ilcd/archives/selection/churchill/.

44. Raymond Poidevin, ed., *Histoire des Débuts de la Construction Européenne, mars 1948–mai 1950* (Brussels: Bruylant, 1986); Geoffrey Warner and Anne Deighton, "British Perceptions of Europe in the Postwar Period," in *Les Europes des Européens*, ed. Rene Girault (Paris: Publications de la Sorbonne, 1993). For the policy implications of British independence from Europe, see Lord Christopher, "'With But Not Of:' Britain and the Schuman Plan," *Journal of European Integration History* 4, no. 2 (1998); Edmund Dell, *The Schuman Plan and the British Abdication of Leadership in Europe* (Oxford: Oxford University Press, 1995). For the American role in this episode, see Pierre Melandri, *Les États-Unis face à l'Unification de l'Europe, 1945–1954* (Paris: Pedone, 1980).

45. Eric Pace, "Charles M. Spofford is Dead at 88," *New York Times*, March 25, 1991.

46. North Atlantic Council Deputies, Document D-D/18, "A Proposal for Action by Council Deputies," August 4, 1950; Ismay, *NATO*, 31.

47. North Atlantic Council, Document C5-D/2, "Report of the North Atlantic Council Deputies," New York, September 14, 1950. North Atlantic Council, C5-R/1, "Summary Record of the First Meeting," New York, September 15, 1950.

48. North Atlantic Council, C5-VR/2, "Statement by the Chairman of the Council [Dean Acheson]," New York, September 15, 1950.

49. An integrated military command was both familiar and an easy point of consensus, as it recalled experience from World War II and from the Brussels Treaty's nascent cooperative efforts in the Western Union Defence Organization. Lawrence S. Kaplan, *NATO 1948: The Birth of the Transatlantic Alliance* (Lanham, MD: Rowman & Littlefield, 2007), 139–65.

50. North Atlantic Council, Document C5-VR/6, "Verbatim Text of the Fifth Session of the North Atlantic Council," New York, September 18, 1950.

51. Fursdon, *The European Defence Community*, 82–83.

52. Ibid.

53. Raymond Aron and Daniel Lerner, eds., *France Defeats E.D.C.* (London: Thames and Hudson, 1957).

54. North Atlantic Council, "Final Communiqué," September 26, 1950.

55. Jean Monnet, *Mémoires* (Paris: Fayard, 1976), 401.

56. René Pleven, Speech to the French National Assembly, Paris, October 24, 1950.

57. Aron and Lerner, *France Defeats E.D.C.*, 4.

58. Traité instituant la Communauté européenne de défense [EDC Treaty], Paris, May 27, 1952.

59. Alan S. Milward, *The Frontier of National Sovereignty: History and Theory* (London: Routledge, 1993).

60. European political cooperation has been a persistent challenge and theme in European integration, as discussed in David Allen, Reinhardt Rummel, and Wolfgang Wessels, eds., *European Political Cooperation: Towards a Foreign Policy for Western Europe* (London: Butterworth Scientific, 1981); Panagiotes Ifestos, *European Political Cooperation: Towards a Framework of Supranational Diplomacy?* (Aldershot, England: Avebury, 1987); European Communities, *European Political Cooperation (EPC)* (Luxembourg: Office for Official Publications of the European Communities, 1988).

61. See reflections in Konrad Adenauer, *Erinnerungen: 1945–1953* (Stuttgart: Deutsche Verlags-Anstalt, 1976). See also Hans-Peter Schwarz, *Adenauer: Der Aufstieg, 1876–1952* (Stuttgart: Deutsche Verlags-Anstalt, 1986); and Hans-Peter Schwarz, *Adenauer: Der Staatsmann, 1952–1967* (Stuttgart: Deutsche Verlags-Anstalt, 1991).

62. The CDU gained over one hundred seats in the September 1953 elections, increasing its share from 139 to 243. See Ronald J. Granieri, *The Ambivalent Alliance: Konrad Adenauer, the CDU/CSU, and the West, 1949–1966* (New York: Berghahn Books, 2003).

63. French political instability as it applies to the EDC is covered in Aron and Lerner's *France Defeats E.D.C.* For broader patterns of French political instability during this period of the Fourth Republic, see Robert Gildea, *France since 1945* (New York: Oxford University Press, 1997); and Gordon Wright, *France in Modern Times*, 5th ed. (New York: W. W. Norton, 1995), especially chapter 33.

64. Raymond Aron described this set of expectations as unrealistic from the start, since close British participation and a supranational political structure were "mutually exclusive." Aron and Lerner, *France Defeats E.D.C.*, 7.

65. Quoted in Fursdon, *The European Defence Community*, 211.

66. Jules Moch, *Alerte! Le problème crucial de la Communauté européenne de défense* (Paris: R. Laffont, 1954).

67. For analysis of allied reaction to the French decision, see Sloan, *NATO's Future*, 25–27.

68. Perhaps a sign of these uncertain and volatile times, the man introducing the European army concept to NATO was French Defence Minister Jules Moch, the same man whose book *Alerte!* would undermine French support for the EDC in 1954.

69. North Atlantic Council Deputies, Document D-R/33, "Summary Record of the Thirty-Third Meeting of the Council Deputies," London, November 25, 1950; North Atlantic Council Deputies, Document D-D/174, "Contribution of Germany to the Defence of Western Europe: Statement Made by the French Deputy at the 28th Meeting of the Council Deputies," November 14, 1950; North Atlantic Council Deputies, Document D-D/190, "Provisional Arrangements for the Participation of Germany in the Defence of Western Europe: Memorandum by the United States Deputy," November 22, 1950.

70. North Atlantic Council, Document C6-D/1 (also DC 29/1), "Joint Report on the German Contribution to the Defence of Western Europe by the North Atlantic Council Deputies and the Military Committee to the North Atlantic Council and the Defence Committee [Spofford Report]," Brussels, December 13, 1950.

71. Ibid.; Norrin M. Ripsman, *Peacemaking by Democracies: The Effect of State Autonomy on the Post-World War Settlements* (University Park: Pennsylvania State University Press, 2002), 200–201.

72. Charles M. Spofford, "NATO's Growing Pains," *Foreign Affairs* 31, no. 1 (October 1952): 95–105.

73. North Atlantic Council, "Final Communiqué," December 18–19, 1950.

74. North Atlantic Council, Document C6-D/7, "Resolution on the Creation of an Integrated Force," December 19, 1950.

75. North Atlantic Council, "Final Communiqué," September 26, 1950.

76. North Atlantic Council, Document C5-D/11, "Resolution on the Defence of Western Europe," New York, September 26, 1950; emphasis added.

77. Ismay, *NATO*, 35. One cannot avoid remarking on Ismay's use of the term *critical juncture*, which although not used in the same social science methodological sense as appears elsewhere throughout this study still accurately reflects the significance of these events.

78. North Atlantic Council, Document C6-D/9, "Résolution Approuvant la Nomination d'un Commandant Suprême," December 19, 1950.

79. North Atlantic Council, "Final Communiqué," December 18–19, 1950.

80. North Atlantic Council Deputies, Document D-D(51)123, "NATO Reorganization: Press Communiqué," May 4, 1951.

81. Ismay, *NATO*, 41.

82. Ibid.

83. North Atlantic Council Deputies, Document D-D(51)44, "Establishment of an International Staff for NATO," February 13, 1951. North Atlantic Council Deputies, Document D-R(51)9, "Summary Record of Council Deputies Meeting of 12 February 1951 in London," February 14, 1951.

84. A military structure had been developed under the auspices of the Brussels Treaty in September 1948. NATO co-opted not only Western Union reports and practices but also structures: the central region headquarters subordinate to SHAPE had been originally established in 1948 under the Western Union. See Kaplan, *NATO 1948*, 139–65.

85. Ismay, *NATO*, 38.

86. Diary of Dwight D. Eisenhower, October 28, 1950, DDE Diary series, Eisenhower Library, Abilene, Kansas.

87. Diary of Dwight D. Eisenhower, July 6, 1960, Ann Whitman file, Eisenhower Library, Abilene, Kansas.

88. Dwight D. Eisenhower, Testimony of February 1, 1951, Hearings, Committee on Foreign Relations and Armed Services, Records of the US Senate; "Notes on a Meeting at the White House," January 31, 1951, in *Foreign Relations of the United States, 1951, Vol. III* (Washington, DC: Government Printing Office, 1979), 449–58; Stephen E. Ambrose with Morris Honick, "Eisenhower: Rekindling the Spirit of the West," in *Generals in International Politics: NATO's Supreme Allied Commander, Europe*, ed. Robert S. Jordan (Lexington: University Press of Kentucky, 1987), 11–15; James McAllister, *No Exit: America and the German Problem, 1943–1954* (Ithaca, NY: Cornell University Press, 2002), 209–12.

89. Andrew J. Goodpaster, "The Development of SHAPE: 1950–1953," in *Generals in International Politics: NATO's Supreme Allied Commander, Europe*, ed. Robert S. Jordan (Lexington: University Press of Kentucky, 1987), 2.

90. Ismay, *NATO*, 43.

91. North Atlantic Council, "Seventh Session Final Communiqué," Ottawa, Canada, September 15–20, 1951.

92. Not to be confused with another NATO group known as the "Three Wise Men," consisting of foreign ministers Lester Pearson (Canada), Gaetano Martino (Italy), and Halvard Lange (Norway), which was convened in 1956 to assess the potential for improved nonmilitary consultation within the Alliance.

93. Ismay, *NATO*, 45.

94. North Atlantic Treaty Organization, "Final Report of the Temporary Council Committee," December 18, 1951, Para 83, Roll 86, Appendix 4, NATO Document Series, Brussels.

95. Ismay, *NATO*, 46.

96. North Atlantic Council, Document D-D(52)35(Final), "Report by the Council Deputies on Relations between EDC and NATO," February 20, 1952; and North Atlantic Council, Document C-M(52)20, "NATO-EDC Relations: Report by the Committee to Examine the EDC Treaty," May 26, 1952.

97. North Atlantic Council, Document C9-D/19, "Resolution on German Participation in Western Defence," February 22, 1952.

98. North Atlantic Council, Document C9-D/4(Final), "Reorganization of the North Atlantic Treaty Organization," March 17, 1952.

99. North Atlantic Council Deputies, Document D-D(52)67, "Resolution on the Appointment of Lord Ismay as Vice-Chairman of the North Atlantic Council and Secretary-General of the North Atlantic Treaty Organization," March 13, 1952.

100. Ismay, *NATO*, 35, 40.

101. This, of course, was part of a wider military buildup in which the total size of the US armed forces doubled to 2.9 million in the nine months following the outbreak of the Korean War. Paul Kennedy, *The Rise and Fall of the Great Powers* (New York: Random House, 1987), 382–86.

102. Supreme Allied Commander, General of the Army Dwight D. Eisenhower, *First Annual Report of the Supreme Commander, Allied Powers Europe* (Paris: Public Information Division, SHAPE, April 1952).

103. Hervé Alphand, February 1951, quoted in Ismay, *NATO*, 41.

104. Hew Strachan, "Les armées européennes ne peuvent-elles mener que des guerres limitées?," *Politique Étrangère* 76, no. 2 (2011).

105. Kennedy, *Rise and Fall of the Great Powers*, 369; and David Singer and Melvin Small, *The Wages of War, 1816–1965: A Statistical Handbook* (New York: John Wiley, 1972).

106. The Off-Shore Procurement program allowed for military equipment being purchased by the United States to be manufactured and acquired outside the United States, providing the added benefit that this sort of aid would not only increase the stocks of military hardware in European arsenals but also support European defense industries manufacturing that materiel. Ismay, *NATO*, 135–38.

107. North Atlantic Council, "Report on the Annual Review for 1953," Paris, December 14–16, 1953; North Atlantic Council, "Report on the Annual Review for 1954," Paris, December 17–18, 1954.

108. Kennedy, *Rise and Fall of the Great Powers*, 384, 436; and Singer and Small, *The Wages of War, 1816–1965*.

109. North Atlantic Council, Document C-R(52)1, "Summary Record of the Meeting of the Council," Paris, April 29, 1952.

110. US National Security Council, Document NSC 162/2, "Basic National Security Policy," in *Foreign Relations of the United States, 1952–1954, Vol. II, Part 1*, October 30, 1953 (Washington, DC: US Government Printing Office, 1979), 577.

111. Gregory W. Pedlow, "The Evolution of NATO Strategy, 1949–1969," in *NATO Strategy Documents 1949–1969*, ed. Gregory W. Pedlow (Mons, Belgium: Supreme Headquarters Allied Powers Europe, 1997), 17. Robert Wampler, "NATO Strategic Planning and Nuclear Weapons," Nuclear History Program Occasional Paper 6 (College Park: University of Maryland, 1990), 9.

112. George Eugene Pellitier, "Ridgway: Trying to Make Good on the Promises," in *Generals in International Politics: NATO's Supreme Allied Commander, Europe*, ed. Robert S. Jordan (Lexington: University Press of Kentucky, 1987), 50–52.

113. North Atlantic Council, Document C-M(53)166(Final), "Resolution on the 1954 Annual Review and Related Problems," December 15, 1953.

114. Military Committee, Document MC 14/2(Rev)(Final Decision), "Overall Strategic Concept for the Defense of the North Atlantic Treaty Organization Area," May 23, 1957. Several other documents coming out of the New Approach foreshadowed this development, most notably Military Committee, Document MC 48(Final), "The Most Effective Pattern of NATO Military Strength for the Next Few Years," November 22, 1954. For a detailed history, see Marc Trachtenberg, "La formation du système de défense occidentale: Les États-Unis, la France, et MC 48," in *France et l'OTAN, 1949–1996*, ed. Maurice Vaisse (Paris: Centre d'études d'histoire de la défense, 1996), 115–26.

115. Ismay, *NATO*, 103–104, 112.

116. Robert S. Jordan, *The NATO International Staff/Secretariat, 1952–1957* (London: Oxford University Press, 1967), 33–42; and Robert S. Jordan, *Political Leadership in NATO* (Boulder, CO: Westview Press, 1979), 13–14.

117. North Atlantic Council, "Reorganization of the North Atlantic Treaty Organization"; NATO Historical Officer, Document NHO/63/1, "The Evolution of NATO Political Consultation, 1949–1962," May 2, 1963, paragraph 16.

118. Ryan C. Hendrickson, "NATO's Secretaries-General: Organizational Leadership in Shaping Alliance Strategy," in *NATO in Search of a Vision*, ed. Gülnur Aybet and Rebecca R. Moore (Washington, DC: Georgetown University Press, 2010), 52–53.

119. North Atlantic Council, Document C-R(52)16, Record of Meeting on July 16, 1952, paragraph 44. NATO Historical Officer, "The Evolution of NATO Political Consultation, 1949–1962," paragraph 19.

120. Ibid., paragraph 35.

121. Ibid., paragraph 22.

122. North Atlantic Council, Document C-M(53)87, June 25, 1953; North Atlantic Council, Document C-R(53)32, n.d. [1953]; NATO Historical Officer, "The Evolution of NATO Political Consultation, 1949–1962," paragraph 33; North Atlantic Council, "Report on the Annual Review for 1953."

123. Lord Ismay's role as observer at the Bermuda Conference foreshadowed an official decision in the Long-Term Planning Report of 1961 that the secretary-general be represented at other similar consultations among member-states only for the purpose

of facilitating work within NATO. North Atlantic Council, Document C-M(61)30, "Long Term Planning," April 18, 1961.

124. "NATO Allies Astonished at Switch," *Washington Post*, April 15, 1956, A13; Jordan, *The NATO International Staff/Secretariat, 1952–1957*, 77.

125. Standing Group, Document SG 80/2, "Report by the International Working Team to the Standing Group on Association of Turkey and Greece with NATO Military Planning," November 29, 1950.

126. Military Committee [North Atlantic], Document SGM-1136-51, "Memorandum for the Standing Group [on] Association of Greece and Turkey with NATO," July 18, 1951.

127. North Atlantic Council, Document C7-D/23(Final), "Resolution on the Accession of Greece and Turkey to the North Atlantic Treaty," October 17, 1951; North Atlantic Council Deputies, Document D-D(51)280, "Protocol to the North Atlantic Treaty on the Accession of Greece and Turkey," November 9, 1951.

128. The title "Western European Union" did not appear in the actual text of the final act. The name was decided at the Paris Conference following London, but the substance of the agreement is the same. The Western European Union ceased to exist as a treaty-based international organization on June 30, 2011. For an analysis of the WEU's ultimately limited role, see Anne Deighton, ed., *Western European Union 1954–1997: Defence, Security, Integration* (Oxford: European Interdependence Research Unit, 1997).

129. "Final Act of the London Conference," London, October 3, 1954, in Ismay, *NATO*, supplementary appendix 1.

130. Final Communiqué of the Meeting of the North Atlantic Council attended by Foreign and Defence Ministers, Paris, October 22, 1954. Protocol to the North Atlantic Treaty on the Accession of the Federal Republic of Germany, Paris, October 23, 1954. The additional treaties implementing the London Conference agreement were drawn up at the conference in Paris, October 20–22, 1954. Ismay, *NATO*, supplementary appendices.

131. René Massigli, quoted in Fursdon, *The European Defence Community*, 322.

Chapter 5 · *Flexible Response and the Future Tasks of the Alliance, 1962–1967*

1. Vasiliĭ Danilovich Sokolovskiy, *Soviet Military Strategy* (Moscow: Voenizdat, 1963).

2. A point acknowledged in the West too: Bernard Brodie, ed., *The Absolute Weapon: Atomic Power and World Order* (New York: Harcourt, Brace, 1946), 76.

3. See A. W. DePorte, *Europe between the Superpowers: The Enduring Balance*, 2nd ed. (London: Yale University Press, 1986); and Robert S. Jordan, ed., *Europe and the Superpowers: Essays on European International Politics* (London: Pinter Publishers, 1991).

4. Lawrence Freedman, *The Evolution of Nuclear Strategy* (London: Macmillan, 1981), 52.

5. US National Security Council, Document NSC 30, "United States Policy on Atomic Warfare," September 10, 1948, in *Foreign Relations of the United States, 1948*, vol.1, part 2 (Washington, DC: Government Printing Office, 1976), 624–28.

6. In contrast to his views in 1945, Truman now said of nuclear weapons: "You have to understand that this isn't a military weapon. It is used to wipe out women, children and unarmed people, and not for military use. So we have to treat this differently from rifles and cannon and ordinary things like that." David McCullough, *Truman* (New York: Simon & Schuster, 1992), 650, 441–42.

7. In reality, the US nuclear arsenal was not large enough in 1948 to equip these B-29s with weapons, and thus they did not carry any. Although the lack of armament was a

closely guarded secret shared between the United States and the United Kingdom, Soviet intelligence probably also knew that the bomb bays were empty. Nevertheless, there could be no mistaking the aim of the American show of force.

8. US National Security Council, Document NSC 162/2, "Basic National Security Policy," October 30, 1953, in *Foreign Relations of the United States, 1952–54*, vol. 2, part 1 (Washington, DC: Government Printing Office, 1979), 577–97.

9. John Foster Dulles, "The Evolution of Foreign Policy," *The Department of State Bulletin* 30 (January 25, 1954): 107–10.

10. John Foster Dulles, "Policy for Security and Peace," *Foreign Affairs* 32, no. 3 (April 1954): 353–64; Samuel F. Wells Jr., "The Origins of Massive Retaliation," *Political Science Quarterly* 96, no. 1 (Spring 1981): 31–52.

11. Quoted in Stephen E. Ambrose and Douglas G. Brinkley, *Rise to Globalism: American Foreign Policy since 1938*, 8th rev. ed. (New York: Penguin, 1997), 131. A February 1947 report by the American Air Staff, *Strategic Implications of the Atomic Bomb on Warfare*, officially confirmed this; see Freedman, *The Evolution of Nuclear Strategy*, 54.

12. A fact NSC 162/2 foresaw in acknowledging a likely future "stalemate" as Soviet nuclear capabilities grew.

13. A number of historians have remarked that thermonuclear weapons developed by 1955, even more than the first atomic bombs created in 1945, were the truly revolutionary technologies that made war unendurable. Richard Rhodes, *The Making of the Atomic Bomb* (New York: Simon & Schuster, 1986), 749–78; Marc Trachtenberg, *History and Strategy* (Princeton, NJ: Princeton University Press, 1991), 4–6; and André Beaufre, *NATO and Europe*, trans. Joseph Green and R. H. Barry (London: Faber and Faber, 1967), 51–54.

14. In reality, fears about the bomber and missile gap were overblown. Most of the Soviet Bison bombers were concentrated at a single airbase, giving the false illusion that all airbases were similarly well equipped when in fact they were empty. Soviet missile production was slow, and the United States still maintained more nuclear warheads. Eisenhower knew this from secret U-2 reconnaissance flights over the Soviet Union but refused to divulge this secret information. For most Americans, therefore, the Soviet superiority and threat seemed alarmingly real. Christopher A. Preble, "Who Ever Believed in the 'Missile Gap'? John F. Kennedy and the Politics of National Security," *Presidential Studies Quarterly* 33, no. 4 (December 2003): 801–26.

15. Gregory W. Pedlow, "The Evolution of NATO's Command Structure, 1951–2009," n.d., 6–7, Historical Office of the Supreme Headquarters Allied Powers Europe, Mons, Belgium.

16. Standing Group, Document SG 80/2, "Report by the International Working Team to the Standing Group on Association of Turkey and Greece with NATO Military Planning," November 29, 1950; and Pierre Guillen, "Les chefs militaires français, le réarmement de l'Allemagne, et la CED (1950–1954)," *Revue d'histoire de la Deuxième Guerre mondiale et des conflits contemporains* 33, no. 129 (January 1983): 3–33.

17. North Atlantic Council, Document C-M(53)166(Final), "Resolution on the 1954 Annual Review and Related Problems," December 15, 1953.

18. "Statement by the Secretary of State to the North Atlantic Council Closed Ministerial Session," Paris, April 23, 1954, in *Foreign Relations of the United States, 1952–1953, Vol. V, Part 1* (Washington, DC: Government Printing Office, 1979), 511–12.

19. Joint Planning Staff, Document JP(54)76(Final), "Capabilities Study—Allied Com-

mand Europe, 1957," September 2, 1954; Military Committee, Document MC 48(Final), "The Most Effective Pattern of NATO Military Strength for the Next Few Years," November 22, 1954.

20. Military Committee, Document MC 14/1(Final), "Strategic Guidance [*supersedes DC 13 and MC 14*]," December 9, 1952, 10.

21. Military Committee, "The Most Effective Pattern of NATO Military Strength for the Next Few Years"; emphasis added.

22. Ibid. For a detailed history, see Marc Trachtenberg, "La formation du système de défense occidentale: Les États-Unis, la France, et MC 48," in *France et l'OTAN, 1949–1996*, ed. Maurice Vaisse (Paris: Centre d'études d'histoire de la défense, 1996), 115–26.

23. North Atlantic Council, Document CM(54)118(Final), "Resolution on the 1955 Annual Review and Related Problems," December 17, 1954.

24. Military Committee, Document MC 48/1, "The Most Effective Pattern of NATO Military Strength for the Next Few Years—Report No. 2," December 9, 1955.

25. Military Committee, Document MC 14/2(Rev)(Final Decision), "Overall Strategic Concept for the Defense of the North Atlantic Treaty Organization Area," May 23, 1957.

26. North Atlantic Council, Document C-M(56)138(Final), "Directive to the NATO Military Authorities from the North Atlantic Council," December 13, 1956.

27. Beatrice Heuser, *NATO, Britain, France, and the FRG: Nuclear Strategies and Forces for Europe, 1949–2000* (London: Macmillan, 1997), 40–53; John S. Duffield, *Power Rules: The Evolution of NATO's Conventional Force Posture* (Stanford, CA: Stanford University Press, 1995), 112–14, 121–30; and Marc Trachtenberg, *A Constructed Peace* (Princeton, NJ: Princeton University Press, 1999), 188–89.

28. Military Committee, "Overall Strategic Concept for the Defense of the North Atlantic Treaty Organization Area."

29. Gregory W. Pedlow, "The Evolution of NATO Strategy, 1949–1969," in *NATO Strategy Documents 1949–1969*, ed. Gregory W. Pedlow (Mons, Belgium: Supreme Headquarters Allied Powers Europe, 1997), 17; Robert Wampler, "NATO Strategic Planning and Nuclear Weapons," Nuclear History Program Occasional Paper 6 (College Park: University of Maryland, 1990), 9.

30. Robert S. Jordan, "Gruenther: Attempts to Retain NATO Solidarity," in *Generals in International Politics: NATO's Supreme Allied Commander, Europe*, ed. Robert S. Jordan (Lexington: University Press of Kentucky, 1987), 53.

31. North Atlantic Council, "Directive to the NATO Military Authorities from the North Atlantic Council." Recent scholarship suggests that social norms entrenched during the Suez Crisis had a long-term impact on NATO's twenty-first-century out-of-area operations, but this long view contrasts with the limited impact of the crisis on NATO organization and strategy in the short term. Veronica M. Kitchen, "NATO's Out-of-Area Norm from Suez to Afghanistan," *Journal of Transatlantic Studies* 8, no. 2 (2010): 105–17.

32. An exception to this was the creation of the so-called committee of the "Three Wise Men" to explore additional avenues for enhanced political consultation within the Alliance as a result of the Suez Crisis. This was an important initiative, but an essentially intergovernmental one. See Halvard Lange, Gaetano Martino, and Lester B. Pearson, "Report of the Committee of Three on Non-Military Co-operation," December 13, 1956.

33. Preble, "Who Ever Believed in the 'Missile Gap'?," 801–26.

34. Jack Raymond, "Kennedy Defense Study Finds No Evidence of a 'Missile Gap,'" *New York Times*, February 7, 1961, A1.

35. Jeremy Isaacs and Taylor Downing, *Cold War* (New York: Little, Brown, 1998), 183.

36. As Sean Maloney explains, "The second Berlin Crisis (1958–62) was a complicated series of diplomatic, domestic political, and military manoeuvres. In effect, Berlin was an anti-climactic grand showdown between the Soviet Union and the Western NATO allies that flowed into a sharper, possibly more dangerous situation, the Cuban Missile Crisis of 1962." Sean M. Maloney, "Berlin Contingency Planning: Prelude to Flexible Response, 1958–63," *The Journal of Strategic Studies* 25, no. 1 (March 2002): 99.

37. Sean M. Maloney, "Notfallplanung für Berlin: Vorläufer der Flexible Response, 1958–1963," *Militärgeschichte* Jahrgang 7, Heft 1 (1997): 3–15; and Gregory W. Pedlow, "Flexible Response before MC 14/3: General Lauris Norstad and the Second Berlin Crisis 1958–62," *Storia delle Relazioni Internationali* 13, no. 1 (1998): 235–68.

38. But an attack on the United States would have triggered the mutual defense clause of the North Atlantic Treaty. The assumed purpose of the clause was to provide guarantees in case of an attack in Europe, but that did not prevent the reverse from occurring. The first and, to date, only invocation of this portion of the treaty was after the attacks on the United States on September 11, 2001.

39. Exclusive for President of the United States from GEN Norstad, October 22, 1962, Papers of John F. Kennedy, Folder: NATO: Norstad correspondence, 1962: July–December, John F. Kennedy Presidential Library, Boston, Mass.

40. Norstad, USNMR Shape Paris to POTUS White House, October 27, 1962, Papers of John F. Kennedy, Folder: NATO: Norstad correspondence, 1962: July–December, John F. Kennedy Presidential Library, Boston, Mass.

41. Robert S. Jordan, *Political Leadership in NATO* (Boulder, CO: Westview Press, 1979), 118.

42. North Atlantic Council, "Final Communiqué," December 13–15, 1962; emphasis added.

43. President Kennedy through Joint Chiefs of Staff to General Norstad, Message CAPS492-62, October 22, 1962, Papers of John F. Kennedy, Folder: NATO: Norstad correspondence, 1962: July–December, John F. Kennedy Presidential Library, Boston, Mass.

44. General Norstad to President Kennedy, Report on London Visit, October 24, 1962, Papers of John F. Kennedy, Folder: NATO: Norstad correspondence, 1962: July–December, John F. Kennedy Presidential Library, Boston, Mass.; Barton J. Bernstein, "The Cuban Missile Crisis: Trading the Jupiters in Turkey?," *Political Science Quarterly* 95, no. 1 (Spring 1980): 97–125.

45. General Norstad to President Kennedy, Preparations for a NAC Meeting on Cuban Missile Crisis, Message No. PRS 2634, October 24, 1962, Papers of John F. Kennedy, Folder: NATO: Norstad correspondence, 1962: July–December, John F. Kennedy Presidential Library, Boston, Mass.

46. President Kennedy to General Norstad, Response to Report on London Visit, October 24, 1962, Papers of John F. Kennedy, Folder: NATO: Norstad correspondence, 1962: July–December, John F. Kennedy Presidential Library, Boston, Mass.

47. For a history into the origins and later development of the British nuclear pro-

gram, see Andrew J. Pierre, *Nuclear Politics: The British Experience with an Independent Strategic Force, 1939–1970* (London: Oxford University Press, 1972); Heuser, *NATO, Britain, France, and the FRG*; Beatrice Heuser, *Nuclear Mentalities? Strategies and Beliefs in Britain, France, and the FRG* (London: Macmillan, 1998); and Ranya Ogilvie-White, *On Nuclear Deterrence: The Correspondence of Sir Michael Quinlan* (London: International Institute for Strategic Studies, 2011).

48. Ian Clark, *Nuclear Diplomacy and the Special Relationship: Britain's Deterrent and America, 1957–1962* (Oxford: Clarendon Press, 1994), 21–30.

49. Philip Nash, *The Other Missiles of October: Eisenhower, Kennedy, and the Jupiters, 1957–1963* (Chapel Hill: University of North Carolina Press, 1997), 9–16.

50. Jan Melissen, "The Politics of US Missile Deployment in Britain 1955–59," *Storia delle Relazioni Internationali* 13, no. 1 (1998): 151–85; and Ralph Dietl, "In Defence of the West: General Lauris Norstad, NATO Nuclear Forces and Transatlantic Relations 1956–1963," *Diplomacy & Statecraft* 17, no. 2 (2006): 354.

51. Robert Gildea, *France since 1945* (Oxford: Oxford University Press, 1996), 201–2.

52. As de Gaulle explained, "A great state," which allows other states to develop nuclear weapons without developing any of its own, "does not command its own destiny." Quoted in Wilfred L. Kohl, *French Nuclear Diplomacy* (Princeton, NJ: Princeton University Press, 1971), 129. See also Pierre M. Gallois, *Stratégie de l'âge Nucléaire* (Paris: Calmann-Lévy, 1960); and Raymond Aron, *Le Grand Débat: Initiation à la Stratégie Atomique* (Paris: Calmann-Lévy, 1963).

53. For more on the British nuclear weapons program, see Lawrence Freedman, *Britain and Nuclear Weapons* (London: Royal Institute of International Affairs, 1980); and Jeff McMahan, *British Nuclear Weapons: For and Against* (London: Junction Books, 1981).

54. Dietl, "In Defence of the West," 347–92.

55. France: De Gaulle press conference, January 14, 1963, Papers of John F. Kennedy, Presidential Papers, President's Office Files, Countries Series, John F. Kennedy Presidential Library, Boston, Mass.

56. Lawrence S. Kaplan, *NATO Divided, NATO United: The Evolution of an Alliance* (London: Praeger, 2004), 39.

57. Treaty Establishing the European Atomic Energy Community [Euratom], Rome, March 25, 1957, 2010 OJ (C84) 1 (signed concurrently with the treaty establishing the EEC). Treaty Establishing a Single Council and a Single Commission of the European Communities [Merger Treaty], Brussels, April 8, 1965 (with effect from July 1, 1967), 1967 OJEC (152).

58. Dietl, "In Defence of the West," 351–53.

59. Franco-German Treaty of Friendship [Élysée Treaty], Paris, January 22, 1963.

60. Dietl, "In Defence of the West," 347–92.

61. North Atlantic Council, "Final Communiqué," December 16–18, 1960.

62. For an interesting insight into American views, see *Nonproliferation Treaty: Hearings before the Committee on Foreign Relations, United States Senate, 10 July–20 February 1969* (Washington, DC: United States Government Printing Office, 1968–69). See also Michael J. Brenner, *Nuclear Power and Non-Proliferation: The Remaking of US Policy* (Cambridge: Cambridge University Press, 1981).

63. Alastair Buchan, "The Multilateral Force: A Study in Alliance Politics," *International Affairs (Royal Institute of International Affairs 1944–)* 40, no. 4 (October 1964): 619–37;

Robert E. Osgood, *The Case for the MLF: A Critical Evaluation* (Washington, DC: Washington Center for Foreign Policy Research, 1964); Wilfred L. Kohl, "Nuclear Sharing in NATO and the Multilateral Force," *Political Science Quarterly* 80, no. 1 (March 1965): 88–109.

64. The United Kingdom also acceded to the Partial Test Ban Treaty, but France did not.

65. See "The Fissuring of the Bipolar World" in Paul Kennedy, *The Rise and Fall of the Great Powers* (New York: Random House, 1987), 395–413.

66. See Angela Stent, *From Embargo to Ostpolitik, 1955–1980* (Cambridge: Cambridge University Press, 1981). Also Willi Brandt, "German Policy towards the East," *Foreign Affairs* 46, no. 3 (April 1968).

67. For a concise summary of British national priorities, see "Britain: Better Times and Retreat from Empire," in J. A. S. Grenville, *A History of the World in the Twentieth Century* (Cambridge, MA: Belknap Press, 1994).

68. Gordon Wright, *France in Modern Times*, 5th ed. (New York: W. W. Norton, 1995), 418.

69. Daniel J. Mahoney, *De Gaulle: Statesmanship, Grandeur, and Modern Democracy* (London: Transaction Publishers, 2000), 136.

70. Helga Haftendorn, *NATO and the Nuclear Revolution: A Crisis of Credibility, 1966–1967* (Oxford: Clarendon Press, 1996), 9.

71. See, for example, Raymond Aron, *Paix et Guerre entre les Nations* (Paris: Calmann-Lévy, 1962).

72. See, for example, Victor-Yves Ghebali, *La France en Guerre et les Organisations Internationales, 1939–1945* (Paris: La Haye, Mouton, 1969).

73. Ibid. The relationship between European integration and de Gaulle's vision of grandeur for France is strongly nationalist. Unlike other Europeanists, de Gaulle's vision was one of a *Europe des patries* in which the unique national character of France would be preserved, rather than a more homogeneous "united Europe." By leading the integration project, France could continue to pursue its own national interests but do so with the resources of an integrated Europe.

74. Many senior French figures shared de Gaulle's views on the proper roles of France, Europe, and the Atlantic Alliance, and welcomed these moves against NATO. See, for example, André Beaufre, *L'O.T.A.N. et l'Europe* (Paris: Calmann-Lévy, 1966).

75. Gildea, *France since 1945*, 202.

76. Jordan, *Political Leadership in NATO*, 194.

77. Ibid., 193.

78. The impact of this decision on the United States was the most strong, as the United States maintained more than twenty-five bases and over 750,000 tons of military equipment in France in 1966.

79. Jordan, *Political Leadership in NATO*, 195–96.

80. Ibid., 196.

81. Ibid.

82. Ibid., 197.

83. The subsequent understanding, known as the Lemnitzer-Ailleret agreement of 1967, served as the basis for the possible participation of French forces in NATO operations, including a detailed specification of the role French forces could play in a war in Germany. Peter Schmidt, "Germany, France, and NATO," paper presented at Strategic

Outreach Roundtable, Strategic Studies Institute, US Army War College, Carlisle, PA, 1994; Pierre Melandri, "La France et les États-Unis," *Politique Étrangère* 51, no. 1 (1986): 219–46.

84. Jordan, *Political Leadership in NATO*, 198.

85. Ibid., 198–201.

86. North Atlantic Council, "Final Communiqué," December 15–16, 1966.

87. Jordan, *Political Leadership in NATO*, 202–203.

88. Haftendorn, *NATO and the Nuclear Revolution*, 168.

89. Jordan, *Political Leadership in NATO*, 233.

90. The body was also known as the McNamara Committee, and McNamara did insist on many details, including a certain bespoke style of table for these meetings that would force attendees to interact and reduce the proximity or access of secondary staff members.

91. Jordan, *Political Leadership in NATO*, 233–36.

92. North Atlantic Council, "Final Communiqué," December 15–16, 1966.

93. For more on how the work of the NPG occurred in practice, see Paul Buteux, *The Politics of Nuclear Consultation in NATO, 1965–1980* (London: Cambridge University Press, 1983).

94. Haftendorn, *NATO and the Nuclear Revolution*, 175. For more on the relationship between nuclear policy and flexible response, see Shaun R. Gregory, *Nuclear Command and Control in NATO: Nuclear Weapons Operation and the Strategy of Flexible Response* (London: Macmillan, 1996).

95. "Address by Secretary of Defence McNamara at the Ministerial Meeting of the North Atlantic Council, Athens, May 5, 1962," in *Foreign Relations of the United States, 1961–1963*, vol. 3 (Washington, DC: Government Printing Office, 1986), 278.

96. "Address by Secretary of Defence McNamara at the Ministerial Meeting of the North Atlantic Council, Paris, December 14, 1962," in *Foreign Relations of the United States, 1961–1963*, vol. 3 (Washington, DC: Government Printing Office, 1986), 440, 445–46.

97. *Differentiated response* is the term that Beatrice Heuser uses to distinguish the thinking in MC 14/2 from the more pure expressions of "massive retaliation" in MC 48 and "flexible response" as outlined in the Strategic Concept document MC 14/3. Heuser, *NATO, Britain, France, and the FRG*, 40.

98. North Atlantic Council, "Final Communiqué," May 8–10, 196; emphasis added.

99. North Atlantic Council, "Final Communiqué," December 13–15, 1961.

100. Secretary-General, Document CM(62)48, "Report on NATO Defence Policy," April 17, 1962.

101. Buteux, *The Politics of Nuclear Consultation in NATO, 1965–1980*, 102–103.

102. Secretary-General, Document NDP/62/10, "NATO Defence Policy" ["Stikker Paper"], September 3, 1962.

103. Pedlow, "The Evolution of NATO Strategy, 1949–1969," 23.

104. Although MC 14/3 is most commonly known as the Strategic Concept that fully develops "flexible response," Beatrice Heuser perhaps more accurately refers to it as a strategy of "flexible escalation," since some flexibility alone had been in evidence in the earlier MC 14/2 normally associated with "massive retaliation." Heuser, *NATO, Britain, France, and the FRG*, 53.

105. Military Committee, Document MC 14/3 (Final), "A Report by the Military Committee to the Defence Planning Committee on Overall Strategic Concept for the Defense of the North Atlantic Treaty Organization Area," January 16, 1968.

106. Indeed, throughout NATO's history, strategy documents often have been better at reflecting new realities rather than creating them. The obstacles to swift agreement under the consensus model of NATO decision-making contribute significantly to the long time needed for adaptation.

107. Several of these problems were exogenous to NATO institutions and bore on the international and domestic politics of Alliance members more generally. Chief among these were bilateral arms control negotiations the United States had undertaken with the Soviet Union, leaving European allies to fear the worst at being left out of such discussions, and, conversely, American concerns about the success of the Soviet peace campaign propaganda in encouraging European states to seek their own rapprochement. These factors help explain the relative prominence of national actors in the events leading to the Harmel Report. Stanley R. Sloan, *Permanent Alliance? NATO and the Transatlantic Bargain from Truman to Obama* (New York: Bloomsbury, 2013), 51.

108. Manlio Brosio, "Secretary General Address to Eleventh NATO Parliamentarians' Conference, October 4, 1965," in *The Atlantic Alliance: Allied Comment* (Washington, DC: US Government Printing Office, 1966), 53–64.

109. North Atlantic Council, "Final Communiqué," December 15–16, 1966.

110. Jordan, *Political Leadership in NATO*, 204.

111. North Atlantic Council, "The Future Tasks of the Alliance: Report of the Council [Harmel Report]" (Brussels: North Atlantic Treaty Organization, December 13–14, 1967).

112. Haftendorn, *NATO and the Nuclear Revolution*, 399.

Chapter 6 · *NATO and the New World Order, 1992–1997*

1. Peter J. Katzenstein, *The Culture of National Security* (New York: Columbia University Press, 1996), xi; Michael Barnett and Kathryn Sikkink, "From International Relations to Global Society," in *The Oxford Handbook of International Relations*, ed. Christian Reus-Smith and Duncan Snidal (Oxford: Oxford University Press, 2008), 66; and Richard Ned Lebow and Thomas Risse-Kappen, eds., *International Relations Theory and the End of the Cold War* (New York: Columbia University Press, 1995).

2. Consider, for example, Soviet support to the Marxist People's Liberation Army in Angola and US support of the mujahedin fighting Soviet occupation of Afghanistan. See Michael E. Latham, "The Cold War in the Third World, 1963–1975," in *The Cambridge History of the Cold War*, vol.2, *Crises and Détente*, ed. Melvin P. Leffler and Odd Arne Westad (Cambridge: Cambridge University Press, 2010), 258–80; and Robert W. Clawson, ed., *East-West Rivalry in the Third World: Security Issues and Regional Perspectives* (Wilmington, DE: Scholarly Resources, 1986).

3. Military competition continued, but fewer entirely new kinds of weapons were developed when compared to groundbreaking developments such as the hydrogen bomb and ICBMs during the early Cold War. On arms control, the Partial Test Ban Treaty and Non-Proliferation Treaty in the 1960s, the Anti-Ballistic Missile (ABM) Treaty and Strategic Arms Limitation Talks (SALT) in the 1970s, the Mutual and Balanced Force Reductions (MBFR) process between 1973 and 1989, and the 1987 Intermediate Nuclear Forces (INF) Treaty all served to temper the radical and rapid militarization of the early

Cold War. See John Lewis Gaddis, ed., *Cold War Statesmen Confront the Bomb: Nuclear Diplomacy since 1945* (Oxford: Oxford University Press, 1999). See also the Foreign and Commonwealth Office series *Notes on Arms Control* (London: Foreign and Commonwealth Office, 1990–1992), and later *Notes on Security and Arms Control* (London: Foreign and Commonwealth Office, 1993–).

4. Pavel Podvig and Theodore Postol, "Did 'Star Wars' Win the Cold War? Evidence from Newly Discovered Soviet Documents," seminar, Stanford University, Stanford, CA, April 19, 2007.

5. John Lewis Gaddis, *We Now Know: Rethinking Cold War History* (New York: Oxford University Press, 1997), 191.

6. Kenneth Dyson, ed., *European Détente: Case Studies of the Politics of East-West Relations* (London: Pinter, 1986); and Richard Davy, ed., *European Détente: A Reappraisal* (London: Royal Institute of International Affairs, 1992). On *Ostpolitik*, see Julia von Dannenberg, *The Foundations of Ostpolitik: The Making of the Moscow Treaty between West Germany and the USSR* (Oxford: Oxford University Press, 2008); and Horst Ehmke, Karlheinz Koppe, and Herbert Wehner, eds., *Zwanzig Jahre Ostpolitik: Bilanz und Perspektiven* (Bonn: Neue Gesellschaft, 1986).

7. Victor-Yves Ghebali, *La Diplomatie de la Détente: La CSCE, d'Helsinki à Vienne (1973–89)* (Brussels: Bruylant, 1989).

8. "We Will Bury You!," *Time*, November 26, 1956; and William Taubman, *Khrushchev: The Man and His Era* (New York: W. W. Norton, 2003), 427–28. On how Gorbachev's political and economic reforms (*glasnost* and *perestroika*) in the Soviet Union further contributed to a decline in ideological confrontation, see Mikhail Sergeevich Gorbachev, *Perestroika: New Thinking for Our Country and the World* (Moscow: Izd-vo polit. lit-ry, 1987); and Anthony D'Agostino, *Gorbachev's Revolution, 1985–1991* (Basingstoke: Macmillan, 1998).

9. Allen Lynch, *The Cold War Is Over—Again* (Oxford: Westview, 1992).

10. Adam Roberts, "An 'Incredibly Swift Transition': Reflections on the End of the Cold War," in *The Cambridge History of the Cold War*, vol. 3, *Endings*, ed. Melvin P. Leffler and Odd Arne Westad (Cambridge: Cambridge University Press, 2010), 513–34. For a contemporaneous analysis, see Alex Pravda, ed., *The End of the Outer Empire: Soviet-East European Relations in Transition, 1985–1990* (London: Royal Institute for International Affairs, 1992).

11. Michael Dobbs, "Slavic Republics Declare Soviet Union Liquidated," *Washington Post*, December 9, 1991, A01. See also Boris Pankin, *The Last Hundred Days of the Soviet Union*, trans. Alexei Pankin (London: Tauris, 1996).

12. Josef Joffe, "Once More: The German Question," *Survival* 32, no. 2 (1990): 129–40. Josef Joffe, "The Security Implications of a United Germany," *The Adelphi Papers* 30, no. 257 (1990): 84–91. See also the chapter in this study on NATO in the 1950s.

13. Quoted in George H. W. Bush and Brent Scowcroft, *A World Transformed* (New York: Knopf, 1998), 201.

14. See, for instance, Philip Zelikow and Condoleeza Rice, *Germany Unified and Europe Transformed: A Study in Statecraft* (London: Harvard University Press, 1995).

15. Archie Brown, "The Gorbachev Revolution and the End of the Cold War," in *The Cambridge History of the Cold War*, vol. 3, *Endings*, ed. Melvin P. Leffler and Odd Arne Westad (Cambridge: Cambridge University Press, 2010), 253–54.

16. Although he initially deployed troops to the Baltics and the Caucasus to prevent the breakup of the Soviet Union itself, even these moves were ultimately abandoned.

17. Roberts, "An 'Incredibly Swift Transition,'" 513–34; and Peter M. R. Stirk, *A History of European Integration since 1914* (London: Continuum, 2001), 252–56.

18. North Atlantic Council, Document C-M(91)88, "The Alliance's New Strategic Concept," November 7–8, 1991.

19. Moreover, it was not immediately clear that the West would readily assist in these transitions. As G. John Ikenberry observed, "In the years that followed the end of the Cold War, more than a few Russians remarked—only half jokingly—that reform and reconstruction in the former Soviet Union would have been more successful if Russia had actually been invaded and defeated by the West; the United States and its allies might have been more generous in extending assistance." G. John Ikenberry, *After Victory: Institutions, Strategic Restraint, and the Rebuilding of Order after Major Wars* (Princeton, NJ: Princeton University Press, 2001), 215.

20. Václav Havel, "Speech at NATO Headquarters, Brussels, March 21, 1991," in *NATO, Europe, and the Security of Democracy: Václav Havel, Selected Speeches, Articles, and Interviews, 1990–2002* (Prague: Theo Publishing Pardubice, 2002), 28.

21. Josef Joffe, "The New Europe: Yesterday's Ghosts," *Foreign Affairs* 72, no. 1 (1993): 31.

22. Anne Deighton, "The European Union, Multilateralism, and the Use of Force," in *The Changing Character of War*, ed. Hew Strachan and Sibylle Scheipers (Oxford: Oxford University Press, 2011), 321. In many ways, the popular impression that the end of the Cold War deprived NATO of its main organizing principle continues to this day. See, for example, Mark Mardell, "NATO: What Is It For?," *BBC News*, May 20, 2012, http://www.bbc.co.uk/news/world-us-canada-18135456.

23. Madeleine Albright, in discussion with the author, Chicago, May 20, 2012.

24. United Nations, Department of Public Information, "Former Yugoslavia—UNPROFOR, Department of Peacekeeping Operations," http://www.un.org/Depts/DPKO/Missions/unprof_b.htm.

25. United Nations General Assembly, Document A/54/549, "Report of the Secretary-General Pursuant to General Assembly Resolution 53/35: The Fall of Srebrenica," November 15, 1999.

26. Quoted in Charles Cogan, *The Third Option: The Emancipation of European Defense, 1989–2000* (Westport, CT: Praeger, 2001), 24. Also see Charles Cogan, "Florentine in Winter: François Mitterrand and the Ending of the Cold War, 1989–1991," in *NATO and the Warsaw Pact: Intrabloc Conflicts*, ed. Mary Ann Heiss and S. Victor Papacosma (Kent, OH: Kent State University Press, 2008), 131–32.

27. Quoted in Cogan, *The Third Option*, 24.

28. Andrew Moravcsik, "De Gaulle between Grain and Grandeur: The Political Economy of French EC Policy, 1958–1970," *Journal of Cold War Studies* 2, no. 2 (2000): 3–43.

29. EPC was later given legal status within the 1986 Single European Act, but the general language simply read that states would "endeavour jointly to formulate and implement a European foreign policy." Stirk, *A History of European Integration since 1914*.

30. The Dublin European Council also approved the incorporation of the former GDR into the EC, extending the application of EC law to the East German *Länder* on the same date that they were unified with the Federal Republic.

31. Treaty on European Union [TEU, Maastricht Treaty], February 7, 1992, 1992 O.J. (C191) 1, Article J.4.

32. The WEU demonstrated some modest success in coordinating European mine-sweeping efforts from 1987 to 1990 in connection with the Iran-Iraq War, but the lack of a common European foreign policy position on the Iraqi invasion of Kuwait in 1990 prevented consideration of a WEU role in the Gulf War. Willem van Eekelen, "WEU and the Gulf Crisis," *Survival* 32, no. 6 (1990): 519–32.

33. See the chapter in this study on NATO in the 1950s.

34. The Eurocorps was later brought into the EU under the Treaty of Strasbourg, which took effect February 26, 2009. The Franco-German brigade comprises approximately five thousand troops, and the Eurocorps has included nominally pledged force levels of up to sixty thousand. NATO force levels in the Central European Region, by comparison, numbered over one million during the year the Franco-German brigade was established. John S. Duffield, "International Regimes and Alliance Behavior: Explaining NATO Conventional Force Levels," *International Organization* 46, no. 4 (Autumn 1992): 819–55.

35. Deighton, "The European Union, Multilateralism, and the Use of Force," 315–32.

36. Josip Glaurdić, *The Hour of Europe: Western Powers and the Breakup of Yugoslavia* (New Haven, CT: Yale University Press, 2011), 1.

37. As Josef Joffe has argued, Germany's recognition of these new countries actually contributed to the likelihood of civil war over Bosnia by legitimizing Yugoslavia's breakup and encouraging Serbia especially to fight for territory. Joffe, "The New Europe."

38. Unlike Bosnia or Croatia, Slovenia was ethnically quite homogeneous and lacked a substantial Serb population. Slovenia is also on the geographic fringe of the former Yugoslavia, making its territorial boundaries relatively distinct.

39. James B. Steinberg, "International Involvement in the Yugoslavia Conflict," in *Enforcing Restraint: Collective Intervention in Internal Conflicts*, ed. Lori Fisler Damrosch (New York: Council on Foreign Relations, 1993), 36–46.

40. Victor-Yves Ghebali, *L'OSCE dans l'Europe post-communiste, 1990–1996: vers une identité paneuropéenne de sécurité* (Brussels: Bruylant, 1996); and Harald Löberbauer, *The OSCE System: Institutional Design and Conflict Management in the 21st Century* (Munich: Grin Verlag, 2007).

41. David S. Yost, *NATO Transformed: The Alliance's New Role in International Security* (Washington, DC: United States Institute of Peace Press, 1998), 47.

42. Ibid., 48.

43. Warsaw Treaty of Friendship, Cooperation, and Mutual Assistance [Warsaw Pact], Bulgaria-USSR, May 14, 1955, 6 I.L.M. 906 (1967), Article 11.

44. Joint Declaration of Twenty-Two States, Treaty on Conventional Armed Forces in Europe [CFE Treaty] signing conference, Paris, November 19, 1990. See United Nations General Assembly, Document A/46/48, January 16, 1991.

45. Conference for Security and Co-operation in Europe, Charter of Paris for a New Europe, November 21, 1990. See *International Legal Materials* 30 (1991): 190ff.

46. The Treaty on Open Skies was legally separate from the non-treaty-based CSCE, but the two were closely associated.

47. Conference for Security and Co-operation in Europe, "Towards a Genuine Partnership in a New Era" [Budapest Document], December 5–6, 1994.

48. Victor-Yves Ghebali, "The OSCE between Crisis and Reform: Towards a New

Lease on Life," Policy Paper no. 10, Geneva Centre for the Democratic Control of Armed Forces, Geneva, November 2005.

49. Alexandra Gheciu, *Securing Civilization* (Oxford: Oxford University Press, 2008).

50. This exclusive approach runs counter to the overlapping "mutually reinforcing" institutional logic later adopted among Western institutions but remained the approach Russia employed later in the CSTO.

51. Havel, "Speech at NATO Headquarters, Brussels, March 21, 1991."

52. The "consensus minus one" exception to the OSCE rule of consensus in decision-making can only be used in clear cases of gross and uncorrected violations of CSCE commitments. This is the only occasion it has been used. *OSCE Handbook* (Vienna: OSCE Press and Public Information Section, 2007), 14.

53. Gheciu, *Securing Civilization*, 121.

54. OSCE Conflict Prevention Centre Secretariat, OSCE Document SEC.GAL/171/11/Corr.1, "Survey of OSCE Field Operations," Vienna, October 28, 2011.

55. Yost, *NATO Transformed*, 5–9.

56. Ikenberry, *After Victory*, 17.

57. See, for example, Richard Caplan, *International Governance of War-Torn Territories: Rule and Reconstruction* (Oxford: Oxford University Press, 2005), 33–34.

58. Military Committee, Document MC 314, "Military Committee Policy Guidelines for Ensuring Security during a Changing East/West Relationship," November 23, 1989.

59. Rob de Wijk, *NATO on the Brink of the New Millennium* (London: Brassey's, 1997), 7, 13–15.

60. Ibid., 16.

61. North Atlantic Council, "Declaration of the Heads of State and Government," May 29, 1989.

62. North Atlantic Council, "Final Communiqué," June 8–9, 1989.

63. Nuclear Planning Group, "Final Communiqué," October 24–25, 1989.

64. North Atlantic Council, "Final Communiqué," December 14–15, 1989; emphasis added.

65. Defence Planning Committee, "Final Communiqué," May 22–23, 1990. It is worth further emphasizing that this decision took place within the institutional format of the DPC. France continued to maintain political reservations about the need for strategic adaptation longer than the political leadership of other member-states. The ability of NATO's political leadership to take the initial steps toward strategic adaptation in the DPC exemplifies the durability of the two-tiered institutional arrangement established for political decision-making in NATO following France's withdrawal from NATO's defense-related institutions in 1966.

66. North Atlantic Council, "Final Communiqué," Turnberry, June 7–8, 1990.

67. North Atlantic Council, "Declaration on a Transformed North Atlantic Alliance" [London Declaration], July 5–6, 1990.

68. Michael Legge, "The Making of NATO's New Strategy," *NATO Review* 39, no. 6 (December 1991): 9–14.

69. Ibid.

70. Ibid.

71. North Atlantic Council, "NATO's Core Security Functions in the New Europe," Copenhagen, June 6–7, 1991.

72. Although writing did proceed quickly by historical standards, NATO leaders at one point forecast even more rapid completion, saying: "Work on the strategy review is proceeding well and we expect to be in a position to approve the new strategic concept next Spring [*sic*]." Defence Planning Committee and Nuclear Planning Group, "Final Communiqué," December 6–7, 1990.

73. North Atlantic Council, "The Alliance's New Strategic Concept."

74. Ibid.

75. As if to indicate the continuing preeminence of collective defense in strategy, a separate classified paper on defense and nuclear strategy accompanied the publicly disclosed Strategic Concept. Military Committee, Document MC 317, "NATO Force Structures for the Mid-1990s and Beyond," December 16, 1991.

76. Member-states had agreed to the broad outlines of the Strategic Concept in the London Declaration already, which helped minimize further differences among them. Legge, "The Making of NATO's New Strategy."

77. Ibid.

78. Yost, *NATO Transformed*, 75.

79. North Atlantic Council, "The Alliance's New Strategic Concept."

80. Ibid.

81. A good example of the practice preceding the theory of NATO strategy was the de facto implementation of flexible response with the BERCON plans during the second Berlin crisis, several years before the adoption of the MC 14/3 Strategic Concept in 1967.

82. Hew Strachan, "Deterrence Theory: The Problems of Continuity," *Journal of Strategic Studies* 7, no. 4 (1984): 400. Hew Strachan, "The Lost Meaning of Strategy," *Survival* 47, no. 3 (Autumn 2005): 43–44.

83. Manfred Wörner, Speech by the Secretary-General at the Centro Alti Studi Difesa, Rome, May 10, 1993.

84. Ibid.

85. Ibid.

86. Craig R. Whitney, "NATO's Leadership Gap; Washington's Seeming Confusion on Bosnia Throws Alliance into Crisis of Relevance," *New York Times*, May 29, 1993; Ivo Daalder, *Getting to Dayton: The Making of America's Bosnia Policy* (Washington, DC: Brookings Institution Press, 2000), 15–17; and Jane M. O. Sharp, "Les relations anglo-américaines a l'épreuve de la crise yougoslave," *Les Notes de l'IFRI*, no. 9 (December 1998): 38–39.

87. General George A. Joulwan, Statement of Commander, US European Command, Armed Services Committee, US House of Representatives, March 23, 1994; Yost, *NATO Transformed*, 194.

88. North Atlantic Council, "Final Communiqué," June 4, 1992.

89. North Atlantic Council, "Final Communiqué," December 17, 1992; Defence Planning Committee and Nuclear Planning Group, "Ministerial Communiqué," May 26, 1993.

90. North Atlantic Council, "Final Communiqué," December 17, 1992.

91. Manfred Wörner, "A New NATO for a New Era," Speech by the Secretary-General of NATO, National Press Club, Washington, DC, October 6, 1993.

92. Ryan C. Hendrickson, *Diplomacy and War at NATO: The Secretary General and Military Action after the Cold War* (Columbia: University of Missouri Press, 2006), 57–58.

93. Yost, *NATO Transformed*, 194.

94. Hendrickson, *Diplomacy and War at NATO*, 60.

95. Ibid., 81.

96. Richard Holbrooke, *To End a War* (New York: Random House, 1998), 99.

97. Claes assumed some risk in so doing. France, Canada, Greece, and Spain were concerned about the use of cruise missiles but ultimately regarded the matter as a fait accompli. Hendrickson, *Diplomacy and War at NATO*, 83.

98. Hendrickson, *Diplomacy and War at NATO*, 82.

99. Yost, *NATO Transformed*, 195.

100. This experience clashes with conventional wisdom about highly intertwined or micro-managerial politico-military relations during NATO's later air campaign over Kosovo in 1999. See, for example, Wesley K. Clark, *Waging Modern War: Bosnia, Kosovo, and the Future of Conflict* (New York: Public Affairs, 2001).

101. NATO's first operational deployment of expeditionary forces may be the deployment of the Allied Command Europe (ACE) Mobile Force, established in 1960, to Turkey in January 1991 to guard against possible threats to Turkey from the Gulf War. North Atlantic Treaty Organization, *NATO Handbook*, 62, 112.

102. Notably, the head of the French military mission was also present at this meeting and agreed to the proposal. De Wijk, *NATO on the Brink of the New Millennium*, 22.

103. A memorable quote on the out-of-area debate from this period was that of US Senator Richard Lugar, who argued that NATO would either go "out of area or out of business." Richard Lugar, "NATO: Out of Area or Out of Business," Remarks at the Overseas Writers Club, Washington, DC, June 24, 1993.

104. De Wijk, *NATO on the Brink of the New Millennium*, 15.

105. Military Committee, "NATO Force Structures for the Mid 1990s and Beyond." Originally classified NATO CONFIDENTIAL, unlike the Strategic Concept.

106. Nuclear Planning Group, "Final Communiqué," October 17–18, 1991.

107. Defence Planning Committee, "Final Communiqué," December 12–13, 1991.

108. North Atlantic Council, "Declaration of the Heads of State and Government [Brussels Summit Declaration]," January 11, 1994; emphasis added.

109. Ibid.

110. Thomas-Durell Young, *Reforming NATO's Military Structures: The Long-Term Study and its Implications for Land Forces* (Carlisle, PA: Strategic Studies Institute, 1998).

111. The implementation of the new Regional Commands North and South Europe occurred in 1999–2000 and remain relatively unchanged.

112. Despite the better-known association of this term with twenty-first-century US-led military operations after the September 11, 2001, terrorist attacks, "coalitions of the willing" was in occasional use during the 1990s as well.

113. North Atlantic Council, "Declaration of the Heads of State and Government [Brussels Summit Declaration]."

114. Ibid.

115. Ibid.

116. Yost, *NATO Transformed*, 203.

117. North Atlantic Council, "Final Communiqué," June 3, 1996. The so-called Berlin Plus agreements of March 17, 2003, that allow the use of NATO assets for EU-led operations retained this principle of the NAC's primary decision-making role.

118. Stanley R. Sloan, *NATO's Future: Beyond Collective Defense*, McNair Paper 46 (Washington, DC: Institute for National Strategic Studies, National Defense University, December 1995), 27, 34–37.

119. Stanley R. Sloan, *Permanent Alliance? NATO and the Transatlantic Bargain from Truman to Obama* (New York: Bloomsbury, 2013), 157–58.

120. North Atlantic Council, Document M-NAC(DM)-2(96)89, "Final Communiqué," June 13, 1996.

121. North Atlantic Treaty Organization, *NATO Handbook*, 16–17.

122. North Atlantic Council, "Declaration of Peace and Cooperation [Rome Declaration]," November 8, 1991.

123. North Atlantic Cooperation Council, "Statement on Dialogue, Partnership and Cooperation," December 20, 1991.

124. David Yost's observation of the French position regarding the NACC is worth repeating: "In order to signify their vague disapproval of NACC, it seems, the French at the outset used a faintly ridiculous, even sarcastic, acronym—COCONA—for the Conseil de Coopération Nord-Atlantique. . . . To understand the significance of the original acronym, it should be noted that most of the meanings in French of *coco* are less than entirely dignified. The acronym COCONA conveyed accurately the opinion some French observers expressed about the NACC: that it was a 'political gadget' of doubtful seriousness." Yost, *NATO Transformed*, 358.

125. The first to propose the EAPC was US Secretary of State Warren Christopher in September 1996. Yost, *NATO Transformed*, 158.

126. Ibid., 97.

127. North Atlantic Council/North Atlantic Cooperation Council, Document M-1 (94)2, "Partnership for Peace: Framework Document," NATO Headquarters, Brussels, January 10–11, 1994.

128. Ibid. The North Atlantic Treaty's Article 4 is virtually identical: "The Parties will consult together whenever, in the opinion of any of them, the territorial integrity, political independence or security of any of the Parties is threatened."

129. The PfP format was informally known as "16 + 1" to represent the relationship between a single partnership country and the then-sixteen Alliance members acting as one through NATO.

130. North Atlantic Council/North Atlantic Cooperation Council, "Partnership for Peace: Framework Document."

131. Quoted in Yost, *NATO Transformed*, 98. Nicholas Williams, "The Future of Partnership for Peace," Konrad Adenauer Stiftung, Arbeitspapier, April 1996, 18.

132. Nick Williams, "Partnership for Peace: Permanent Fixture or Declining Asset?," *Survival* 38, no. 1 (1996): 98.

133. North Atlantic Treaty Organization, "A More Ambitious and Expanded Framework for the Mediterranean Dialogue," NATO Official Texts Series, June 28, 2004.

134. Vesna Pusic, Foreign Minister, Republic of Croatia, in discussion with the author, Chicago, May 20, 2012.

135. North Atlantic Council, "Declaration of the Heads of State and Government [Brussels Summit Declaration]."

136. North Atlantic Treaty [Washington Treaty], Washington, DC, April 4, 1949, Article 10.

137. North Atlantic Council/North Atlantic Cooperation Council, "Partnership for Peace: Invitation," NATO Headquarters, Brussels, January 10–11, 1994.

138. North Atlantic Treaty Organization, "Study on NATO Enlargement," September 1995.

139. Ibid.

140. They also reaffirmed that NATO would remain open to new members. NATO extended additional invitations to new members at its 2002 Prague Summit and 2008 Bucharest Summit and has continued to maintain its willingness to consider additional members.

141. Yost, *NATO Transformed*, 136.

142. North Atlantic Council, "Final Communiqué," December 10, 1996.

143. Ibid.

144. Ibid.

145. North Atlantic Treaty Organization, "The Founding Act on Mutual Relations, Co-operation and Security between NATO and the Russian Federation," Paris, May 27, 1997. In 2002, the parties replaced the PJC with a NATO-Russia Council. Whereas the PJC shared the same "NATO+1" format as the PfP, the NRC operated on an intergovernmental basis in which states met as equals.

146. North Atlantic Treaty Organization, "NATO-Ukraine Charter on a Distinctive Partnership," Madrid, July 9, 1997.

147. Manfred Wörner, "A Vigorous Alliance: A Motor for Peaceful Change in Europe," *NATO Review* 40, no. 6 (December 1992): 3–9; emphasis added.

148. Yost, *NATO Transformed*, 161.

149. Hendrickson, *Diplomacy and War at NATO*, 52, 56.

Chapter 7 · *NATO Adaptation into the Twenty-First Century, 1999–2012*

1. Alexander L. George and Andrew Bennett, *Case Studies and Theory Development in the Social Sciences* (Cambridge, MA: MIT Press, 2005), 181–85.

2. Ivo H. Daalder and Michael E. O'Hanlon, *Winning Ugly: NATO's War to Save Kosovo* (Washington, DC: Brookings Institution Press, 2000).

3. Ellen Hallams, *The United States and NATO since 9/11* (New York: Routledge, 2010), 35–53.

4. Patrick Barkham, "The Banana Wars Explained," *The Guardian*, March 5, 1999; Charles Krauthammer, "The Unipolar Moment," *Foreign Affairs* 70, no. 1 (1990/1991): 23–33.

5. North Atlantic Council, Document S-1(99)62, "Statement on Kosovo," Washington, DC, April 23, 1999.

6. Jean-Marie Colombani, "Nous Sommes Tous Américains," *Le Monde*, September 12, 2001.

7. Ryan C. Hendrickson, *Diplomacy and War at NATO: The Secretary General and Military Action after the Cold War* (Columbia: University of Missouri Press, 2006), 120.

8. To be sure, the September 12, 2001, decision was contingent on evidence that the attacks originated from a foreign source. When US officials confirmed this to the NAC early in October, invocation of Article 5 became official. North Atlantic Council, "Statement by the North Atlantic Council," September 12, 2001; George Robertson, "Statement by NATO Secretary General," October 2, 2001.

9. Hendrickson, *Diplomacy and War at NATO*, 120.

10. Bob Woodward and Dan Balz, "At Camp David, Advise and Dissent," Ten Days in September [series], *Washington Post*, January 31, 2002.

11. G. John Ikenberry, "America's Imperial Ambition," *Foreign Affairs* 81, no. 5 (September/October 2002): 54.

12. Ibid.

13. NATO's initial involvement in the Iraq war was indirect, as Turkey invoked Article 4 of the North Atlantic Treaty to discuss concerns about the security of its border with Iraq, and the Alliance ultimately agreed to the deployment of PATRIOT air defense missile systems to Turkey.

14. See, for example, George W. Bush, "Remarks by the President at 2002 Graduation Exercise of the United States Military Academy," June 1, 2002; and *National Security Strategy of the United States*, The White House, Washington, DC, September 2002.

15. Foreign and Commonwealth Office of the United Kingdom, "Joint Declaration on European Defence," Joint Declaration Issued at the British-French Summit, Saint-Malo, December 3–4, 1998.

16. See chapter 6 of this study on NATO after the Cold War.

17. European Council, Document SN 300/1/01, "Presidency Conclusions: European Council Meeting in Laeken," December 14–15, 2001.

18. European Council, "A Secure Europe in a Better World: European Security Strategy," Brussels, December 12–13, 2003.

19. George W. Bush, "Address to a Joint Session of Congress and the American People," Washington, DC, September 20, 2001; Donald H. Rumsfeld, "Secretary Rumsfeld Briefs at Foreign Press Center," US Department of Defense News Transcript, January 22, 2003; Hubert Védrine, "Le monde au tournant du siècle," *Politique Étrangère* 64, no. 4 (1999): 813–21; and Dominique de Villepin, Minister of Foreign Affairs (France), Speech to the United Nations Security Council, New York, March 19, 2003.

20. "Jacques and George, Friends Again (Sort of): France and America Make Up," *The Economist*, November 18, 2005.

21. What to do about those threats remained a matter of debate, however, as the Madrid bombing is widely credited with influencing the outcome of impending Spanish elections and the subsequent withdrawal of Spanish forces from the coalition in Iraq. But decorum and discretion had also markedly returned to transatlantic relations at this point, as the Spanish decision drew nothing of the kind of public bickering that characterized relations leading to the start of the Iraq war in 2003.

22. Thomas E. Ricks, *Fiasco: The American Military Adventure in Iraq* (New York: Penguin, 2006).

23. The command nominally changed from Allied Command Europe (ACE) to Allied Command Operations (ACO), though both SACEUR and the SHAPE headquarters retained their titles and acronyms despite the change to the ACO name that more accurately described the command's responsibilities.

24. Madeleine Albright, informal remarks at the NATO Chicago Summit, Chicago, May 20, 2012.

25. North Atlantic Council, "The Alliance's Strategic Concept," Washington, DC, April 24, 1999.

26. North Atlantic Treaty Organization, "NATO-EU: A Strategic Partnership," November 15, 2011, http://www.nato.int/cps/en/natolive/topics_49217.htm.

27. The 1991 version was titled "The Alliance's *New* Strategic Concept"; emphasis added.

28. United Nations Security Council, Document S/RES/1386(2001), Resolution 1386, December 20, 2001.

29. Jean Edward Smith, "Beware Generals Bearing a Grudge," *New York Times*, February 13, 2004.

30. Judy Dempsey, "France Bars Moves for Greater Alliance Role," *Financial Times*, February 10, 2003.

31. Theo Farrell and Sten Rynning, "NATO's Transformation Gaps: Transatlantic Differences and the War in Afghanistan," *Journal of Strategic Studies* 33, no. 5 (October 2010): 673–99.

32. North Atlantic Council, "Statement," February 22, 2005; and North Atlantic Treaty Organization, "About ISAF," n.d., http://www.isaf.nato.int/history.html.

33. North Atlantic Treaty Organization, "International Security Assistance Force: Key Facts and Figures," October 25, 2010.

34. See, for example, Andrew R. Hoehn and Sarah Harting, *Risking NATO: Testing the Limits of the Alliance in Afghanistan* (Santa Monica, CA: RAND Corporation, 2010).

35. North Atlantic Treaty Organization, "NATO Training Mission—Afghanistan," April 4, 2009, http://www.nato.int/cps/en/natolive/news_52802.htm?selectedLocale=en.

36. North Atlantic Treaty Organization, "Active Engagement, Modern Defence: Strategic Concept for the Defence and Security of the Members of the North Atlantic Treaty Organization," Lisbon, November 19–20, 2010; emphasis added.

37. North Atlantic Council, "Chicago Summit Declaration," May 20, 2012.

38. North Atlantic Treaty Organization, "Operation UNIFIED PROTECTOR: Final Mission Stats," November 2, 2011.

Chapter 8 · How NATO Adapts

1. Further study could evaluate the role of perceived plausibility and severity of consequence as factors in the potential loosening of structural constraints in critical juncture analysis generally.

2. John Lewis Gaddis, *We Now Know: Rethinking Cold War History* (Oxford: Oxford University Press, 1997), 52; emphasis original.

3. Anders Fogh Rasmussen, "NATO's Chicago Summit," Remarks by the Secretary-General of NATO, Chicago, May 19, 2012.

4. This is not to say that all states necessarily embraced the secretary-general's agenda, but the appropriateness of his having one in the first place was not in dispute.

5. See chapter 5 of this study.

6. Jens Stoltenberg, Remarks by the Secretary-General of NATO at the 60th Anniversary of the NATO Parliamentary Assembly, Stavanger, Norway, October 12, 2015.

NATO Documents

Defence Planning Committee. "Final Communiqué." May 22–23, 1990.

Defence Planning Committee. "Final Communiqué." December 12–13, 1991.

Defence Planning Committee and Nuclear Planning Group. "Final Communiqué." December 6–7, 1990.

Defence Planning Committee and Nuclear Planning Group. "Ministerial Communiqué." May 26, 1993.

Joint Planning Staff, Document JP(54)76(Final). "Capabilities Study—Allied Command Europe, 1957." September 2, 1954.

Military Committee. Document MC 14/1(Final). "Strategic Guidance [supersedes DC 13 and MC 14]." December 9, 1952.

Military Committee. Document MC 48(Final). "The Most Effective Pattern of NATO Military Strength for the Next Few Years." November 22, 1954.

Military Committee. Document MC 48/1. "The Most Effective Pattern of NATO Military Strength for the Next Few Years—Report No. 2." December 9, 1955.

Military Committee. Document MC 14/2(Rev)(Final Decision). "Overall Strategic Concept for the Defense of the North Atlantic Treaty Organization Area." May 23, 1957.

Military Committee. Document MC 314. "Military Committee Policy Guidelines for Ensuring Security during a Changing East/West Relationship." November 23, 1989.

Military Committee. Document MC 317. "NATO Force Structures for the Mid-1990s and Beyond." December 16, 1991.

Military Committee [North Atlantic]. Document SGM-1136-51. "Memorandum for the Standing Group [on] Association of Greece and Turkey with NATO." July 18, 1951.

NATO Historical Officer. Document NHO/63/1. "The Evolution of NATO Political Consultation, 1949–1962." May 2, 1963.

North Atlantic Cooperation Council. "Statement on Dialogue, Partnership and Cooperation." December 20, 1991.

North Atlantic Council. Document D-4/1. "Report of the International Working Group on Review of Progress in Implementing the North Atlantic Treaty in the Year since Its Signature." London, May 15, 1950.

North Atlantic Council. Fourth Session. "Final Communiqué." London, May 15–18, 1950.

North Atlantic Council. Document C5-D/2. "Report of the North Atlantic Council Deputies." New York, September 14, 1950.

North Atlantic Council. Document C5-R/1. "Summary Record of the First Meeting." New York, September 15, 1950.

North Atlantic Council. Document C5-VR/2. "Statement by the Chairman of the Council [Dean Acheson]." New York, September 15, 1950.

North Atlantic Council. Document C5-VR/6. "Verbatim Text of the Fifth Session of the North Atlantic Council." New York, September 18, 1950.

North Atlantic Council. Document C5-D/11. "Resolution on the Defence of Western Europe." New York, September 26, 1950.

North Atlantic Council. "Final Communiqué." September 26, 1950.

North Atlantic Council. Document C6-D/1 (also DC 29/1). "Joint Report on the German Contribution to the Defence of Western Europe by the North Atlantic Council Deputies and the Military Committee to the North Atlantic Council and the Defence Committee [Spofford Report]." Brussels, December 13, 1950.

North Atlantic Council. "Final Communiqué." December 18–19, 1950.

North Atlantic Council. Document C6-D/7. "Resolution on the Creation of an Integrated Force." December 19, 1950.

North Atlantic Council. Document C6-D/9. "Résolution Approuvant la Nomination d'un Commandant Suprême." December 19, 1950.

North Atlantic Council. "Seventh Session Final Communiqué." Ottawa, September 15–20, 1951.

North Atlantic Council. Document C7-D/23(Final). "Resolution on the Accession of Greece and Turkey to the North Atlantic Treaty." October 17, 1951.

North Atlantic Council. Document D-D(52)35(Final). "Report by the Council Deputies on Relations between EDC and NATO." February 20, 1952.

North Atlantic Council. Document C9-D/19. "Resolution on German Participation in Western Defence." February 22, 1952.

North Atlantic Council. Document C9-D/4(Final). "Reorganization of the North Atlantic Treaty Organization." March 17, 1952.

North Atlantic Council. Document C-R(52)1. "Summary Record of the Meeting of the Council." Paris, April 29, 1952.

North Atlantic Council. Document C-M(52)20. "NATO-EDC Relations: Report by the Committee to Examine the EDC Treaty." May 26, 1952.

North Atlantic Council, Document C-R(52)16. Record of Meeting on July 16, 1952.

North Atlantic Council. Document C-M(53)87. June 25, 1953.

North Atlantic Council. Document C-R(53)32. n.d. [1953].

North Atlantic Council. "Report on the Annual Review for 1953." Paris, December 14–16, 1953.

North Atlantic Council. Document C-M(53)166(Final). "Resolution on the 1954 Annual Review and Related Problems." December 15, 1953.

North Atlantic Council. Final Communiqué of the Meeting of the North Atlantic Council Attended by Foreign and Defence Ministers. Paris, October 22, 1954.

North Atlantic Council. Document CM(54)118(Final). "Resolution on the 1955 Annual Review and Related Problems." December 17, 1954.

North Atlantic Council. "Report on the Annual Review for 1954." Paris, December 17–18, 1954.

North Atlantic Council. Document C-M(56)138(Final). "Directive to the NATO Military Authorities from the North Atlantic Council." December 13, 1956.

North Atlantic Council. "Final Communiqué." December 16–18, 1960.

North Atlantic Council. Document C-M(61)30. "Long Term Planning." April 18, 1961.

North Atlantic Council. "Final Communiqué." May 8–10, 1961.

North Atlantic Council. "Final Communiqué." December 13–15, 1961.

North Atlantic Council. "Final Communiqué." December 13–15, 1962.

North Atlantic Council. "Final Communiqué." December 15–16, 1966.

North Atlantic Council. "The Future Tasks of the Alliance: Report on the Council [Harmel Report]." Brussels, North Atlantic Treaty Organization, December 13–14, 1967.

North Atlantic Council. "Declaration of the Heads of State and Government." May 29, 1989.

North Atlantic Council. "Final Communiqué." June 8–9, 1989.

North Atlantic Council. "Final Communiqué." December 14–15, 1989.

North Atlantic Council. "Final Communiqué." Turnberry, June 7–8, 1990.

North Atlantic Council. "Declaration on a Transformed North Atlantic Alliance [London Declaration]." July 5–6, 1990.

North Atlantic Council. "NATO's Core Security Functions in the New Europe." Copenhagen, June 6–7, 1991.

North Atlantic Council. Document C-M(91)88. "The Alliance's New Strategic Concept." November 7–8, 1991.

North Atlantic Council. "Declaration of Peace and Cooperation [Rome Declaration]." November 8, 1991.

North Atlantic Council. "Final Communiqué." June 4, 1992.

North Atlantic Council. "Final Communiqué." December 17, 1992.

North Atlantic Council. "Declaration of the Heads of State and Government [Brussels Summit Declaration]." January 11, 1994.

North Atlantic Council. "Final Communiqué." June 3, 1996.

North Atlantic Council. Document M-NAC(DM)-2(96)89. "Final Communiqué." June 13, 1996.

North Atlantic Council. "Final Communiqué." December 10, 1996.

North Atlantic Council. Document S-1(99)62. "Statement on Kosovo." Washington, DC, April 23, 1999.

North Atlantic Council. "The Alliance's Strategic Concept." Washington, DC, April 24, 1999.

North Atlantic Council. "Statement by the North Atlantic Council." September 12, 2001.

North Atlantic Council. "Statement." February 22, 2005.

North Atlantic Council. "Chicago Summit Declaration." Chicago, May 20, 2012.

North Atlantic Council / North Atlantic Cooperation Council. "Partnership for Peace: Invitation." NATO Headquarters, Brussels, January 10–11, 1994.

North Atlantic Council / North Atlantic Cooperation Council. Document M-1(94)2. "Partnership for Peace: Framework Document." NATO Headquarters, Brussels, January 10–11, 1994.

North Atlantic Council Deputies. Document D-D/18. "A Proposal for Action by Council Deputies." August 4, 1950.

North Atlantic Council Deputies. Document D-D/174. "Contribution of Germany to the Defence of Western Europe: Statement Made by the French Deputy at the 28th Meeting of the Council Deputies." November 14, 1950.

North Atlantic Council Deputies. Document D-D/190. "Provisional Arrangements for the Participation of Germany in the Defence of Western Europe: Memorandum by the United States Deputy." November 22, 1950.

North Atlantic Council Deputies. Document D-R/33. "Summary Record of the Thirty-Third Meeting of the Council Deputies." London, November 25, 1950.

North Atlantic Council Deputies. Document D-D(51)44. "Establishment of an International Staff for NATO." February 13, 1951.

North Atlantic Council Deputies. Document D-R(51)9. "Summary Record of Council Deputies Meeting of 12 February 1951 in London." February 14, 1951.

North Atlantic Council Deputies. Document D-D(51)123. "NATO Reorganization: Press Communiqué." May 4, 1951.

North Atlantic Council Deputies. Document D-D(51)280. "Protocol to the North Atlantic Treaty on the Accession of Greece and Turkey." November 9, 1951.

North Atlantic Council Deputies. Document D-D(52)67. "Resolution on the Appointment of Lord Ismay as Vice-Chairman of the North Atlantic Council and Secretary-General of the North Atlantic Treaty Organization." March 13, 1952.

North Atlantic Defense Committee. Document DC 6/1. "The Strategic Concept for the Defense of the North Atlantic Area." December 1, 1949.

North Atlantic Defense Committee. Document DC 13. "North Atlantic Treaty Organization Medium Term Plan." March 28, 1950.

North Atlantic Treaty Organization. "About ISAF." N.d., http://www.isaf.nato.int/history.htm.

North Atlantic Treaty Organization. "Final Report of the Temporary Council Committee." December 18, 1951, Para 83, Roll 86, Appendix 4, NATO Document Series, Brussels.

North Atlantic Treaty Organization. *NATO Handbook*. Brussels: NATO Office of Information and Press, 1991.

North Atlantic Treaty Organization. *NATO Handbook*. Brussels: North Atlantic Treaty Organization, 1992.

North Atlantic Treaty Organization. "Study on NATO Enlargement." September 1995.

North Atlantic Treaty Organization. "The Founding Act on Mutual Relations, Co-operation and Security between NATO and the Russian Federation." Paris, May 27, 1997.

North Atlantic Treaty Organization. "NATO-Ukraine Charter on a Distinctive Partnership." Madrid, July 9, 1997.

North Atlantic Treaty Organization. "A More Ambitious and Expanded Framework for the Mediterranean Dialogue." NATO Official Texts Series, June 28, 2004.

North Atlantic Treaty Organization. "NATO Training Mission—Afghanistan." April 4, 2009, http://www.nato.int/cps/en/natolive/news_52802.htm?selectedLocale=en.

North Atlantic Treaty Organization. "International Security Assistance Force: Key Facts and Figures." October 25, 2010.

North Atlantic Treaty Organization. "Active Engagement, Modern Defence: Strategic

Concept for the Defence and Security of the Members of the North Atlantic Treaty Organization." Lisbon, November 19–20, 2010.

North Atlantic Treaty Organization. "Operation UNIFIED PROTECTOR: Final Mission Stats." November 2, 2011.

North Atlantic Treaty Organization. "NATO-EU: A Strategic Partnership," November 15, 2011, http://www.nato.int/cps/en/natolive/topics_49217.htm.

North Atlantic Treaty Organization [Halvard Lange, Gaetano Martino, and Lester B. Pearson]. "Report of the Committee of Three on Non-Military Co-operation." December 13, 1956.

Nuclear Planning Group. "Final Communiqué." October 24–25, 1989.

Nuclear Planning Group. "Final Communiqué." October 17–18, 1991.

Pedlow, Gregory W. "The Evolution of NATO's Command Structure, 1951–2009." n.d. Historical Office of the Supreme Headquarters Allied Powers Europe, Mons, Belgium.

Secretary General. Document CM(62)48. "Report on NATO Defence Policy." April 17, 1962.

Secretary General. Document NDP/62/10. "NATO Defence Policy [Stikker Paper]." September 3, 1962.

Standing Group. Document SG 80/2. "Report by the International Working Team to the Standing Group on Association of Turkey and Greece with NATO Military Planning." November 29, 1950.

Supreme Allied Commander, General of the Army Dwight D. Eisenhower. *First Annual Report of the Supreme Commander, Allied Powers Europe*. Paris: Public Information Division, SHAPE, April 1952.

Treaties, International Legal Materials, and Documents

Treaty of Alliance and Mutual Assistance between His Majesty in Respect of the United Kingdom of Great Britain and Northern Ireland and the President of the French Republic [Dunkirk Treaty], Dunkirk, March 4, 1947. In *Treaties and International Agreements Registered or Filed and Recorded with the Secretariat of the United Nations*. New York: United Nations, 1947.

Treaty of Economic, Social and Cultural Collaboration and Collective Self-Defence [Brussels Treaty], Brussels, March 17, 1948, Ministère des Affaires Étrangères—Traités et Conventions (1732–1998), AE TC 365, Archives Nationales du Luxembourg.

North Atlantic Treaty [Washington Treaty]. Washington, DC, April 4, 1949.

United Nations Security Council, Resolution 82. June 25, 1950

United Nations Security Council, Resolution 83. June 27, 1950.

United Nations Security Council, Resolution 84. July 7, 1950.

Council of Europe Parliamentary Assembly, Document AS(2)52. "Recommendation 5 Relative to the Creation of a European Army, Adopted 11th August 1950, on the Conclusion of the Debate on the Report and Message from the Committee of Ministers to the Assembly." Strasbourg, France.

Traité Instituant la Communauté Européenne de Défense [EDC Treaty]. Paris, May 27, 1952.

Protocol to the North Atlantic Treaty on the Accession of the Federal Republic of Germany. Paris, October 23, 1954.

Warsaw Treaty of Friendship, Cooperation, and Mutual Assistance [Warsaw Pact]. Bulgaria-USSR, May 14, 1955, 6 I.L.M. 906 (1967).

Treaty Establishing the European Atomic Energy Community [Euratom]. Rome, March 25, 1957, 2010 OJ (C84).

Franco-German Treaty of Friendship [Élysée Treaty]. Paris, January 22, 1963.

Treaty Establishing a Single Council and a Single Commission of the European Communities [Merger Treaty]. Brussels, April 8, 1965, 1967 OJEC (152).

European Communities. *European Political Cooperation (EPC)*. Luxembourg: Office for Official Publications of the European Communities, 1988.

Joint Declaration of Twenty-Two States, Treaty on Conventional Armed Forces in Europe [CFE Treaty] Signing Conference. Paris, November 19, 1990.

Conference for Security and Co-operation in Europe, Charter of Paris for a New Europe. November 21, 1990.

United Nations General Assembly, Document A/46/48. January 16, 1991.

Treaty on European Union [TEU, Maastricht Treaty]. February 7, 1992, 1992 O.J. (C191) 1, Article J.4.

Conference for Security and Co-operation in Europe. "Towards a Genuine Partnership in a New Era" [Budapest Document]. December 5–6, 1994.

United Nations, Department of Public Information. "Former Yugoslavia—UNPROFOR, Department of Peacekeeping Operations," http://www.un.org/Depts/DPKO/Missions/unprof_b.htm.

United Nations General Assembly, Document A/54/549. "Report of the Secretary-General Pursuant to General Assembly Resolution 53/35: The Fall of Srebrenica." November 15, 1999.

European Council, Document SN 300/1/01. "Presidency Conclusions: European Council Meeting in Laeken." December 14–15, 2001.

United Nations Security Council, Document S/RES/1386(2001), Resolution 1386. December 20, 2001.

European Council. "A Secure Europe in a Better World: European Security Strategy." Brussels, December 12–13, 2003.

Organization for Security and Cooperation in Europe. *OSCE Handbook*. Vienna: OSCE Press and Public Information Section, 2007.

OSCE Conflict Prevention Centre Secretariat, OSCE Document SEC.GAL/171/11/Corr.1. "Survey of OSCE Field Operations." Vienna, October 28, 2011.

Books and Articles

Abbott, Kenneth W., and Duncan Snidal. "Why States Act through Formal International Organizations." *The Journal of Conflict Resolution* 42, no. 1 (February 1998): 3–32.

Adenauer, Konrad. *Erinnerungen: 1945–1953*. Stuttgart: Deutsche Verlags-Anstalt, 1976.

Adler, Emanuel, and Michael N. Barnett. *Security Communities*. Cambridge: Cambridge University Press, 1998.

Allen, David, Reinhardt Rummel, and Wolfgang Wessels, eds. *European Political Cooperation: Towards a Foreign Policy for Western Europe*. London: Butterworth Scientific, 1981.

Allison, Graham T. "Conceptual Models and the Cuban Missile Crisis." *The American Political Science Review* 63, no. 3 (September 1969): 689–718.

Allison, Graham T. *Essence of Decision: Explaining the Cuban Missile Crisis.* Boston: Little, Brown, 1971.

Allison, Graham T., and Philip Zelikow. *Essence of Decision: Explaining the Cuban Missile Crisis.* 2nd ed. New York: Longman, 1999.

Alsop, Stewart. "We Are Losing Asia Fast." *Saturday Evening Post* 222, no. 37 (March 11, 1950): 11.

Ambrose, Stephen E., and Douglas G. Brinkley. *Rise to Globalism: American Foreign Policy since 1938.* 8th rev. ed. New York: Penguin, 1997.

Ambrose, Stephen E., with Morris Honick. "Eisenhower: Rekindling the Spirit of the West." In *Generals in International Politics: NATO's Supreme Allied Commander, Europe,* edited by Robert S. Jordan, 8–30. Lexington: University Press of Kentucky, 1987.

Aron, Raymond. *Le Grand Débat: Initiation à la Stratégie Atomique.* Paris: Calmann-Lévy, 1963.

Aron, Raymond. *Paix et Guerre entre les Nations.* Paris: Calmann-Lévy, 1962.

Aron, Raymond, and Daniel Lerner, eds. *France Defeats E.D.C.* London: Thames and Hudson, 1957.

Arthur, W. Brian. "Competing Technologies, Increasing Returns, and Lock-In by Historical Events." *Economic Journal* 99, no. 394 (March 1989): 116–31.

Arthur, W. Brian. *Increasing Returns and Path Dependence in the Economy.* Ann Arbor: University of Michigan Press, 1994.

Asmus, Ronald D. "Rebuilding the Atlantic Alliance." *Foreign Affairs* 82, no. 5 (September/October 2003): 20–31.

Barany, Zoltan, and Robert Rauchhaus. "Explaining NATO's Resilience: Is International Relations Theory Useful?" *Contemporary Security Policy* 32, no. 2 (August 2011): 286–307.

Barkham, Patrick. "The Banana Wars Explained." *The Guardian,* March 5, 1999.

Barnett, Michael, and Martha Finnemore. *Rules for the World: International Organizations in Global Politics.* Ithaca, NY: Cornell University Press, 2004.

Barnett, Michael N., and Martha Finnemore. "The Politics, Power, and Pathologies of International Organizations." *International Organization* 53, no. 4 (Autumn 1999): 699–732.

Barnett, Michael, and Kathryn Sikkink. "From International Relations to Global Society." In *The Oxford Handbook of International Relations,* edited by Christian Reus-Smith and Duncan Snidal, 62–83. Oxford: Oxford University Press, 2008.

Beaufre, André. *L'O.T.A.N. et l'Europe.* Paris: Calmann-Lévy, 1966.

Beaufre, André. *NATO and Europe.* Translated by Joseph Green and R. H. Barry. London: Faber and Faber, 1967.

Berger, Thomas U. "Norms, Identity, and National Security in Germany and Japan." In *The Culture of National Security,* edited by Peter J. Katzenstein, 317–56. New York: Columbia University Press, 1996.

Bernstein, Barton J. "The Cuban Missile Crisis: Trading the Jupiters in Turkey?" *Political Science Quarterly* 95, no. 1 (Spring 1980): 97–125.

Berridge, Geoff R. *Diplomacy: Theory and Practice.* 4th ed. Basingstoke: Palgrave Macmillan, 2010.

Betts, Richard K. "Is Strategy an Illusion?" *International Security* 25, no. 2 (Fall 2000): 5–50.

Blau, Peter Michael, and W. Richard Scott. *Formal Organizations: A Comparative Approach.* San Francisco: Chandler Publishing, 1962; Stanford, CA: Stanford University Press, 2003.

Brandt, Willy. "German Policy towards the East." *Foreign Affairs* 46, no. 3 (April 1968): 476–86.

Brenner, Michael J. *Nuclear Power and Non-Proliferation: The Remaking of US Policy.* Cambridge: Cambridge University Press, 1981.

Brodie, Bernard, ed. *The Absolute Weapon: Atomic Power and World Order.* New York: Harcourt, Brace, 1946.

Brown, Archie. "The Gorbachev Revolution and the End of the Cold War." In *The Cambridge History of the Cold War.* Vol. 3, *Endings,* edited by Melvin P. Leffler and Odd Arne Westad, 244–66. Cambridge: Cambridge University Press, 2010.

Buchan, Alastair. "The Multilateral Force: A Study in Alliance Politics." *International Affairs (Royal Institute of International Affairs 1944–)* 40, no. 4 (October 1964): 619–37.

Burgess, Philip M., and James A. Robinson. "Alliances and the Theory of Collective Action: A Simulation of Coalition Processes." *Midwest Journal of Political Science* 13, no. 2 (May 1969): 194–218.

Bush, George H. W., and Brent Scowcroft. *A World Transformed.* New York: Knopf, 1998.

Buteux, Paul. *The Politics of Nuclear Consultation in NATO, 1965–1980.* London: Cambridge University Press, 1983.

Calleo, David. *The German Problem Reconsidered: Germany and the World Order, 1870 to the Present.* New York: Cambridge University Press, 1978.

Caplan, Richard. *International Governance of War-Torn Territories: Rule and Reconstruction.* Oxford: Oxford University Press, 2005.

Capoccia, Giovanni, and R. Daniel Kelemen. "The Study of Critical Junctures: Theory, Narrative, and Counterfactuals in Historical Institutionalism." *World Politics* 59, no. 3 (April 2007): 341–69.

Clark, Ian. *Nuclear Diplomacy and the Special Relationship: Britain's Deterrent and America, 1957–1962.* Oxford: Clarendon Press, 1994.

Clark, Wesley K. *Waging Modern War: Bosnia, Kosovo, and the Future of Conflict.* New York: Public Affairs, 2001.

Clawson, Robert W., ed. *East-West Rivalry in the Third World: Security Issues and Regional Perspectives.* Wilmington, DE: Scholarly Resources, 1986.

Cogan, Charles. "Florentine in Winter: François Mitterrand and the Ending of the Cold War, 1989–1991." In *NATO and the Warsaw Pact: Intrabloc Conflicts,* edited by Mary Ann Heiss and S. Victor Papacosma, 122–40. Kent, OH: Kent State University Press, 2008.

Cogan, Charles. *The Third Option: The Emancipation of European Defense, 1989–2000.* Westport, CT: Praeger, 2001.

Cohen, Morris C., and Ernest Nagel. *An Introduction to Logic and Scientific Method.* New York: Harcourt, Brace, 1934.

Collier, Ruth Berins, and David Collier. *Shaping the Political Arena: Critical Junctures, the Labor Movement, and Regime Dynamics in Latin America.* Princeton, NJ: Princeton University Press, 1991.

Colombani, Jean-Marie. "Nous Sommes Tous Américains." *Le Monde,* September 12, 2001.

Daalder, Ivo. *Getting to Dayton: The Making of America's Bosnia Policy.* Washington, DC: Brookings Institution Press, 2000.

Daalder, Ivo H., and Michael E. O'Hanlon. *Winning Ugly: NATO's War to Save Kosovo.* Washington, DC: Brookings Institution Press, 2000.

D'Agostino, Anthony. *Gorbachev's Revolution, 1985–1991.* Basingstoke: Macmillan, 1998.

David, Paul. "Clio and the Economics of QWERTY." *American Economic Review* 75 (May 1985): 332–37.

Davy, Richard, ed. *European Détente: A Reappraisal.* London: Royal Institute of International Affairs, 1992.

Deighton, Anne. "The European Union, Multilateralism, and the Use of Force." In *The Changing Character of War*, edited by Hew Strachan and Sibylle Scheipers, 315–32. Oxford: Oxford University Press, 2011.

Deighton, Anne, ed. *Western European Union 1954–1997: Defence, Security, Integration.* Oxford: European Interdependence Research Unit, 1997.

Dell, Edmund. *The Schuman Plan and the British Abdication of Leadership in Europe.* Oxford: Oxford University Press, 1995.

Dempsey, Judy. "France Bars Moves for Greater Alliance Role." *Financial Times*, February 10, 2003.

DePorte, A. W. *Europe between the Superpowers: The Enduring Balance.* 2nd ed. London: Yale University Press, 1986.

Deutsch, Karl Wolfgang. *Political Community and the North Atlantic Area: International Organization in the Light of Historical Experience.* Princeton, NJ: Princeton University Press, 1957.

De Wijk, Rob. *NATO on the Brink of the New Millennium.* London: Brassey's, 1997.

Dietl, Ralph. "In Defence of the West: General Lauris Norstad, NATO Nuclear Forces and Transatlantic Relations 1956–1963." *Diplomacy & Statecraft* 17, no. 2 (2006): 347–92.

DiMaggio, Paul J., and Walter W. Powell. "The Iron Cage Revisited: Institutional Isomorphism and Collective Rationality in Organizational Fields." *American Sociological Review* 28 (April 1983): 147–60.

Dobbs, Michael. "Slavic Republics Declare Soviet Union Liquidated." *Washington Post*, December 9, 1991, p. A1.

Dower, John W. *Embracing Defeat: Japan in the Wake of World War II.* London: Allen Lane, 1999.

Doyle, Michael. "Liberalism and World Politics." *American Political Science Review* 80, no. 4 (December 1986): 1151–69.

Duffield, John. "What Are International Institutions?" *International Studies Review* 9, no. 1 (Spring 2007): 1–22.

Duffield, John S. "International Regimes and Alliance Behavior: Explaining NATO Conventional Force Levels." *International Organization* 46, no. 4 (Autumn 1992): 819–55.

Duffield, John S. *Power Rules: The Evolution of NATO's Conventional Force Posture.* Stanford, CA: Stanford University Press, 1995.

Dulles, John Foster. "Policy for Security and Peace." *Foreign Affairs* 32, no. 3 (April 1954): 353–64.

Dyson, Kenneth, ed. *European Détente: Case Studies of the Politics of East-West Relations.* London: Pinter, 1986.

Ehmke, Horst, Karlheinz Koppe, and Herbert Wehner, eds. *Zwanzig Jahre Ostpolitik: Bilanz und Perspektiven.* Bonn: Neue Gesellschaft, 1986.

Eldredge, Niels, and Stephen Jay Gould. "Punctuated Equilibria: An Alternative to Phyletic Gradualism." In *Models in Paleobiology*, edited by Thomas J. M. Schopf, 82–115. San Francisco: Freeman, Cooper, 1972.

Elster, Jon, and Aanund Hylland, eds. *Foundations of Social Choice Theory*. Cambridge: Cambridge University Press, 1986.

Farrell, Theo, and Sten Rynning. "NATO's Transformation Gaps: Transatlantic Differences and the War in Afghanistan." *Journal of Strategic Studies* 33, no. 5 (October 2010): 673–99.

Finnemore, Martha. *National Interests in International Society*. Ithaca, NY: Cornell University Press, 1996.

Fioretos, Orfeo. "Historical Institutionalism in International Relations." *International Organization* 65, no. 2 (April 2011): 367–99.

Flint, Roy K. "Task Force Smith and the 24th Division: Delay and Withdraw, 5–19 July 1950." In *America's First Battles, 1776–1965*, edited by Charles E. Heller and William A Stofft, 266–99. Lawrence: University Press of Kansas, 1986.

Freedman, Lawrence. *Britain and Nuclear Weapons*. London: Royal Institute of International Affairs, 1980.

Freedman, Lawrence. *The Evolution of Nuclear Strategy*. London: Macmillan, 1981.

"French Economic Recovery: The Monnet Plan." *The World Today* 3, no. 3 (March 1947): 132–41.

Fursdon, Edward. *The European Defence Community: A History*. London: Macmillan, 1980.

Gaddis, John Lewis, ed. *Cold War Statesmen Confront the Bomb: Nuclear Diplomacy since 1945*. Oxford: Oxford University Press, 1999.

Gaddis, John Lewis. *Strategies of Containment: A Critical Appraisal of Postwar American National Security Policy*. New York: Oxford University Press, 1982.

Gaddis, John Lewis. *The United States and the Origins of the Cold War, 1941–1947*. New York: Columbia University Press, 1972.

Gaddis, John Lewis. *We Now Know: Rethinking Cold War History*. New York: Oxford University Press, 1997.

Gallois, Pierre M. *Stratégie de l'âge Nucléaire*. Paris: Calmann-Lévy, 1960.

George, Alexander L., and Andrew Bennett. *Case Studies and Theory Development in the Social Sciences*. Cambridge, MA: MIT Press, 2005.

Ghebali, Victor-Yves. *La Diplomatie de la Détente: La CSCE, d'Helsinki à Vienne (1973–89)*. Brussels: Bruylant, 1989.

Ghebali, Victor-Yves. *La France en Guerre et les Organisations Internationales, 1939–1945*. Paris: La Haye, Mouton, 1969.

Ghebali, Victor-Yves. *L'OSCE dans l'Europe post-communiste, 1990–1996: vers une identité paneuropéenne de sécurité*. Brussels: Bruylant, 1996.

Ghebali, Victor-Yves. "The OSCE between Crisis and Reform: Towards a New Lease on Life." Policy Paper No. 10, Geneva Centre for the Democratic Control of Armed Forces, Geneva, November 2005.

Gheciu, Alexandra. *Securing Civilization*. Oxford: Oxford University Press, 2008.

Gildea, Robert. *France since 1945*. Oxford: Oxford University Press, 1996.

Glaurdić, Josip. *The Hour of Europe: Western Powers and the Breakup of Yugoslavia*. New Haven, CT: Yale University Press, 2011.

Golden, James R., Daniel J. Kaufman, Asa A. Clark IV, and David H. Petraeus, eds. *NATO at Forty: Change, Continuity and Prospects*. London: Westview, 1989.

Goodpaster, Andrew J. "The Development of SHAPE: 1950–1953." In *Generals in International Politics: NATO's Supreme Allied Commander, Europe*, edited by Robert S. Jordan, 1–7. Lexington: University Press of Kentucky, 1987.

Gorbachev, Mikhail Sergeevich. *Perestroika: New Thinking for Our Country and the World*. Moscow: Izd-vo polit. lit-ry, 1987.

Gourevitch, Peter. *Politics in Hard Times: Comparative Responses to International Economic Crises*. Ithaca, NY: Cornell University Press, 1986.

Granieri, Ronald J. *The Ambivalent Alliance: Konrad Adenauer, the CDU/CSU, and the West, 1949–1966*. New York: Berghahn Books, 2003.

Gray, Colin S. *Modern Strategy*. Oxford: Oxford University Press, 1999.

Gray, Colin S. *The Strategy Bridge: Theory for Practice*. Oxford: Oxford University Press, 2010.

Greenberg, Jerald, and Robert A. Barron. *Behavior in Organizations*. 9th ed. London: Pearson, 2008.

Gregory, Shaun R. *Nuclear Command and Control in NATO: Nuclear Weapons Operation and the Strategy of Flexible Response*. London: Macmillan, 1996.

Greif, Avner, and David Laitin. "A Theory of Endogenous Institutional Change." *American Political Science Review* 98 (2004): 633–52.

Grenville, J. A. S. *A History of the World in the Twentieth Century*. Cambridge, MA: Belknap Press, 1994.

Grieco, Joseph M. "Anarchy and the Limits of Cooperation: A Realist Critique of the Newest Liberal Institutionalism." *International Organization* 42, no. 3 (Summer 1988): 485–507.

Grieco, Joseph, Robert Powell, and Duncan Snidal. "The Relative-Gains Problem for International Cooperation." *The American Political Science Review* 87, no. 3 (September 1993): 729–43.

Grossman, Sanford J., and Oliver D. Hart. "An Analysis of the Principal-Agent Problem." *Econometrica* 51, no. 1 (January 1983): 7–45.

Guillen, Pierre. "Les chefs militaires français, le réarmement de l'Allemagne, et la CED (1950–1954)." *Revue d'histoire de la Deuxième Guerre mondiale et des conflits contemporains* 33, no. 129 (January 1983): 3–33.

Gulick, Edward Vose. *Europe's Classical Balance of Power: A Case History of Theory and Practice of One of the Great Concepts of European Statecraft*. Ithaca, NY: Cornell University Press, 1955.

Gutner, Tamar, and Alexander Thompson. "The Politics of IO Performance: A Framework." *Review of International Organizations* 5, no. 3 (September 2010): 227–48.

Haas, Ernst B. *The Uniting of Europe: Political, Social, and Economical Forces, 1950–1957*. 2nd ed. Stanford, CA: Stanford University Press, 1968.

Haas, Peter M., Robert O. Keohane, and Marc A. Levy, eds. *Institutions for the Earth: Sources of Effective International Environmental Protection*. Cambridge, MA: MIT Press, 1993.

Haftendorn, Helga. *NATO and the Nuclear Revolution: A Crisis of Credibility, 1966–1967*. Oxford: Clarendon Press, 1996.

Haftendorn, Helga, Robert O. Keohane, and Celeste Wallander, eds. *Imperfect Unions: Security Institutions over Time and Space*. Oxford: Oxford University Press, 1999.

Hall, Peter A. "Historical Institutionalism in Rationalist and Sociological Perspective." In *Explaining Institutional Change: Ambiguity, Agency, and Power*, edited by James Mahoney and Kathleen Thelen, 204–23. Cambridge: Cambridge University Press, 2010.

Hall, Peter A. "Preference Formation as a Political Process: The Case of Monetary Union in Europe." In *Preferences and Situations*, edited by Ira Katznelson and Barry Weingast, 129–60. New York: Russell Sage Foundation, 2005.

Hall, Peter A., and Rosemary C. R. Taylor. "Political Science and the Three New Institutionalisms." *Political Studies* 44, no. 5 (1996): 936–57.

Hallams, Ellen. *The United States and NATO since 9/11*. New York: Routledge, 2010.

Hendrickson, Ryan C. *Diplomacy and War at NATO: The Secretary General and Military Action after the Cold War*. Columbia: University of Missouri Press, 2006.

Hendrickson, Ryan C. "NATO's Secretaries-General: Organizational Leadership in Shaping Alliance Strategy." In *NATO in Search of a Vision*, edited by Gülnur Aybet and Rebecca R. Moore. Washington, DC: Georgetown University Press, 2010.

Herrmann, Richard, and Richard Ned Lebow, eds. *Ending the Cold War*. New York: Palgrave Macmillan, 2004.

Heuser, Beatrice. *NATO, Britain, France, and the FRG: Nuclear Strategies and Forces for Europe, 1949–2000*. London: Macmillan, 1997.

Heuser, Beatrice. *Nuclear Mentalities? Strategies and Beliefs in Britain, France, and the FRG*. London: Macmillan, 1998.

Heuser, Beatrice. "Stalin as Hitler's Successor: Western Interpretations of the Soviet Threat." In *Securing Peace in Europe, 1945–62*, edited by Beatrice Heuser and Robert O'Neill, 17–40. London: Macmillan, 1992.

Hoehn, Andrew R., and Sarah Harting. *Risking NATO: Testing the Limits of the Alliance in Afghanistan*. Santa Monica, CA: RAND Corporation, 2010.

Hogan, Michael. *Marshall Plan: America, Britain, and the Reconstruction of Western Europe, 1947–52*. New York: Cambridge University Press, 1987.

Holbrooke, Richard. *To End a War*. New York: Random House, 1998.

Ifestos, Panagiotes. *European Political Cooperation: Towards a Framework of Supranational Diplomacy?* Aldershot, England: Avebury, 1987.

Ikenberry, G. John. *After Victory: Institutions, Strategic Restraint, and the Rebuilding of Order after Major Wars*. Princeton, NJ: Princeton University Press, 2001.

Ikenberry, G. John. "America's Imperial Ambition." *Foreign Affairs* 81, no. 5 (September/October 2002): 44–60.

Isaacs, Jeremy, and Taylor Downing. *Cold War*. New York: Little, Brown, 1998.

Ismay, Hastings. *NATO: The First Five Years*. Paris: North Atlantic Treaty Organization, 1955.

Jackson, Scott. "Prologue to the Marshall Plan: The Origins of the American Commitment for a European Recovery Program." *Journal of American History* 65, no. 4 (March 1979): 1043–68.

"Jacques and George, Friends Again (Sort of): France and America Make Up." *The Economist*, November 18, 2005.

Jervis, Robert. "Cooperation under the Security Dilemma." *World Politics* 30, no. 2 (January 1978): 167–214.

Joffe, Josef. "The New Europe: Yesterday's Ghosts." *Foreign Affairs* 72, no. 1 (1993): 29–43.

Joffe, Josef. "Once More: The German Question." *Survival* 32, no. 2 (1990): 129–40.

Joffe, Josef. "The Security Implications of a United Germany." *The Adelphi Papers* 30, no. 257 (1990): 84–91.

Johnston, Seth A. "NATO Is a Global Organization in All but Name." *Yale Journal of International Affairs* 8, no. 2 (Summer 2013): 131–32.

Johnston, Seth A. "Safeguarding the Freedom, Common Heritage, and Civilization of the Peoples: President Truman and the North Atlantic Treaty." In A *Dialogue on the Presidency with a New Generation of Leaders*, edited by Robert E. Henderson, 23–34. Washington, DC: Center for the Study of the Presidency, 2003.

Jordan, Robert S., ed. *Europe and the Superpowers: Essays on European International Politics*. London: Pinter Publishers, 1991.

Jordan, Robert S., ed. *Generals in International Politics: NATO's Supreme Allied Commander, Europe*. Lexington: University Press of Kentucky, 1987.

Jordan, Robert S. "Gruenther: Attempts to Retain NATO Solidarity." In *Generals in International Politics: NATO's Supreme Allied Commander, Europe*, edited by Robert S. Jordan, 53–72. Lexington: University Press of Kentucky, 1987.

Jordan, Robert S. *The NATO International Staff/Secretariat, 1952–1957: A Study in International Administration*. London: Oxford University Press, 1967.

Jordan, Robert S. *Political Leadership in NATO: A Study in Multinational Diplomacy*. Boulder, CO: Westview Press, 1979.

Kagan, Robert. *Paradise and Power: America and Europe in the New World Order*. London: Atlantic Books, 2003.

Kaplan, Lawrence S. *The Long Entanglement: NATO's First Fifty Years*. London: Praeger, 1999.

Kaplan, Lawrence S. *NATO 1948: The Birth of the Transatlantic Alliance*. Lanham, MD: Rowman & Littlefield, 2007.

Kaplan, Lawrence S. *NATO Divided, NATO United: The Evolution of an Alliance*. London: Praeger, 2004.

Karber, Phillip A., and Jerald A. Combs. "The United States, NATO, and the Soviet Threat to Western Europe: Military Estimates and Policy Options, 1945–1963." *Diplomatic History* 22, no. 3 (Summer 1998): 399–429.

Katzenstein, Peter J. "Alternative Perspectives on National Security." In *The Culture of National Security*, edited by Peter J. Katzenstein, 1–32. New York: Columbia University Press, 1996.

Katzenstein, Peter J. *The Culture of National Security*. New York: Columbia University Press, 1996.

Kennan, George F. [X, pseud.]. "The Sources of Soviet Conduct." *Foreign Affairs* 25, no. 4 (July 1947): 566–82.

Kennedy, Craig, and Marshall M. Bouton. "The Real Trans-Atlantic Gap." *Foreign Policy*, no. 133 (October/November 2002): 66.

Kennedy, Paul. *The Rise and Fall of the Great Powers*. New York: Random House, 1987.

Keohane, Robert O. *After Hegemony: Cooperation and Discord in the World Economy*. Princeton, NJ: Princeton University Press, 1984.

Keohane, Robert O. "Institutional Theory and the Realist Challenge after the Cold War." In *Neorealism and Neoliberalism: The Contemporary Debate*, edited by David A. Baldwin, 284–91. New York: Columbia University Press, 1993.

Kitchen, Veronica M. "NATO's Out-of-Area Norm from Suez to Afghanistan." *Journal of Transatlantic Studies* 8, no. 2 (2010): 105–17.

Knight, Jack. *Institutions and Social Conflict.* Cambridge: Cambridge University Press, 1992.

Kohl, Wilfrid L. *French Nuclear Diplomacy.* Princeton, NJ: Princeton University Press, 1971.

Kohl, Wilfrid L. "Nuclear Sharing in NATO and the Multilateral Force." *Political Science Quarterly* 80, no. 1 (March 1965): 88–109.

Koremenos, Barbara, Charles Lipson, and Duncan Snidal, eds. *The Rational Design of International Institutions.* Cambridge: Cambridge University Press, 2003.

Krasner, Stephen D., ed. *International Regimes.* Ithaca, NY: Cornell University Press, 1983.

Krasner, Stephen D. "Structural Causes and Regime Consequences: Regimes as Intervening Variables." *International Organization* 36, no. 2 (Spring 1982): 185–205.

Krauthammer, Charles. "The Unipolar Moment." *Foreign Affairs* 70, no. 1 (1990): 23–33.

Laffont, Jean-Jacques, and David Martimort. *The Theory of Incentives: The Principal-Agent Model.* Princeton, NJ: Princeton University Press, 2002.

Lang, Kurt. "Military Organizations." In *Handbook of Organizations,* edited by James G. March, 838–78. Chicago: Rand McNally, 1965.

Langer, William L. *European Alliances and Alignments: 1871–1890.* 2nd ed. New York: Alfred A. Knopf, 1962.

Latham, Michael E. "The Cold War in the Third World, 1963–1975." In *The Cambridge History of the Cold War.* Vol. 2, *Crises and Détente,* edited by Melvin P. Leffler and Odd Arne Westad, 258–80. Cambridge: Cambridge University Press, 2010.

Lebow, Richard Ned, and Thomas Risse-Kappen, eds. *International Relations Theory and the End of the Cold War.* New York: Columbia University Press, 1995.

Leffler, Melvyn. "The United States and the Strategic Dimensions of the Marshall Plan." *Diplomatic History* 12, no. 3 (Summer 1988): 277–306.

Legge, Michael. "The Making of NATO's New Strategy." *NATO Review* 39, no. 6 (December 1991): 9–14.

Lipset, Seymour M., and Stein Rokkan. "Cleavage Structures, Party Systems and Voter Alignments: An Introduction." In *Party Systems and Voter Alignments: Cross-National Perspectives,* edited by Lipset and Rokkan, 1–64. New York: Free Press, 1967.

Liska, George F. *Nations in Alliance: The Limits of Interdependence.* Baltimore: Johns Hopkins Press, 1962.

Löberbauer, Harald. *The OSCE System: Institutional Design and Conflict Management in the 21st Century.* Munich: Grin Verlag, 2007.

Lord, Christopher. "'With But Not Of:' Britain and the Schuman Plan." *Journal of European Integration History* 4, no. 2 (1998): 23–46.

Lunn, Simon. *Burden Sharing in NATO.* London: Royal Institute for International Affairs, 1983.

Lynch, Allen. *The Cold War Is Over—Again.* Oxford: Westview, 1992.

Lynch, Frances M. B. "Resolving the Paradox of the Monnet Plan: National and International Planning in French Reconstruction." *The Economic History Review* 37, no. 2 (May 1984): 229–43.

Mahoney, Daniel J. *De Gaulle: Statesmanship, Grandeur, and Modern Democracy.* London: Transaction Publishers, 2000.

Mahoney, James. *The Legacies of Liberalism: Path Dependence and Political Regimes in Central America.* Baltimore: Johns Hopkins University Press, 2002.

Mahoney, James, and Kathleen Thelen, eds. *Explaining Institutional Change: Ambiguity, Agency, and Power.* Cambridge: Cambridge University Press, 2010.

Maloney, Sean M. "Berlin Contingency Planning: Prelude to Flexible Response, 1958–63." *The Journal of Strategic Studies* 25, no. 1 (March 2002): 99–134.

Maloney, Sean M. "Notfallplanung für Berlin: Vorläufer der Flexible Response, 1958–1963." *Militärgeschichte* 7, no. 1 (1997): 3–15.

Mardell, Mark. "NATO: What Is It For?" *BBC News*, May 20, 2012, http://www.bbc.co.uk/news/world-us-canada-18135456.

McAllister, James. *No Exit: America and the German Problem, 1943–1954.* Ithaca, NY: Cornell University Press, 2002.

McCalla, Robert B. "NATO's Persistence after the Cold War." *International Organization* 50, no. 3 (Summer 1996): 445–75.

McCullough, David. *Truman.* New York: Simon & Schuster, 1992.

McMahan, Jeff. *British Nuclear Weapons: For and Against.* London: Junction Books, 1981.

Mearsheimer, John J. "Back to the Future: Instability in Europe after the Cold War." *International Security* 15, no. 1 (Summer 1990): 5–56.

Mearsheimer, John J. *The Tragedy of Great Power Politics.* New York: Norton, 2001.

Melandri, Pierre. "La France et les États-Unis." *Politique Étrangère* 51, no. 1 (1986): 219–46.

Melandri, Pierre. *Les États-Unis face à l'Unification de l'Europe, 1945–1954.* Paris: Pedone, 1980.

Melissen, Jan. "The Politics of US Missile Deployment in Britain 1955–59." *Storia delle Relazioni Internationali* 13, no. 1 (1998): 151–85.

Menon, Anand, and Jennifer Welsh. "Understanding NATO's Sustainability: The Limits of Institutionalist Theory." *Global Governance* 17, no. 1 (January–March 2011): 81–94.

Mill, John Stuart. "Of the Four Methods of Experimental Inquiry." In *A System of Logic*, 9th ed. London: Longmans, Green, Reader, and Dyer, 1875.

Milward, Alan S. *The Frontier of National Sovereignty: History and Theory.* London: Routledge, 1993.

Mitrany, David. "The Functional Approach to World Organisation." *International Affairs* 24, no. 3 (July 1948).

Moch, Jules. *Alerte! Le problème crucial de la Communauté européenne de défense.* Paris: R. Laffont, 1954.

Moe, Terry. "Power and Political Institutions." *Perspectives on Politics* 3, no. 2 (June 2005): 215–33.

Monnet, Jean. *Mémoires.* Paris: Fayard, 1976.

Moore, Barrington. *Social Origins of Dictatorship and Democracy.* Boston: Beacon Press, 1966.

Moore, Rebecca R. *NATO's New Mission: Projecting Stability in a Post–Cold War World.* Westport, CT: Praeger Security International, 2007.

Moravcsik, Andrew. "De Gaulle between Grain and Grandeur: The Political Economy of French EC Policy, 1958–1970." *Journal of Cold War Studies* 2, no. 2 (2000): 4–68.

Moravcsik, Andrew. "Taking Preferences Seriously: A Liberal Theory of International Politics." *International Organization* 51, no. 4 (Autumn 1997): 513–53.

Morgenthau, Hans J. *Politics among Nations: The Struggle for Power and Peace.* New York: Knopf, 1949.

Nash, Philip. *The Other Missiles of October: Eisenhower, Kennedy, and the Jupiters, 1957– 1963.* Chapel Hill: University of North Carolina Press, 1997.

"NATO Allies Astonished at Switch." *Washington Post,* April 15, 1956, p. A13.

Nielsen, Suzanne C. *An Army Transformed: The US Army's Post-Vietnam Recovery and the Dynamics of Change in Military Organizations.* The Letort Papers. Carlisle, PA: Strategic Studies Institute, US Army War College, 2010.

Nye, Joseph S., Jr. "Power and Foreign Policy." *Journal of Political Power* 4, no. 1 (April 2011): 9–24.

Ogilvie-White, Ranya. *On Nuclear Deterrence: The Correspondence of Sir Michael Quinlan.* London: International Institute for Strategic Studies, 2011.

Olson, Mancur. *The Logic of Collective Action.* Cambridge, MA: Harvard University Press, 1965.

O'Neal, John R., and Mark A. Elrod. "NATO Burden Sharing and the Forces of Change." *International Studies Quarterly* 33, no. 4 (December 1989): 435–56.

Osgood, Robert E. *The Case for the MLF: A Critical Evaluation.* Washington, DC: Washington Center for Foreign Policy Research, 1964.

Pace, Eric. "Charles M. Spofford Is Dead at 88." *New York Times,* March 25, 1991.

Pankin, Boris. *The Last Hundred Days of the Soviet Union.* Translated by Alexei Pankin. London: Tauris, 1996.

Pedlow, Gregory W. "The Evolution of NATO Strategy, 1949–1969." In *NATO Strategy Documents 1949–1969,* edited by Gregory W. Pedlow, ix–xxv. Mons, Belgium: Supreme Headquarters Allied Powers Europe, 1997.

Pedlow, Gregory W. "Flexible Response before MC 14/3: General Lauris Norstad and the Second Berlin Crisis 1958–62." *Storia delle Relazioni Internationali* 13, no. 1 (1998): 235–68.

Pellitier, George Eugene. "Ridgway: Trying to Make Good on the Promises." In *Generals in International Politics: NATO's Supreme Allied Commander, Europe,* edited by Robert S. Jordan, 31–52. Lexington: University Press of Kentucky, 1987.

Peters, B. Guy. *Institutional Theory in Political Science: The "New Institutionalism."* 2nd ed. London: Continuum, 2005.

Pfeffer, Jeffrey, and Gerald R. Salancik. *The External Control of Organizations: A Resource Dependence Perspective.* New York: Harper & Row, 1978.

Pierre, Andrew J. *Nuclear Politics: The British Experience with an Independent Strategic Force, 1939–1970.* London: Oxford University Press, 1972.

Pierson, Paul. "Increasing Returns, Path Dependence, and the Study of Politics." *American Political Science Review* 92, no. 4 (2000): 251–67.

Pierson, Paul. *Politics in Time: History, Institutions, and Social Analysis.* Princeton, NJ: Princeton University Press, 2003.

Poidevin, Raymond, ed. *Histoire des Débuts de la Construction Européenne, mars 1948–mai 1950.* Brussels: Bruylant, 1986.

Posen, Barry. *The Sources of Military Doctrine: France, Britain, and Germany between the World Wars.* Ithaca, NY: Cornell University Press, 1984.

Powell, Walter W., and Paul J. DiMaggio, eds. *The New Institutionalism in Organizational Analysis.* Chicago: University of Chicago Press, 1991.

Pravda, Alex, ed. *The End of the Outer Empire: Soviet-East European Relations in Transition, 1985–1990*. London: Royal Institute for International Affairs, 1992.

Preble, Christopher A. "Who Ever Believed in the 'Missile Gap'? John F. Kennedy and the Politics of National Security." *Presidential Studies Quarterly* 33, no. 4 (December 2003): 801–26.

Ragin, Charles C. *The Comparative Method: Moving beyond Qualitative and Quantitative Strategies*. Berkeley: University of California Press, 1987.

Raymond, Jack. "Kennedy Defense Study Finds No Evidence of a 'Missile Gap.'" *New York Times*, February 7, 1961, p. A1.

Reiter, Dan. "Learning, Realism, and Alliances: The Weight of the Shadow of the Past." *World Politics* 46, no. 4 (July 1994): 490–526.

Rhodes, Richard. *The Making of the Atomic Bomb*. New York: Simon & Schuster, 1986.

Ricks, Thomas E. *Fiasco: The American Military Adventure in Iraq*. New York: Penguin, 2006.

Ripsman, Norrin M. *Peacemaking by Democracies: The Effect of State Autonomy on the Post-World War Settlements*. University Park: Pennsylvania State University Press, 2002.

Risse-Kappen, Thomas. "Collective Identity in a Democratic Community." In *The Culture of National Security*, edited by Peter J. Katzenstein. New York: Columbia University Press, 1996: 357–99.

Riste, Olaf. *Western Security—The Formative Years: European and Atlantic Defence, 1947–1953*. New York: Columbia University Press, 1985.

Roberts, Adam. "An 'Incredibly Swift Transition': Reflections on the End of the Cold War." In *The Cambridge History of the Cold War, Vol. III: Endings*, edited by Melvin P. Leffler and Odd Arne Westad, 513–34. Cambridge: Cambridge University Press, 2010.

Röpke, Wilhelm. *Die Deutsche Frage*. Erlenbach-Zürich: E. Rentsch, 1945.

Rosen, Stephen Peter. "New Ways of War: Understanding Military Innovation." *International Security* 13, no. 1 (Summer 1988): 134–68.

Rosenberg, David Alan. "The Origins of Overkill: Nuclear Weapons and American Strategy, 1945–1960." *International Security* 7, no. 4 (Spring 1983): 3–71.

Ruggie, John Gerard. "International Responses to Technology: Concepts and Trends." *International Organization* 29, no. 3 (Summer 1975): 557–83.

Scheffer, Jaap de Hoop. "Towards Fairer Burden-Sharing in NATO." *Europe's World* 9 (Summer 2008): 68–73.

Schmidt, Gustav. *A History of NATO: The First Fifty Years*. Basingstoke: Palgrave, 2001.

Schwarz, Hans-Peter. *Adenauer: Der Aufstieg, 1876–1952*. Stuttgart: Deutsche Verlags-Anstalt, 1986.

Schwarz, Hans-Peter. *Adenauer: Der Staatsmann, 1952–1967*. Stuttgart: Deutsche Verlags-Anstalt, 1991.

Schweller, Randall L. "Bandwagoning for Profit: Bringing the Revisionist State Back In." *International Security* 19, no. 1 (Summer 1994): 72–107.

Selznick, Philip. *TVA and the Grass Roots: A Study in the Sociology of Formal Organization*. Berkeley: University of California Press, 1949.

Sharp, Jane M. O. "Les relations anglo-américaines à l'épreuve de la crise yougoslave." *Les Notes de l'IFRI*, no. 9 (December 1998).

Shepsle, Kenneth. "Institutional Equilibrium and Equilibrium Institutions." In *Political Science: The Science of Politics*, edited by Herbert Weisberg, 51–81. New York: Agathon, 1986.

Singer, David, and Melvin Small. *The Wages of War, 1816–1965: A Statistical Handbook.* New York: John Wiley, 1972.

Sloan, Stanley R. *NATO's Future: Beyond Collective Defense.* McNair Paper 46. Washington, DC: Institute for National Strategic Studies, National Defense University, December 1995.

Sloan, Stanley R. *NATO's Future: Toward a New Transatlantic Bargain.* Washington, DC: National Defense University Press, 1985.

Sloan, Stanley R. *Permanent Alliance? NATO and the Transatlantic Bargain from Truman to Obama.* New York: Bloomsbury, 2013.

Smith, Jean Edward. "Beware Generals Bearing a Grudge." *New York Times,* February 13, 2004.

Snidal, Duncan. "Rational Choice and International Relations." In *Handbook of International Relations,* edited by Walter Carlsnaes, Thomas Risse, and Beth A. Simmons, 73–94. London: Sage, 2002.

Snyder, Glenn H. "Alliance Theory: A Neorealist First Cut." *Journal of International Affairs* 44, no. 1 (Spring 1990): 103–23.

Snyder, Glenn H. "The Security Dilemma in Alliance Politics." *World Politics* 36, no. 4 (July 1984): 461–95.

Sokolovskiy, Vasiliĭ Danilovich. *Soviet Military Strategy.* Moscow: Voenizdat, 1963.

Soutou, Georges-Henri. "France." In *The Origins of the Cold War in Europe: International Perspectives,* edited by David Reynolds. New Haven, CT: Yale University Press, 1994.

Soutou, Georges-Henri. *L'Alliance incertaine—Les rapports politico-stratégiques franco-allemands (1954–1996).* Paris: Fayard, 1996.

Spofford, Charles M. "NATO's Growing Pains." *Foreign Affairs* 31, no. 1 (October 1952): 95.

Steel, Ronald. *The End of Alliance: America and the Future of Europe.* New York: Viking, 1964.

Steinberg, James B. "International Involvement in the Yugoslavia Conflict." In *Enforcing Restraint: Collective Intervention in Internal Conflicts,* edited by Lori Fisler Damrosch, 27–76. New York: Council on Foreign Relations, 1993.

Stent, Angela. *From Embargo to Ostpolitik, 1955–1980.* Cambridge: Cambridge University Press, 1981.

Stirk, Peter M. R. *A History of European Integration since 1914.* London: Continuum, 2001.

Stone, David R. *A Military History of Russia: From Ivan the Terrible to the War in Chechnya.* Westport, CT: Praeger Security International, 2006.

Strachan, Hew. "Les armées européennes ne peuvent-elles mener que des guerres limitées?" *Politique Étrangère* 76, no. 2 (2011): 305–17.

Strachan, Hew. "Deterrence Theory: The Problems of Continuity." *Journal of Strategic Studies* 7, no. 4 (1984): 394–405.

Strachan, Hew. "The Lost Meaning of Strategy." *Survival* 47, no. 3 (Autumn 2005): 33–54.

Strachan, Hew. "Strategy and Contingency." *International Affairs* 87, no. 6 (2011): 1281–96.

Taubman, William. *Khrushchev: The Man and His Era.* New York: W. W. Norton, 2003.

Taylor, A. J. P. *The Struggle for Mastery in Europe, 1858–1918.* Oxford: Oxford University Press, 1954.

Thelen, Kathleen. "Historical Institutionalism in Comparative Politics." *Annual Review of Political Science* 2 (1999): 369–404.

Thelen, Kathleen. *How Institutions Evolve.* Cambridge: Cambridge University Press, 2004.

Thelen, Kathleen, and Sven Steinmo. "Historical Institutionalism in Comparative Politics." In *Structuring Politics: Historical Institutionalism in Comparative Analysis,* edited by Sven Steinmo, Kathleen Thelen, and Frank Longstreth, 1–32. Cambridge: Cambridge University Press, 1992.

Thies, Wallace J. *Why NATO Endures.* Cambridge: Cambridge University Press, 2009.

Thompson, James D. *Organizations in Action: Social Science Bases of Administrative Theory.* London: McGraw-Hill, 1967.

Trachtenberg, Marc. *A Constructed Peace.* Princeton, NJ: Princeton University Press, 1999.

Trachtenberg, Marc. "La formation du système de défense occidentale: Les États-Unis, la France, et MC 48." In *France et l'OTAN, 1949–1996,* edited by Maurice Vaisse. Paris: Centre d'études d'histoire de la défense, 1996.

Trachtenberg, Marc. *History and Strategy.* Princeton, NJ: Princeton University Press, 1991.

True, James, Bryan Jones, and Frank Baumgartner. "Punctuated Equilibrium Theory." In *Theories of the Policy Process,* edited by Paul Sabatier. Boulder, CO: Westview Press, 1999.

Tsouras, Peter G., ed. *The Greenhill Dictionary of Military Quotations.* London: Greenhill, 2000.

Van Dyke, Nella, and Holly J. McCammon. *Strategic Alliances: Coalition Building and Social Movements.* Minneapolis: University of Minnesota Press, 2010.

Van Eekelen, Willem. "WEU and the Gulf Crisis." *Survival* 32, no. 6 (1990): 519–32.

Van Evera, Stephen. *Guide to Methods for Students of Political Science.* Ithaca, NY: Cornell University Press, 1997.

Védrine, Hubert. "Le monde au tournant du siècle." *Politique Étrangère* 64, no. 4 (1999): 813–21.

Von Clausewitz, Carl. *On War.* Translated and edited by Michael Howard and Peter Paret. Princeton, NJ: Princeton University Press, 1976.

Von Dannenberg, Julia. *The Foundations of Ostpolitik: The Making of the Moscow Treaty between West Germany and the USSR.* Oxford: Oxford University Press, 2008.

Von Moltke, Helmuth Graf. *Militarische Werke,* Vol. 2, Part 2. Berlin: E. S. Mittler, 1892–1912.

Walt, Stephen M. *The Origins of Alliances.* Ithaca, NY: Cornell University Press, 1987.

Walt, Stephen M. "The Ties That Fray: Why Europe and America Are Drifting Apart." *The National Interest,* no. 54 (Winter 1998–99): 3–11.

Waltz, Kenneth N. "The Emerging Structure of International Politics." *International Security* 18, no. 2 (Autumn 1993): 44–79.

Waltz, Kenneth N. *Man, the State, and War.* New York: Columbia University Press, 1954.

Waltz, Kenneth N. *Theory of International Politics.* Reading, MA: Addison-Wesley, 1979.

Warner, Geoffrey, and Anne Deighton. "British Perceptions of Europe in the Postwar Period." In *Les Europes des Européens,* edited by Rene Girault. Paris: Publications de la Sorbonne, 1993.

"We Will Bury You!" *Time.* November 26, 1956.

Weber, Max. *From Max Weber: Essays in Sociology.* Translated and edited by H. H. Gerth and C. Wright Mills. Oxford: Routledge, 1948.

Wells, Samuel F., Jr. "The Origins of Massive Retaliation." *Political Science Quarterly* 96, no. 1 (Spring 1981): 31–52.

Wendt, Alexander. "Constructing International Politics." *International Security* 20, no. 1 (Summer 1995): 71–81.

Wendt, Alexander. *Social Theory of International Politics*. Cambridge: Cambridge University Press, 1999.

Whitney, Craig R. "NATO's Leadership Gap; Washington's Seeming Confusion on Bosnia Throws Alliance into Crisis of Relevance." *New York Times*, May 29, 1993.

Wiebes, Cees, and Bert Zeeman. "Pentagon Negotiations March 1948: The Launching of the North Atlantic Treaty." *International Affairs* 59, no. 3 (Summer 1983): 351–63.

Williams, Nick. "Partnership for Peace: Permanent Fixture or Declining Asset?" *Survival* 38, no. 1 (1996): 98–110.

Williamson, Oliver E., ed. *Organization Theory: From Chester Barnard to the Present and Beyond*. Oxford: Oxford University Press, 1995.

Wilson, James Q. *Bureaucracy: What Government Agencies Do and Why They Do It*. New York: Basic Books, 1989.

Woodward, Bob, and Dan Balz. "At Camp David, Advise and Dissent." Ten Days in September [series], *Washington Post*, January 31, 2002.

Wörner, Manfred. "A Vigorous Alliance: A Motor for Peaceful Change in Europe." *NATO Review* 40, no. 6 (December 1992): 3–9.

Wright, Gordon. *France in Modern Times*. 5th ed. New York: W. W. Norton, 1995.

Wylie, J. C. *Military Strategy: A General Theory of Power Control*. New Brunswick, NJ: Rutgers University Press, 1967.

Wylie, J. C. "On Maritime Strategy." *Proceedings* 79, no. 5 (May 1953): 467–77.

Yost, David S. *NATO Transformed: The Alliance's New Roles in International Security*. Washington, DC: United States Institute of Peace Press, 1998.

Young, Oran. "Regime Dynamics: The Rise and Fall of International Regimes." In *International Regimes*, edited by Stephen D. Krasner, 93–113. Ithaca, NY: Cornell University Press, 1983.

Young, Thomas-Durell. *Reforming NATO's Military Structures: The Long-Term Study and Its Implications for Land Forces*. Carlisle, PA: Strategic Studies Institute, 1998.

Zelikow, Philip, and Condoleeza Rice. *Germany Unified and Europe Transformed: A Study in Statecraft*. London: Harvard University Press, 1995.

Theses and Unpublished Material

Everts, Steven. "Unilateral America, Lightweight Europe? Managing Divergence in Transatlantic Foreign Policy." Centre for European Reform working paper, February 2001.

Jordan, Robert S. "A Study of the Role of the International Staff/Secretariat of the North Atlantic Treaty Organization during the Tenure of Lord Ismay as Secretary General." DPhil thesis, Oxford University, 1959.

Levy, Jack, and Gary Goertz, eds. "Causal Explanations, Necessary Conditions, and Case Studies: World War I and the End of the Cold War." Unpublished manuscript, 2005.

Nagl, John A. "British and American Army Counterinsurgency Learning during the Malayan Emergency and the Vietnam War." DPhil thesis, Oxford University, 1997.

Parrish, Scott D., and Mikhail M. Narinsky. "New Evidence on the Soviet Rejection of the

Marshall Plan, 1947: Two Reports." Cold War International History Project, Working Paper no. 9. Washington, DC: Woodrow Wilson International Center for Scholars, 1994.

Podvig, Pavel, and Theodore Postol. "Did 'Star Wars' Win the Cold War? Evidence from Newly Discovered Soviet Documents." Seminar, Stanford University, Stanford, CA, April 19, 2007.

Schmidt, Peter. "Germany, France, and NATO." Paper presented at Strategic Outreach Roundtable, Strategic Studies Institute, US Army War College, Carlisle, PA, 1994.

Wampler, Robert. "NATO Strategic Planning and Nuclear Weapons." Nuclear History Program Occasional Paper 6, p. 9. College Park: University of Maryland, 1990.

Williams, Nicholas. "The Future of Partnership for Peace." Konrad Adenauer Stiftung, working paper, April 1996.

Speeches

Albright, Madeleine. Informal Remarks at the NATO Chicago Summit. Chicago, May 20, 2012.

Brosio, Manilo. "Secretary General Address to Eleventh NATO Parliamentarians' Conference, October 4, 1965." In *The Atlantic Alliance: Allied Comment*, 53–64. Washington, DC: Government Printing Office, 1966.

Bush, George W. "Address to a Joint Session of Congress and the American People." Washington, DC, September 20, 2001.

Bush, George W. "Remarks by the President at 2002 Graduation Exercise of the United States Military Academy." West Point, NY, June 1, 2002.

Churchill, Winston. Address to the Council of Europe, August 11, 1950, Reports, Council of Europe Consultative Assembly, 2nd Session, August 7–28, 1950, Strasbourg, France.

Churchill, Winston. Speech to the Academic Youth, Zurich, September 19, 1946. Council of Europe Digital Archive, Strasbourg, France. http://www.coe.int/t/dgal/dit/ilcd/archives/selection/churchill/.

Freedman, Lawrence. "Creating Power." Remarks Delivered at the Oxford Programme on the Changing Character of War Annual Lecture, Oxford, November 29, 2010.

Havel, Václav. "Speech at NATO Headquarters, Brussels, March 21, 1991." In *NATO, Europe, and the Security of Democracy: Václav Havel, Selected Speeches, Articles, and Interviews, 1990–2002*. Prague: Theo Publishing Pardubice, 2002.

Lugar, Richard. "NATO: Out of Area or Out of Business." Remarks at the Overseas Writers Club, Washington, DC, June 24, 1993.

Pleven, René. Speech to the French National Assembly, Paris, October 24, 1950.

Rasmussen, Anders Fogh. "NATO's Chicago Summit." Remarks by the Secretary General of NATO, Chicago, May 19, 2012.

Robertson, George. "Statement by NATO Secretary General," October 2, 2001.

Scheffer, Jaap de Hoop. "A Transforming Alliance." Speech by the secretary-general of NATO, Cambridge Union Society, Cambridge, February 2, 2005.

Schuman, Robert. Declaration, Paris, May 9, 1950. *Histoire de l'Union européenne* / Robert Schuman, Médiathèque centrale de la Commission européenne, Berlaymont 4/363, Brussels.

Stoltenberg, Jens. Remarks by the Secretary General of NATO at the 60th Anniversary of the NATO Parliamentary Assembly, Stavanger, Norway, October 12, 2015.

Villepin, Dominique de. Minister of Foreign Affairs (France), Speech to the United Nations Security Council, New York, March 19, 2003.

Wörner, Manfred. "A New NATO for a New Era." Speech by the Secretary-General of NATO, National Press Club, Washington, DC, October 6, 1993.

Wörner, Manfred. Speech by the Secretary-General at the Centro Alti Studi Difesa, Rome, May 10, 1993.

Government Documents

"Address by Secretary of Defence McNamara at the Ministerial Meeting of the North Atlantic Council, Athens, May 5, 1962." In *Foreign Relations of the United States, 1961–1963*. Vol. 8. Washington, DC: Government Printing Office, 1986.

"Address by Secretary of Defence McNamara at the Ministerial Meeting of the North Atlantic Council, Paris, December 14, 1962." In *Foreign Relations of the United States, 1961–1963*. Vol. 8. Washington, DC: Government Printing Office, 1986.

Bernard Montgomery (Field Marshal), 1st Viscount Montgomery of Alamein. Report to Brussels Treaty Powers on the Military Situation in Germany, June 15, 1950. Archives of the Western European Union, Public Record Office, Kew, Richmond, Surrey, England.

British Embassy to the Department of State, Aide-Mémoire, March 11, 1948. In *Foreign Relations of the United States*. Vol. 3, *Western Europe*, 46–48. Washington, DC: US Government Printing Office, 1974.

Condit, Kenneth W. *History of the Joint Chiefs of Staff: The Joint Chiefs of Staff and National Policy*. Vol. 2. Washington, DC: US Government Printing Office, 1986.

Congressional Budget Office. "Assessing the NATO / Warsaw Pact Military Balance," Budget Issue Paper for Fiscal Year 1979. Washington, DC: Government Printing Office, December 1977.

Dulles, John Foster. "The Evolution of Foreign Policy." *The Department of State Bulletin* 30 (January 25, 1954).

Eisenhower, Dwight D. Testimony of February 1, 1951, Hearings, Committee on Foreign Relations and Armed Services, Records of the US Senate.

Foreign and Commonwealth Office of the United Kingdom. "Joint Declaration on European Defence." Joint Declaration Issued at the British-French Summit, Saint-Malo, December 3–4, 1998.

Foreign and Commonwealth Office of the United Kingdom. *Notes on Arms Control*. London: Foreign and Commonwealth Office, 1990–1992.

Foreign and Commonwealth Office of the United Kingdom. *Notes on Security and Arms Control*. London: Foreign and Commonwealth Office, 1993–.

Joulwan, General George A. Statement of Commander, US European Command, Armed Services Committee, US House of Representatives, March 23, 1994.

Kennan, George, to George Marshall ["Long Telegram"], February 22, 1946, Harry S. Truman Administration File, Elsey Papers, Harry S. Truman Library and Museum, Independence, Missouri.

Memorandum by the Chief of the Division of Central European Affairs, United States Department of State. "Suggested Recommendations on Treatment of Germany from the Cabinet Committee for the President," September 4, 1944. In *Foreign Relations of the United States: The Conference at Quebec*, 86–101. Washington, DC: US Government Printing Office, 1972.

National Security Strategy of the United States. The White House, Washington, DC, September 2002.

Nonproliferation Treaty: Hearings before the Committee on Foreign Relations, United States Senate, 10 July–20 February 1969. Washington, DC: United States Government Printing Office, 1968–69.

"Notes on a Meeting at the White House," January 31, 1951. In *Foreign Relations of the United States, 1951.* Vol. 3. Washington, DC: Government Printing Office, 1979.

"The President's News Conference of April 7, 1954." In *Public Papers of the Presidents: Dwight D. Eisenhower, 1954.* Washington, DC: Government Printing Office, 1960.

Public Papers of the Presidents: Harry S. Truman, 1945–1947. Washington, DC: Government Printing Office, 1961.

Rumsfeld, Donald H. "Secretary Rumsfeld Briefs at Foreign Press Center." US Department of Defense News Transcript, January 22, 2003.

"Statement by the Secretary of State to the North Atlantic Council Closed Ministerial Session," Paris, April 23, 1954. In *Foreign Relations of the United States, 1952–1953.* Vol. 5, Part 1. Washington, DC: Government Printing Office, 1979.

US National Security Council, Document NSC 162/2. "Basic National Security Policy," October 30, 1953. In *Foreign Relations of the United States, 1952–54, Vol. II, Part 1,* 577–97. Washington, DC: Government Printing Office, 1979.

US National Security Council, Document NSC 30. "United States Policy on Atomic Warfare," September 10, 1948. In *Foreign Relations of the United States, 1948.* Vol. 1, Part 2, 624–28. Washington, DC: Government Printing Office, 1976.

Non-NATO Archives

Ann Whitman Files. Dwight D. Eisenhower Presidential Library and Museum, Abilene, Kansas.

Archives of the Western European Union. Public Record Office, Kew, Richmond, Surrey, England.

Central Media Archive of the European Commission. Berlaymont, Brussels.

Dwight D. Eisenhower Diary Series. Dwight D. Eisenhower Presidential Library and Museum, Abilene, Kansas.

Elsey Papers. Harry S. Truman Presidential Library and Museum, Independence, Missouri.

Papers of John F. Kennedy. Norstad Correspondence, 1962. John F. Kennedy Presidential Library, Boston, Massachusetts.

Papers of John F. Kennedy. President's Office Files, France. John F. Kennedy Presidential Library, Boston, Massachusetts.